A REMARKABLE

DAVID J. WHITCOMB

MARRIAGE

JOURNEYFORTH
Greenville, South Carolina

Library of Congress Cataloging-in-Publication Data

Whitcomb, David J., 1953-
  A remarkable marriage / David J. Whitcomb.
     p. cm.
  Summary: "A look at the biblical view of marriage"—Provided by publisher.
  ISBN 978-1-59166-950-0 (perfect bound pbk. : alk. paper)
  1. Marriage—Religious aspects—Christianity. I. Title.
  BV835.W515 2009
  248.4—dc22

                                                     2008036772

Cover Photo Credit: Craig Oesterling

ESV: Scripture quotations marked ESV are from The Holy Bible, English Standard Version®, copyright © 2001 by Crossway Bibles, a publishing ministry of Good News Publishers. Used by permission. All rights reserved.
GOD'S WORD: GOD'S WORD is a copyrighted work of God's Word to the Nations. Quotations are used by permission. Copyright 1995 by God's Word to the Nations. All rights reserved.

All Scripture is quoted from the Authorized King James Version unless otherwise noted.

A Remarkable Marriage

Design by Rita Golden
Page layout by Kelley Moore

© 2009 by BJU Press
Greenville, South Carolina 29614
JourneyForth Books is a division of BJU Press

Printed in the United States of America
All rights reserved

ISBN 978-1-59166-950-0

15   14   13   12   11   10   9   8   7   6   5   4   3   2

To my remarkable family—
my wife of thirty-five years, Patty,
our son Michael and his wife, Christina,
their children, Emma and Elliot,
our son Matthew and his wife, Rachelle,
and our son Mark and his wife, Jennifer

CONTENTS

INTRODUCTION

I grew up in a real "Leave It to Beaver" kind of home. Modern television viewers might chuckle at the normal home life presented in the old television series "Leave It to Beaver" that middle-aged people grew up with in the 1960s. One can hardly imagine, in this fast-paced, technologically advanced society, children who honored their parents, a father who was faithful to his wife, and a wife and mother who was always there when the children came home from school.

But I grew up in a home like that in the 1960s. When I got off the school bus, I knew my mother would be in the house waiting with cookies and milk (really!). I knew that mom would ask about school that day, because she was genuinely interested in my life. In my boyhood home, faithfulness was expected, respect for elders and peers alike was required, and being at home as a family was the norm.

Things have changed. In the fast-paced modern world there are so many experiences that one must be part of that it is difficult for husbands to find time to spend with their wives, and almost impossible for parents to spend time with their children. Now the expected norm is for mother and father to pour themselves into their careers. This is critical in the early years of marriage in order for the husband and wife to advance in their respective vocations. If they do not achieve at a level equal or greater than their peers, they will not have the financial resources available for the family to experience all the things that society insists they experience. How sad it would be for an American family to go through life having never been on a cruise, or having never enjoyed a vacation in Europe, or not having a state-of-the-art personal theater in their home.

So the norm has become Mom and Dad exhausting themselves while chasing their careers. They use much of their hard-earned money to pay other people to educate and influence their children. A couple of times a year, Mom and Dad hurriedly cart the children off to the grand experiences well-adjusted Americans are expected to have. The rest of the year life is a blur of required activities like work, school, soccer, band, camp, and on and on goes the list. Surely in the midst of all the hubbub, well-meaning moms and dads think that the time will come when they have finally achieved a sufficient financial status that will allow them to take time off with the spouse and the family to enjoy life. That utopia never seems to come.

Instead, the common result of the modern American lifestyle is for the children to grow up resenting the absence and distraction of their parents. Worse, the parents grow to resent each other for a number of reasons. One of the chief causes of spousal resentment is the fact that the modern husband and wife hardly know each other because they are so busy with their individual lives. That lack of attention opens the door to another serious cause of marital fractures—the attention experienced at work by a member of the opposite sex. So one of the parents becomes infatuated by a doting co-worker, the marriage breaks up, the children grow to despise both of the parents and grow up to live just like the people they claim they despise.

The foregoing scenario is not uncommon nor is it pleasant. A more positive description of the typical American family would be more palatable, but would it be fair? The facts seem to indicate otherwise. What is a couple to do? Is there hope for this dying institution called the American family? There certainly is. The Designer of the family, God, gave the family a wonderful "owner's manual" that teaches in clear detail all that is necessary for families to be successful according to His standard.

I have had the privilege, during the past twenty-five years of ministry, to counsel scores of young couples before they were married. Early in the process, I discovered that there are many clear and helpful principles in the Bible that map out a road to a successful family. These are tried and proven principles. Of course, God promised that all Scripture is profitable for teaching, reproving, correcting, and instructing in righteousness.

Therefore, one ought to expect that His Word would be profitable for husbands, wives, parents, and children who desire to live according to the way God designed them. I have come to expect the Bible principles to bring about successful families (according to God's standard of success) when the principles are put to work. Nevertheless, I always rejoice when I hear the testimonies of couples who are fast approaching middle age and who have practiced these Bible principles and have discovered that they really work.

This book is a compilation of the stories, truths, and principles the Lord has allowed me to teach to scores of couples. Each chapter is a principle aimed at husbands, or wives, or parents, or children. I pray that you will discover, along with many who have learned and practiced these things, that God's Word is true and profitable to equip His people for every good work. To have a remarkable family is one of the all-time good works.

PRINCIPLE 1
Get to know each other early in the marriage.

When a man is newly married, he shall not go out with the army or be liable for any other public duty. He shall be free at home one year to be happy with his wife whom he has taken. (Deuteronomy 24:5 ESV)

No one naturally likes rules. Rules infringe on our liberties. Rules say that I am not allowed to do what I really want to do, or they insist that I do what my flesh really abhors. For example, medical professionals establish guidelines for good health. One of those guidelines is "Refrain from consuming more than twenty grams of saturated fat in a day." That doesn't sound like a difficult rule to keep until you read the nutrition labels on the packages of all your favorite foods. Do you know how many grams of saturated fat are in good potato chips or a dozen cookies? And how much fat is in that fourteen-ounce sirloin steak?

Another rule for good health requires regular exercise. Many professionals recommend thirty minutes each day. It is difficult to get up in the morning and put forth that kind of effort—especially when your body wants to stay in bed. So we put off exercising until after work only to discover that we are too tired from working all day to exercise. As a result, the best laid plans to exercise fall by the wayside, and, instead of doing right, we sit down to watch television with a bag of potato chips and a half-dozen cookies. What could drive a reasonable person to do such a thing? He craves the chips and cookies to top off the sirloin steak he had for dinner. The next day the guy complains to his doctor that he is tired, lethargic, and unable to lose weight.

People who want to enjoy the rewards of good health must also be people who keep the rules. Some of those rules are simple and foundational. The foundational rules undergird other less important rules.

God's laws for the nation of Israel served a similar function. Many of those old laws are still useful for even non-Jewish people today. While it is true that Christ fulfilled the ceremonial sacrificial laws, many of the other laws still establish good principles for modern husbands and wives. Many of the civil laws in Moses' law code that address personal responsibility still make a lot of sense in a structured society. The laws about marriage are practical and useful. Indeed, societies that still apply God's common sense laws are often more stable and peaceful than societies that ignore His laws.

This is especially true regarding the family. Sinful human nature craves the freedom to do whatever it thinks will bring satisfaction. Sadly, once fulfilled, those desires seldom bring lasting joy. They almost always cause pain to everyone involved. It makes more sense for husbands and wives to exercise self-discipline and keep God's common sense rules about marriage. Like eating well and exercising, God's common sense rules about marriage are sometimes inconvenient to keep, but the result is well worth the effort.

One of those common sense rules is that when a young man marries a young woman, he should put aside all the distractions and responsibilities he possibly can in order for them to learn how they can be happy together. That sounds radical. Is it possible to apply such an archaic-sounding rule today? Does it really have good results? I would certainly think so since the God Who designed us told us that it is a good idea. Will it require discipline? Of course it will. But the value of the rule far exceeds the cost of implementing it. This is a rule that brings excellent health to the marriage relationship.

GOD ESTABLISHED SOME LAWS FOR THE SOCIAL WELL-BEING OF A NATION

Like it or not, all people groups must have laws governing relationships. This applies to every kind of gathering of people. It works for the children's tree house club and for the largest nation in history. Without governing laws, organizations degenerate into chaos. Governing laws are necessary because all people are infected with sin. Sin destroys. Therefore, rules are necessary to counteract the effects of sin. When Adam and Eve opened the door for sin to enter God's creation in the Garden of Eden, that sin disrupted all relationships (Genesis 3:8–13). Suddenly the two humans, who had enjoyed sweet fellowship with God, were now at odds with their

Creator. Eve blamed the serpent for the problem. Adam blamed God because He had given him Eve. Each one was quite sure that someone other than himself or herself was responsible for the big mess called sin.

The primary issue underlying sin is love of self above love of God and others. Because Satan loved himself foremost, he decided to exalt himself into God's place. Because Eve loved herself, she chose to eat fruit that appealed to the lust of her eye, the lust of her flesh, and her pride of life. But what about Adam? What motivated him to disobey God? Adam also loved himself, and maybe he didn't want to live with the pain of having a wife who knew more than he did. So he too sinned.

> **Wise husbands and wives acknowledge and obey God's rules.**

The problem of sin because of self-love has been an insidious part of the human race ever since the fall. Self-love still causes a man to do what he wants to do without regard for his wife's feelings or desires. Self-love still causes a wife to be selfish and controlling, expecting everything to be done according to her desires. Therefore, rules are necessary to govern relationships. Without rules, we will all do what we want to do, which results in hurting or neglecting others.

Governing rules alone are not a magical cure for sin's problems. Often a family, culture, or nation can have well-established rules, but the principles are ineffective because people ignore them. Ignored rules are valueless. God had to establish rules to govern family relationships because sin infects all husbands and all wives. Wise husbands and wives acknowledge and obey God's rules.

History indicates that all successful societies have had laws. The most ancient records available prove that cultures had laws as far back as history knows. Some records are dated as early as 2000 BC. For example the Laws of Eshnunna, which was in Mesopotamia, existed at the time of Jacob's birth. That was six hundred years before God gave His law to Moses. Likewise, the famous Code of Hammurabi is dated somewhere around 1900 BC, five hundred years before Moses. In fact, that law code is so similar to Moses' law that some scholars think that Moses plagiarized the ancient document and passed it off as God's law.

This was not the case. Simple logic dictates that good laws (regardless of when they were written) are rooted in God-given principles. People in every age in the past were familiar with God. God argued (according to

Romans 1) that He has revealed Himself and His way of governing in nature. The person who so desires can understand how to govern wisely by observing God's example. Furthermore, God has revealed His principles in individual's consciences (Romans 2). Therefore, it is not surprising that law codes that preceded Moses' law are very similar to what God required Moses to write.

Whether laws come directly from God or indirectly as wise men learn from God's self-manifestation, laws are necessary in order to protect people from extreme selfishness. Given enough room, natural selfishness becomes anarchy, which brings any society to a colossal failure.

Many of the ancient laws protected marital relationships. One of the statements in the Laws of Eshnunna says, "If [a man] takes the girl and she enters his house, but afterward the young woman should decease, the husband cannot obtain refunded that which he brought to his father-in-law." Another statement found further in the document says, "If a man calls at the house of his father-in-law, and his father-in-law accepts him in servitude, but nevertheless gives his daughter to another man, the father of the girl shall refund the bride-money which he received twofold." The Code of Hammurabi requires, "If the wife of a seignior [lord or noble] has been caught while lying with another man, they shall bind them and throw them into the water. If the husband of the woman wishes to spare his wife, then the king in turn may spare his subject."[1]

Those ancient marriage laws sound a lot like the law God gave to Moses: "If a man be found lying with a woman married to an husband, then they shall both of them die, both the man that lay with the woman, and the woman: so shalt thou put away evil from Israel" (Deuteronomy 22:22). The purpose of the ancient laws as well as God's law was to protect the marriage.

God, being the author of all good law, gave very specific rules for governing marital relationships, which are necessary because human nature tends to destroy relationships. In Israel the rules of common practice often stringently restrained typical human desires. As a result, the Israelite women had few privileges and many obligations. Sometimes a young woman's parents chose her husband for her. Naomi, though she was a mother-in-law and not a mother, ultimately chose Boaz to be Ruth's husband. King Saul clearly exercised this prerogative for his daughter Michal—twice!

In a similar way, parents often chose the brides for their sons. Abraham arranged the marriage of Isaac. Hagar chose a wife for Ishmael. Judah chose a wife for Ur. Sometimes the young man chose a wife himself, but the parents negotiated the deal. That is what the Canaanite Shechem did when he saw Jacob's daughter, Dinah. He was so smitten by her beauty that he knew it was God's will for him to marry her (Genesis 34:4). He begged his father to negotiate with Jacob for Dinah's hand in marriage. That story ended in disaster for Shechem and embarrassment for Jacob. Likewise, Samson, when he had fallen head over heels in lust with a Philistine girl, ordered his father to start negotiations with her father (Judges 14:2). In vivid contrast to this norm, Esau demonstrated rank rebellion when he married foreign wives against his parents' wishes (Genesis 26:34).

The common laws of the culture did not always bring about the best results. Nevertheless, good principles rooted in God's wisdom draw reasonable boundaries for the marriage relationship. God's principles are always good when His people practice them in wisdom.

God gave His guidelines so that His people would demonstrate proper relationships in the home. Therefore, it should be especially true that God's people demonstrate successful relationships. It is important for us to realize that the larger context of the many statements about God's law is always holiness. God gave His rules so that His people would be distinct from the rest of the people in the world. God explained when He gave the law that the purpose of His rules was to make His people holy. When God gave Moses His law on Mount Sinai, He said, "And ye shall be unto me a kingdom of priests, and an holy nation. These are the words which thou shalt speak unto the children of Israel" (Exodus 19:6). Holiness is the primary focus for God's principles regarding marriage.

Does it seem remarkable that this principle about happiness in the marriage (Deuteronomy 24:5) follows immediately the law regarding divorce (Deuteronomy 24:1–4)? Much has been made about this statement regarding divorce in God's law, both in Jesus' day and in our day. Actually the bulk of the divorce statement forbids a husband from remarrying a wife he previously had divorced. But that is seldom the focus in modern discussions of the text. In fact, the rest of the information in the statement is rather vague. Yet the vague and secondary statements are the point of confrontation in discussions. Jesus explained that the only reason God put this rule in His law was that people are stubborn and rebellious. We prove that He was right! It is discouraging to read recent surveys that indicate that divorce among Evangelicals matches or exceeds the rate among unchurched people. What does that say about us? If we are really God's people, we should be obviously distinct in such areas. Our statistics ought to be different. God has given a law that lays a solid foundation for marriage. When men lay this foundation with God's help, the marriage will likely weather those tempestuous storms that tend to wreck other marriages along the way.

THIS LAW CONTRIBUTES TO THE STRENGTH OF THE FAMILY

The law that a man should avoid as much distraction as possible the first year of marriage establishes a very simple rule that is simple to state but difficult to follow. According to God's law for His nation, the new husband was untouchable to society as a whole for a year. The authorities were not allowed to force the man to go to war during the first year of marriage. This was a very important prohibition in a culture where war was so predictable. Israel was a culture that went to war regularly.

The introduction to the tragic story of David and Bathsheba indicates how common war was in Israel: "In the spring of the year, the time when kings go out to battle, David sent Joab, and his servants with him, and all Israel. And they ravaged the Ammonites and besieged Rabbah. But David remained at Jerusalem" (2 Samuel 11:1 ESV). Apparently, war was an annual event for those people. The timing made sense. Because spring was after rainy season, the roads would be passable and the fields would provide plenty of fodder for animals. Nevertheless, war or no war, the officials were not allowed to force a husband to do any public service during the first year of marriage.

It makes sense not to send a bride's new husband off to war where he might well be killed before they had hardly finished the honeymoon. However, the law also protected the new husband from any public duty for a year. What more could authorities expect of the young husband? A statement about King Solomon's reign helps us see the problem: "The account of the forced labor that King Solomon drafted to build the house of the LORD and his own house and the Millo and the wall of Jerusalem and Hazor and Megiddo and Gezer" (1 Kings 9:15 ESV). Obviously, the king was allowed to conscript young husbands to build a temple, to build a palace, to build supporting terraces (i.e., Millo), to build a wall, or to build two cities but not during the first year of his marriage. He was untouchable to the society.

This common sense principle should still be practiced by new husbands today as much as it is practically possible. Husbands should make themselves untouchable for a year after they marry. A new bridegroom is wise to make himself unavailable for extracurricular stuff. Hanging out with the "buds" must quickly become something in the past. A

> **Husbands should make themselves untouchable for a year after they marry.**

new husband has a new "bud," who needs as much time as he can possibly give her. This is why continuing education makes me uneasy. Most of the young couples I marry plan for the husband, if not both the husband and wife, to continue their college education. It is hard to make this principle work in such cases. But it can work. It must work!

A new bridegroom needs to make himself off-limits during the first year of marriage so that he can establish a foundation of happiness for the marriage. The common interpretation "that he should learn how to make his wife happy" is a fair interpretation of the original Hebrew. A man is required to spend as much time as possible learning how to make his new bride happy. Why is this so necessary?

The groom needs to understand that he has just taken a young woman away from the only male authority figure she has known. Generally, the girl has probably lived under Dad's authority for twenty years or more. During that long period of time, she had learned how to be happy in her circumstances. When she stands before witnesses dressed as a beautiful bride and says, "I do," everything changes rapidly. Suddenly she needs to learn to be happy with a new male authority figure.

In spite of the fact that the young man might have courted the young woman for many days, he really does not know her. He must learn about her emotional cycle. He must learn what makes her sad and what makes her laugh. God wants the husband to bring joy to the bride. How can the young man learn this important truth? It does not happen in a few minutes, and it surely is not something he can learn by watching ESPN.

The only way for the new husband to learn critical truths about his new wife is by spending time with her. Spending time together does not just happen. It requires the man to discipline himself to block out chunks of time from his calendar. Each husband has twenty-four hours allotted to him each day. We are all alike in that sense. No one gets more than the other guy. In that amount of time, the new husband must maintain his normal job (most cannot take a year's vacation) and still have time to learn about his wife. The fellow will need to mark out special time on the calendar each day and each week learning how to make his wife happy.

Why is her happiness so important? Is the T-shirt accurate when it says, "If momma isn't happy, no one is happy"? No. The reason a man must spend time learning how to make his wife happy is that God commanded it.

A possible alternative translation of this text can require that the man spend much time with his wife in order for him to learn how he can be happy with his wife. Essentially, that says the same thing as the previous option. There is no doubt that God commands the husband to be happy with his wife. Solomon told his son, "Let thy fountain be blessed: and rejoice with the wife of thy youth" (Proverbs 5:18). This is not a recommendation but a command. So is the command of this text. Husbands must learn how to be happy with their wives. It means that the man will need to adjust his likes and dislikes. It means that he must be willing to change. The world says, "Don't let the woman change you." God says, "You must be willing to learn how to be happy with her."

It takes time to learn how to do this. Lots of it. Time is a precious commodity much like money. We all get the same amount. Life is like a game of Monopoly; at the beginning each player is given the same amount of money, and he or she must budget it wisely. In the game of life, we each receive twenty-four hours each day, seven days each week, three hundred sixty-five days each year. The wise husband budgets his time wisely. He takes much time to learn how to be happy with his wife.

Knowing good governing principles is not the same as practicing good governing principles. Common sense dictates that this is a good principle. However, only the husband who spends time learning how to make his wife happy and how to be happy with his wife will enjoy the results of the principle.

PUT IT TO WORK

1. How much time do you (husband) reserve each month specifically for your wife?

2. Do you (wife) think that it would be impossible for your husband to make you happy?

3. What simple things does it take for you (husband) to please your wife?

4. Have you learned how to be happy with your wife?

5. How many years do you think a man and wife could be married before it is too late for them to learn this principle?

PRINCIPLE 2
God's plan requires single units.

Then the man said, "This at last is bone of my bones and flesh of my flesh; she shall be called Woman, because she was taken out of Man." Therefore a man shall leave his father and his mother and hold fast to his wife, and they shall become one flesh. (Genesis 2:23–24 ESV)

The institution called "family" is under attack. Why it is under attack can be debated. The certainty of attack is obvious in too many areas to allow for denial. One of the clearest fronts of attack is Hollywood. For several years the movers and shakers in Hollywood have produced a steady stream of sitcoms that assail the traditional family from every vantage point imaginable. Way back in the sixties, the kind and folksy family of Sheriff Andy Taylor was presented as typical. The family consisted of the matronly Aunt Bea, who served as matriarch of the home, her nephew Andy, and his son, Opie. Did families like that exist in the mid-twentieth century? Of course. Is that the ideal pattern according to God's Word? No.

Then there were the Beverly Hillbillies. This family from the Ozark Mountains struck it rich when they discovered oil on their land. The whole family moved to Beverly Hills, California. The family consisted of Uncle Jed, Granny, Elly May, and Jethro. Many people watched every episode of this sitcom without realizing that this was a dysfunctional family. Jedediah Clampett was the patriarch. He lived with his mother-in-law, "Granny," his daughter, Elly May, and his cousin's son, Jethro Bodine. Were they related? Yep. Did the family illustrate God's plan for the family? Nope.

These two examples are some of the most family-friendly sitcoms available. Since the midsixties, things in Hollywood have deteriorated to a point that was unimaginable by innocent folks who fed their minds with the antics of dysfunctional families in black and white a generation ago. Now the typical presentation of families is young couples living together out of wedlock, homosexuals cohabiting, lesbians with children, single moms trying to rear rebellious children, and transvestites who wonder why Christians are so weird. Do relationships like this exist in our culture? Sure. Are such relationships the kind of family God describes in the Bible? Not even close!

Hollywood is not the only pawn Satan uses in attacking the family. The family has been assaulted for generations in cultures where wives are considered no better than chattel. Societies and religions that allow or encourage a man to have multiple wives assail God's norm for the family. Cultures that allow easy divorce and encourage it wreak havoc on families. Societies that refuse to outlaw the free display and participation in sexuality contribute to the destruction of families.

But probably the most vicious attack against the family, and yet not perceived as an assault, is the teaching of evolution. If the various theories of evolution were true, there would be no Creator God. If there is no Creator God, He did not create man and woman to be the first family. If God did not establish the family and its governing principles, then we are free to define family any way we choose. Because God's enemies determined fifty years ago that the theory of evolution was true and must be taught to every malleable mind in the school system, they can now build on the foundation of error they laid. Now unregenerate leaders think they are free to define a family as any people (will it also include animals?) who choose to live together. As a result, cities across America are grappling with the definition of family. Does the Constitution allow the owner of rental property to evict six people who are living in an apartment because they are not related and, therefore, not a family?

The further we move away from the standard of God's Word, the more unnecessary problems we cause ourselves. God's Word clearly states that God created the family, it tells us why He created the family, and it tells us how we should respond to His institution of the family. To deny God's creative act opens a Pandora's box of family problems.

A MAN NEEDS A HELPER (Genesis 2:18-23)

It was obvious from the beginning that man should not live alone (vv. 18–20). God's creation was good, but it was not complete without woman (v. 18). This was not man's finding after several years of research made possible by a grant of several million dollars from the government. Adam, in all his perfection, did not come to this conclusion on his own and then inform God that He had made a mistake in creation. God determined that it was not good for man to be alone.

But didn't God already say that everything about His creation was very good (1:31)? This apparent contradiction might be cleared up by viewing the statements in the opening chapters of Genesis as a nonchronological account. For example, in 1:27 Moses wrote that God made both man and woman within the six-day period of creation. That would make the statements here in Genesis 2 an expansion of the details of the creation. Or maybe the statement in 1:27 was just a reference to God's plan to make man and woman—a fact that He carried out after the sixth day.

Did the "aloneness" of man detract from the "very goodness" of creation? No. It is possible to interpret the word *good* in verse 18 (the same Hebrew word as in 1:31) to refer to completeness. The creation was good, but the idea of man living alone left a sense of incompleteness. Did God decide in light of the evidence that He should have made a mate for man? No. The creation of woman was part of God's overall plan from the outset. Man's being alone did not fit with the rest of God's plan for man. God planned all along to make a mate for Adam because He created man to be a communicator, to engage in interaction, and to be a communal creature. God created man with the capacity to reproduce after his kind like the rest of creation. That would be impossible without a mate.

Therefore, God determined to make a suitable helper for the man. The word translated "helper" comes from the similar word that often speaks, in a military sense, of an ally or someone to come alongside and help. God planned to create a support for Adam, but God did not plan only to make a helper. God chose to make a helper like man (this is the word *suitable*). The woman would be a helper that would be similar to man, yet different in many ways. God intended for woman to be a helper that would complement man. He created her to be a helper that provides what man lacks—especially after the fall. In light of God's intent to complement the man with the woman, if a husband and wife are exactly alike in everything, one of them is unnecessary. Maybe this is why some people conclude that opposites attract. Differences in some things are necessary in order to maintain balance.

The rest of creation attested to man's need for companionship (vv. 19–20). God caused all the animals He had created to go to Adam. Through intuitive knowledge, Adam named each of them. I cannot help but wonder if while Adam was naming all the animals he realized that they had mates and he did not. Maybe God required this exercise by Adam to help him realize his need of a mate.

According to God's plan, He created the perfect counterpart for man (vv. 21–23). The text states that God created woman from the side of man (vv. 21–22). Granted, most English translations say that God created woman from the man's rib, but *rib* is a translation too restrictive. The Hebrew word occurs thirty-three times in the Old Testament, and it almost always speaks of a side or a side room. Some strange legends have resulted from translating this Hebrew word *rib* in this one instance in the Old Testament. Some people have claimed that men have one less rib than women. That kind of thinking does damage to God's Word.

> If a husband and wife are exactly alike in everything, one of them is unnecessary.

Furthermore, to translate the Hebrew word with the more common translation of side includes flesh and bones. When God introduced the woman to Adam, he concluded right away that she shared his flesh and bone. While God made every other beast from dust of the ground (2:19), He made woman from the flesh and bone of man. He took her from man's side to show her equality with Him.

He did not take her from man's head so that she would rule over man. He did not take her from man's feet so that he would tread upon her. The creation of woman makes her complementary to the man.

The first man, Adam, certainly understood God's blessing to him through the creation of woman (v. 23). God introduced the woman to man once he awakened from the surgery (v. 22*b*). Immediately upon seeing the woman, Adam exclaimed how complementary she was. She was quite unlike the animals he had just named. This suitable helper was of the same stuff he was made of. She had a body like his. She was his flesh and his bone. This is a significant conclusion in light of the New Testament admonition for the husband to love his wife like he loves himself. God requires, "So ought men to love their wives as their own bodies. He that loveth his wife loveth himself" (Ephesians 5:28). This text reminds the reader that it is natural for men to care for themselves. They should also care for the one who is like them.

The creation of the suitable helper was God's plan. He did it on purpose. The husband/wife relationship flows out of His purposes. Humanity's fall into sin changed mankind's natural desires and responses. Sometimes God permitted a man to live alone, that is without female companionship, such as Paul's case (1 Corinthians 7:7). God also permitted divorce in His law because of the effects of sin. But His original plan for the family He created was for a husband to take a wife and they would hold fast to each other.

A MAN NEEDS TO HOLD FAST TO HIS HELPER (2:24-25)

God's principle is that since God made a partner for the man, the man must leave his parents and hold fast to his wife (v. 24a). This principle of separation from parents is necessary for the health of the new union. However, we must wonder who Adam's parents were. This was a prophetic statement in context because Adam did not have a mother and father to leave. Moses wrote the book of Genesis under the inspiration of the Holy Spirit. While most of the book is historical, this principle had to be a precept that conveys God's plan for the entire history of mankind. In practical terms, the next generation, Cain and Abel, needed to take a wife and leave Adam and Eve.

The idea behind the separation principle is that a new husband/wife unit should separate from the old husband/wife unit. Of course that was also the father/mother unit. In the old unit, the husband lived under the authority of his father and mother. In the new unit, the husband must become the head of his house. He cannot live under dad's authority any longer. In the old unit, the young woman was under the direct authority of her father. In the new unit, the father's authority is exchanged for her husband's authority. More often than not, the problems that arise in this area are from parents who do not want their children to become independent units. Doting mothers seek to keep their sons under their care and protection. Fathers refuse to give their daughters in marriage, though they publicly proclaim that is what they are doing.

I have often wondered how difficult it must be for a father to stand in the presence of God and of multiplied human witnesses and literally give his daughter away. After twenty-plus years of pouring his life into this beautiful, fragile, dependent girl, he just gives her to this immature, nonthinking, hormone-driven boy. I have a friend who tells the story of standing in the side room with his future father-in-law moments before his wedding ceremony. The father-in-law-to-be turned to the young man and said, "Ron, I feel just like a man who is about to hand his Stradivarius violin to a gorilla." Being the father of three sons, I have never had to agonize about that decision. But fathers and mothers must make the decision to give away their children as the children create a new unit. The parents must insist that the new unit practice this principle.

It is also possible that some children do not want to grow up and become the leaders of their homes. Sometimes they find it easy to resort to the old leaders (mom and dad) and get some more of the pampering they miss so much. Frankly, there are times when evil children play their parents for fools and bleed them for all the attention and financial help they can. Shame on parents and children alike when that happens.

Many parents do not understand that their insistent desire to keep things as they have been destroys the new couple's ability to become one. When a person interferes with God's plan, the result is trouble. The trouble such disobedience brings is not at all worth the cost.

This "holding fast" principle is a key requirement for the union. The term *hold fast* means to cling to something or, in this case, to cling to each other. It is a word that also describes the welding process that is common in our age. After a craftsman has welded two pieces of metal together, it is almost impossible to break them apart, if the welder did a sufficient job. That welded piece of metal illustrates God's plan for the man and wife. They who were once two unique individuals have become one.

In fact, God's plan is for the man and the woman to become one flesh as husband and wife (vv. 24b–25). That means that they will be completely and thoroughly identified with each other (v. 24b). It is God's plan for the husband and wife to become united in body and soul. Some people teach that the uniting actually takes place during the sexual consummation of the marriage. That may be so, but becoming one involves more than just the flesh. A husband and his wife should become so much alike that their similarities eclipse the old similarities they once shared with their natural family members. This means that young couples will develop their own traditions and ideas, which might not be the same as those their parents taught them. That is a good thing. It is proof that their single union is working. It is evidence of the individuals' dissolving into the one unit.

God's plan is for the man and woman to become indissolubly united. When a carpenter needs a wide board, he typically glues two or three narrow boards together. When I was building kitchen cabinets, I glued two boards together to make a door. A couple of days later, I realized that the two boards were too wide and decided that if I broke the seam where I had glued them together, one board would be sufficient. When I broke the seam, the grains in the two boards had become so tightly bonded that the two boards splintered leaving part of one with the other. That is what divorce does. It rips part of the person's being away because the couple had become one.

The last verse of this passage pictures the new husband and wife with a clear conscience about their union (v. 25). They were naked, but they did not have any shame. It is sad that many people in our culture become more and more naked in public, and they have no apparent shame because they have seared their consciences. In paradise, nakedness caused no guilt because there was no sin.

This pictures God's standard for the man and wife who have become one flesh. Their relationship is supposed to be pure, leaving them with a perfect conscience. Our culture has moved so far away from God's plan for the family that it is almost impossible to imagine this standard. The "traditional" family is in the minority in America. That does not mean that God has changed His plan or His standard. He created the family unit. He stipulated that one husband should be committed for life to one wife. He determined that such unions should be indissolubly meshed. The result is a clear conscience before God. A clear conscience brings God's peace. God's peace in a family is worth the effort it takes to keep it.

How many people among our peers actually believe that God created man and woman and, therefore, the family? Do you believe that God created the husband and wife to be indissolubly united? If so, how will you teach that truth to your children? The next generation in America will be more perverse in their thinking than this generation unless God brings a miraculous revival. How will your children respond to the pressure? Will they confidently assert that God is the Creator, that as the Creator He has a plan for the man and the woman, that His plan calls for the family to be at least one man with one woman and often children from that union? They will only if parents confidently teach that this is God's plan.

PUT IT TO WORK

1. Do you believe that God created all things including humans?

2. Did God create the family or did it evolve as a necessary process?

3. Since God created the family by making a suitable helper for Adam, what purpose did He have in mind?

4. What does divorce do to God's plan for the family?

5. Did your parents really allow you to leave them and create a new unit by cleaving to your spouse?

PRINCIPLE 3
A wife will have a natural desire to usurp her husband's authority.

To the woman he said, "I will surely multiply your pain in childbearing; in pain you shall bring forth children. Your desire shall be for your husband, and he shall rule over you." (Genesis 3:16 ESV)

I n her first official speech as Speaker of the House, Nancy Pelosi pointed out that she had just broken the marble ceiling. That was a reference to the fact that she is the first female Speaker of the House in our nation's history. Her ascendancy to that high office is viewed as a major accomplishment by people who struggle with a perceived inequality between male and female workers and professionals in almost every venue of American or world culture. These same people look forward to having someone like Hillary Clinton become the first female president of the United States.

Is this a bad thing? Not necessarily. A couple of decades ago "Maggie the Iron Lady," Margaret Thatcher, achieved the highest pinnacle of government in Great Britain (apart from the queen) when she was elected prime minister. Thatcher proved to be a very capable leader. She was well qualified, just, wise, and staunch in her conservative beliefs. It is one thing to promote a woman to a position of authority just because she is a woman and something quite different to have a woman in authority because she is qualified for the position.

Who determines if any particular woman is qualified to serve in any given position of authority? In a democracy, the citizens are supposed to be responsible to express their desires through the electoral process. If the majority of the people want a woman to be the president of our nation, so be it. Let's just pray that she is a qualified leader. In a business or company, the board of directors, administrators, or owners make that decision. In an educational venue, such a decision is the responsibility of the school board, executive board, principal, or president. In the family, who decides whether the man or the woman should be the chief authority?

Who indeed makes this judgment? Does society decide? Maybe we should abide by the law of the Wild West and let the fastest gun rule. Of course, in the family it would be the fastest talker or the fastest thinker. Maybe we should not have an authority in families but let the husband and wife rule equally. Maybe we should allow authority on a rotating basis. The wife can be in charge this week, and the husband can be in charge next week.

This postmodern, post-Christian culture of America is quite sure that the idea of a man, that is the husband, ruling in a position of authority is archaic at best. Try proposing that idea at the local PTA meeting, and you will be howled out of the meeting. People of the modern age are quite sure that such male-dominance thinking died along with the dinosaurs. The feminist movement, which caught fire in the mid-1960s in America, has clearly drawn the lines of battle. They have made it quite clear that women and men are equal. Their idea of equality is that woman should compete for man's position in business, education, sports, and especially in the family. They really do believe that it is good for the wife to go out into the career arena and fight with men for dominance while their husband stays home and cleans the house and watches the children or the television. What a crazy, mixed-up world this modern age has become.

Actually, the ideas of modern feminism have been around for a long time. Twentieth-century America was not the first society to incubate these ideas. Many cultures throughout history have struggled with the equality or inequality of man's and woman's authority. In fact, the whole conflict goes back to the Garden of Eden—which modern thinkers relegate to the same shelf as Mother Goose and Aesop's Fables. However, it is very interesting that the problem with family authority that developed in Eden— according to the Bible—is alive and well today. Husbands and wives still struggle with the promise that the Creator God made because Eve and Adam chose to sin against Him. In response to Eve's choice to sin, God warned the woman that she would struggle with the desire to usurp her husband's authority.

SIN CHANGED EVERYTHING (2:25-3:19)

God finished creating all things and then pronounced His work good. But in time (how much time we do not know) things changed. Sin brought the knowledge of good and evil (2:25–3:13), and suddenly nothing was the same in God's creation. Originally man and woman were innocent (2:25). The statement at the end of the creation story, that the man and woman were naked, says more than first meets the eye. The eternal Word of God could have pointed out hundreds of other characteristics about the circumstances in the garden or about the man and the woman. However, nakedness speaks of innocence, or maybe even pure naiveté. It was a good thing. Before sin barged into God's perfect family, the husband and wife were as innocent and naive as newborns. As far as we can tell, babies do not have opinions about human nakedness. Adults do. Adults know that public nakedness is not acceptable. We are experienced regarding good and evil, and public nakedness qualifies for evil, not good. Before sin ruined God's perfect creation, nakedness caused no shame. It was not evil. That was before.

When the first humans opened the door for sin, the sin caused them to experience evil. The story points out in the first verse of chapter 3 that the source of evil is Satan. He was the first of God's created beings to decide to take God's place of authority (Isaiah 14:14). He was motivated in this dastardly deed by love of self. God judged Satan's wicked devices by relegating him to the earth sphere. Therefore, it is not surprising that this same being, apparently, indwelt a serpent and tempted the woman with the same kind of self-love to which he had yielded (Genesis 3:1).

Satan led the woman down the path of destruction by questioning the authority of God's Word: "Did God actually say . . . ?" (v. 1*b*). As if it was not bad enough to question the authority of God's Word, the next phrase out of the serpent's mouth was a direct contradiction of God's Word (v. 4). God had warned Adam and Eve that if they disobeyed, they would surely die. Satan said, "Ye shall not surely die." Finally, the deceiver closed the deal when he told the truth about God's plan (v. 5). He informed the woman, "Your eyes shall be opened, and ye shall be as gods, knowing good and evil." Notice that this was a direct appeal to her self-love.

The sad news in the last part of verse 6 is that the woman and man fell into sin. She ate the forbidden fruit and was marred by sin (v. 6*b*). Then she gave the same fruit to her husband, and he submitted to her leadership and ate (v. 6*b*). Immediately, they both understood good and evil. After the fall, the confrontation, and the explanation of curses, "the Lord God said, Behold, the man is become as one of us, to know good and evil" (Genesis 3:22). That was not a compliment. The fact that the man and woman had experienced the difference between good and evil is obvious. Now they knew they were naked (v. 7). The innocence was gone. Now the beings God had created to fellowship with Him hid from Him. They no longer wanted God's company because they were aware of their offense against Him (v. 8). Now they feared retribution instead of enjoying the peace and confidence they had known in innocence (v. 10).

Probably the most obvious demonstration of the human's knowledge of good and evil is the fact that when God confronted them about their failure, they blamed others for their choices (vv. 12–13). The man virtually blamed God for giving him Eve (v. 12). The woman blamed the serpent (v. 13). No one stepped up to the Judge and said, "I am guilty, Sir. I chose to offend You." No, because they lost their innocence, they concluded that their sin was someone else's fault. Suddenly, every relationship faltered. The serpent offended the woman, the woman despised the serpent, and the man blamed God and his wife. In a perfect environment, relationships naturally succeed. In an environment tainted by sin (i.e., your family), relationships will fail unless they are hedged about by the firm structure and discipline of God's corrective Word. In a perfect environment, equality thrives as the norm. In an environment swamped by sin, equality must be artificially enforced because self-love precludes it.

Worse than broken relationships is the fact that sin brought God's curse on His own creation (vv. 14–19). Sin marred even the animal life (v. 14). No one can fully explain the extent of the serpent's concession in this scenario, but in His infinite wisdom God cursed the snake to slither on its stomach and eat dirt. The snake is still despised by most people due to God's curse. That part of the curse is still valid—still functioning.

> When the first humans opened the door for sin, the sin caused them to experience evil.

Second, sin marred all natural processes. Because Eve opened the door for sin to enter Paradise, God promised that woman's pain and sorrow would be multiplied in childbearing (v. 16*a*). Is this an indication that there would have been little pain while giving birth to a child in Paradise? It would seem that Paradise would be completely pain free in every circumstance of life. However, this statement is broader than a reference only to the pain a woman experiences in the process of delivering a baby. The word *pain* occurs twice in this single verse (v. 16). Both times the Hebrew word is the same root word and speaks of toil, pain, and/or sorrow. In other words, God's curse included the whole process of motherhood. From pregnancy, through childhood, through the teen years, and beyond, there is sorrow and pain connected with being a mother. What woman has not experienced pain and sorrow because of her children's failures (great or small)? The mother definitely has pain in the birthing process, but after that the mother gives her heart to her child in love. Because of the sin principle, the child, sometimes purposely, often inadvertently, breaks mother's heart with sorrow many times along the way. God's curse is still alive and well.

Even the ground shows the effects of the curse (vv. 17–19). Through toil, labor, sweat, and pain, we produce crops from ground that is naturally prone to grow weeds. The labor principle is still in effect. God still expects the human race to survive through work. That is precisely why natural man does all he possibly can to get around the principle. Paul's letter to the Thessalonians reveals that this is a problem even with people who claim to be followers of Christ. He warned, "For even when we were with you, this we commanded you, that if any would not work, neither should he eat" (2 Thessalonians 3:10). We must work against relentless odds because the earth is subject to sin's curse. No wonder the entire race joins all creation as it groans looking forward to the removal of sin's curse! Paul reminded the Roman Christians, "We know that the whole creation has been groaning together in the pains of childbirth until now. And not only the creation, but we ourselves, who have the firstfruits of the Spirit, groan inwardly as we wait eagerly for adoption as sons, the redemption of our bodies" (Romans 8:22–23 ESV). Every Monday morning most people are very aware that this curse is still in effect.

Sin also created the need for the Redeemer, according to verse 15. God promised that He would provide the Redeemer, Who would be born of woman but not of man (i.e., the seed of the woman). God also promised that the Redeemer would deal a fatal blow to Satan and his work. This part of the promise, unlike the continuing curse, has already been fulfilled on the cross.

Since every other aspect of God's promise and curse in response to creation being thrust into sin is true, surely the promise of the authority struggle is true also.

SIN CREATED THE NEED FOR AN AUTHORITY STRUCTURE (3:16)

One more result of sin in creation is that it was necessary for God to establish the authority structure for the family. Again, in a perfect world, no authority structure would be necessary in the family because husband, wife, and children would all do the right thing all the time, but this is not a perfect world. We live in a sin-struck world where God promised that the wife's desire will be toward her husband. Is that part of the curse? God's promise that the woman's desire will be toward her husband actually sounds pretty good to human wisdom. What husband would not appreciate his wife's desire? The Hebrew word translated "desire" literally means running toward or about. It speaks of a strong desire that can be good or bad. The word is used three times in the Old Testament. Solomon employed the word in Song of Solomon 7:10, where the bride confessed, "I am my beloved's, and his desire is toward me." In that context, the word must refer to a strong, passionate desire. That is a good thing because it comes within the marriage context and talks about the groom's desire for his bride.

The word appears again shortly after the text we are presently considering. In Genesis 4:7 God warned Cain, "If you do well, will you not be accepted? And if you do not do well, sin is crouching at the door. Its desire is for you, but you must rule over it" (ESV). Here the warning is that sin strongly desires to destroy us. It is crouching like a beast to take people unawares. Therefore, the desire in this case is bad because it speaks of failure and horrible consequences.

Now in verse 16 of this text we must decide if the wife's desire for her husband is good or bad. It would be nice if it were positive. What husband would not want a wife who desires him? But since God gave the promise within the context of sin and His curse on sin, it must be bad. Some scholars believe that God promised here that the wife will desire her husband, but he will not respond well. Instead he will rule over her. That is a possibility. But again, that sounds more like a blessing for the wife and the husband than a curse for the woman. The more probable interpretation is that, because of sin, the wife will desire her husband's position of authority. The pain of the curse lies in the fact that, though the wife desires her

God promised that the husband will rule over the wife because it is His plan for orderliness in the family.

husband's position, God has ordained that the husband will rule over her. Obviously, that is a frustrating situation for the wife.

How much latitude is in the promise that the husband will rule over the wife? Sometimes this promise is taken to an extreme, which causes untold suffering for women. This is true in cultures where men despise women, own them, take multiple wives, and generally treat women as if they were a piece of property. It is also true that the concept of "rule" is abused in more refined cultures like our own. Who does not know of a case where a husband claims this verse allows him to act like a tyrant?

God promised that the husband will rule over the wife because it is His plan for orderliness in the family. He put the husband in charge. It was God's plan, not the manipulations of an insecure bully. Paul explained God's plan when he told the Corinthians, "But I would have you know, that the head of every man is Christ; and the head of the woman is the man; and the head of Christ is God" (1 Corinthians 11:3). Since that is true, it must also be true that God expects the wife to submit to the husband, whom He put in charge over her and the family. Indeed, Paul instructed wives to "submit yourselves unto your own husbands, as unto the Lord" (Ephesians 5:22). When a husband rules like Christ, it is easy for the wife to respond appropriately.

The promise is clear. However, the application escapes us too often. Very simply, this text warns God's people that a wife has the natural desire to usurp her husband's position of authority. In real life, it is true that a wife is often wiser than her husband. Even if she is not wiser than her husband, it is inevitable that there will be occasions (sometimes frequently) when the husband does not make the best decisions. At such times the wife's natural desire for usurping the husband's authority becomes almost uncontrollable.

In other cases, it is possible that a wife is very gifted or skilled in various or many ways. She has multiple talents and her husband is a bit of a klutz or dolt. It is difficult for a woman in such circumstances to cheerfully, willingly press down the desire to rule that explodes in her innermost being. Wives in situations like this must always be aware of this natural desire to supplant their husbands' position. It is very easy for women in those scenarios to simply take over and be quite confident that they can do a better job. But that is not God's plan.

Probably a more common problem in our circles is that of a wife who unintentionally turns the marriage on its head. She is just naturally a take-charge person. She is very confident and, therefore, sure that she fully understands what needs to be done and knows the best way to do it. She errantly believes that her opinion is the only one that matters. Incompetence frustrates her, and she is unwilling to allow anything to be left undone. As a result, she usurps her husband's ruling and all the while is convinced that she is doing the family a favor.

Then there is the wife who is in a rut of criticizing. She would not confess that she wants her husband's position of ruling. She just wants to tell him—all the time—how he is failing to fulfill his position of leadership successfully. This wife regularly points out her husband's errors. He must be wrong because he is not performing the way she would if she were given the chance. She errantly believes that her way is not only the best way but the only way.

Another subtle way for a wife to usurp her husband's ruling is to always offer an alternative to whatever he suggests or recommends. In this case, the husband makes a recommendation and, without thinking, the wife responds with an alternative. If she does this on occasion, it is hardly noticed. When this becomes a habit, the family structure is strained. This kind of wife doesn't recognize that her self-love causes her to resist her husband's leadership. This simple expression of her desire to have her husband's position forces him to concede rather than compete with his wife day after day. Eventually he will stop making recommendations at home and concede leadership to the wife. He can lead at work, where his subordinates respect his opinion, so why fight the issue at home? Finally, in order to avoid criticism, he learns that it is best to make no decisions at home or to do very little at home. He prefers to be with the guys (or worse) because they don't criticize him. This beat-down husband hands the reins of leadership over to his take-charge wife because it really is too much work to lead anyway. "If she wants to be in charge, let her," he concludes.

The family is left standing on its head. No one can figure out why there always seems to be tension in the home. No one realizes that the children are learning a perversion of God's plan every day. The root problem is simply that either the wife refuses to acknowledge God's promise about this desire or she refuses to bring her natural desire under control. Is it that important to control the desire? What happens when a woman refuses to bring her natural desire to eat under control? What happens when a man refuses to bring his natural desire to have sex under control? In most cases it is important to control natural desires. Yes, it is very important for the wife to keep this desire under subjection.

At this point women might wonder, "Why was I born a woman?" God has incredibly great and enjoyable plans for the wife as future chapters will reveal. In light of this text, it is important for wives to consider if they really do have a natural desire to usurp their husband's authority. Do you understand why this desire exists? The best solution to the problem is to identify it and then ask God to help you control the desire.

PUT IT TO WORK

1. Why do wives naturally desire to usurp their husband's authority?

2. Have you ever experienced this problem?

3. How does your husband respond when you overrule him?

4. Husband, are you able to help your wife recognize this natural desire?

5. Wives, what do you plan to do to control this desire?

PRINCIPLE 4
The husband must rejoice in the wife of his youth.

Let your fountain be blessed, and rejoice in the wife of your youth.
(Proverbs 5:18 ESV)

According to the 2000 census, there are currently about 9.7 million Americans living with an unmarried different-sex partner. "Forty-one percent of American women ages fifteen to forty-four have cohabited (lived with an unmarried different-sex partner) at some point. This includes 9% of women ages 15–19, 38% of women ages 20–24, 49% of women ages 25–29, 51% of women ages 30–34, 50% of women ages 35–39, and 43% of women ages 40–44."[1] The number of unmarried couples living together increased 72% between 1990 and 2000.[2] The number of unmarried couples living together has increased tenfold between 1960 and 2000.[3]

In the light of such statistics it is not surprising that polyamory is a popular topic of discussion and a common lifestyle in the younger generation. According to an article from the Alternatives to Marriage Project,

> Polyamory means different things to different people . . . but it generally involves honest, responsible non-monogamous relationships. This could take the form of an 'open' relationship, or a group of three or more adults who are 'monogamous' within their group (sometimes called polyfidelity), or a limitless set of other situations. The word *polyamory* means 'many loves' [poly = many + amor = love]. Many people who are exploring polyamory also have an interest in alternatives

to marriage. Some poly people choose not to marry because they feel marriage comes with an assumption of monogamy. . . . Some poly people are married, but consider their relationship to be an 'alternative to marriage.' Polyamory isn't right for everyone. Most people in unmarried relationships want to be monogamous. Among unmarried couples who are living together, 95% say they expect monogamy from their partner, and the percentage for married couples is only a few points higher.[4]

Does our culture have a problem? Yes, and it is about as easy to ignore as a tumor the size of a grapefruit on your forehead. We have a serious problem. Such a low view of marriage stems from a low view of God's Word. God explained His plan like this: "Therefore a man shall leave his father and his mother and hold fast to his wife, and they shall become one flesh" (Genesis 2:24 ESV). That seems simple enough—unless there is no God! What if that standard was just made up by ancient men who did not have the privilege of modern thinking? That is precisely what the theory of evolution teaches. That theory has taught two generations that there is no God; therefore, there is no standard for marriage or the family. No one should be surprised that cohabitation is the most popular lifestyle for adults under the age of forty.

However, the problem goes back many years before the world ever heard of a man named Darwin. Solomon, to whom God had given an unusual measure of wisdom, had 700 wives and 300 concubines. That amounted to 999 women outside God's will. Probably the Shulamite, whom Solomon described with beautiful phrases that gush with love and romance in the Song of Solomon, was his first wife and the one to fulfill God's plan for him according to Genesis 2:24. How did the man with so much wisdom drift so far from his moorings?

At some point in his life, Solomon warned his own son not to follow his path of folly. Ecclesiastes, Solomon's musings at the end of his life, proves that he learned how stupid it was for him to allow his desires to run wild. The words of this text ring true even though Solomon chose to live contrary to his own advice. Indeed, they ring true and prove that Solomon was foolish to ignore his own advice. A wise husband will take heed to this teaching and learn to be satisfied with his own wife.

BE INTOXICATED WITH YOUR WIFE'S LOVE (Proverbs 5:15-19)

God's solution to America's problem is for husbands to drink water from their own cisterns (vv. 15–17). While the command sounds odd to the ears of a twenty-first-century American man, it made perfect sense to husbands in Solomon's day. In that day only privileged men owned a cistern (v. 15). It was his family's supply of water. Water is a chief theme in this passage as the repeated terms *cistern, well, streams,* and *fountain* indicate. No one would argue that water is not an important necessity in anyone's life. Water is naturally satisfying.

The central issue in this command has to do with a natural impulse or natural desire. What could be more natural than a man's physical desire for a woman? God gave that natural desire to men. More than that, God ordained the desire for His own glory. However, God never gets glory when men allow that natural desire to run wild or unchecked. He who gave us the desire for a physical and emotional relationship with a woman also expects us to govern the desire carefully. His rule is simply "Let marriage be held in honor among all, and let the marriage bed be undefiled, for God will judge the sexually immoral and adulterous" (Hebrews 13:4 ESV).

God is very serious about the proper use or directing of this natural desire. We who own the natural desire must be sure to manage it and govern it or it will destroy us. Keeping the picture of the natural desire in mind, we might ask, "Can a man drink too much water?" Drinking is a natural need, but is it possible to let the desire get out of control and drink too much? Yes. Athletes run the risk of drinking too much water if they do not replace electrolytes at the same time. This is called water intoxication, which results in the body's cells swelling to the point that they can even burst. Can a man drink water from the wrong place? Of course. Many years ago while backpacking I found a crystal clear stream of water. No water ever looked purer to my eyes. I foolishly filled my canteen with that water without purifying it first. For two weeks after that foolish choice I suffered from an amoeba in my digestive system. Looks can be deceiving. What appears to be sparkling, refreshing, yea, satisfying to the natural desires can leave the partaker in terrible pain if he gets it from the wrong source.

That is why God warns men to have their desires satisfied from their own source. The wife is a well, a cistern, or a fountain in this text. She is like a source of refreshing, satisfying water. Solomon, the writer of this wisdom principle, concluded this very thing about his beloved Shulamite bride.

He called her "a fountain of gardens, a well of living waters, and streams from Lebanon" (Song of Solomon 4:15). Did he desire her? It sure seems that way. Was that God's blessing? It definitely was. In Solomon's day, most people resorted to the well or cistern located in the center of town to draw water. But the privileged man had his own cistern or well. God pictures the man who has a wife as such a privileged person. Solomon also concluded that, "Whoso findeth a wife findeth a good thing, and obtaineth favour of the Lord" (Proverbs 18:22).

Since husbands are so privileged, according to God's assessment, we ought to find our satisfaction in the source God gave. God told husbands to drink from their own cisterns. It is an imperative, a command for the husband to find satisfaction with his wife. It is also a warning not to seek satisfaction in some other well.

Since the privileged man has his own cistern, he should not have springs running in the street (vv. 16–17). Here is a picture contrasting the private source of satisfaction (your own well) with a public source (streams in the street). Your wife is your well. That is the source of private satisfaction. A prostitute or loose woman, like streams of water in the street, is shared by the public. A woman like this literally "runs in the streets." Later, in chapter 7, Solomon described a poor foolish young man who gets tricked by such a wicked woman. He warned, "And behold, the woman meets him, dressed as a prostitute, wily of heart. She is loud and wayward; her feet do not stay at home; now in the street, now in the market, and at every corner she lies in wait" (Proverbs 7:10–12 ESV). Woe to the fool who walks that path.

Sharing the source of satisfaction is out of the question in God's plan. God said that the satisfaction found in the wife is to be a matter of monogamy. It is not something to be shared. One time I was discussing with a young man about purity before marriage. He argued that because he never bought a pair shoes without trying them on, it was only right that he not marry a woman without going through the same process. I looked at his shoes and asked him how many other men he shared his shoes with. That was the end of the conversation.

In real life, sincere husbands discover that there are plenty of other sources of "water" in our culture. Women roam the mall, pose for magazines, display their wares on television and the Internet, live in your neighborhood, and work in the office next to yours. All of them are off limits! The world tells men that it is acceptable for them to be satisfied from many wells. God warns that a husband must drink water from his own cistern. Period!

When a husband drinks water from his own cistern, he can let his fountain be happy (vv. 18–19). This paves the way for him to rejoice in his well, to rejoice in his wife (vv. 18–19*a*). So far the passage has referred to the wife as a cistern and a well. Here she is called a fountain. This fountain is more likely to be blessed (the Hebrew word for happy) when she is confident of her husband's fidelity. That is why the husband's responses to other women are so important. How he responds when he sees an attractive woman or when he talks with another woman will often determine if his wife's

> God commands the husband to make up his mind that he will rejoice in his wife.

confidence in him is entrenched or eroded. The husband must rejoice in his heart over his "well" if she is ever going to be confident that he does indeed rejoice. The process begins in the heart.

Rejoice is another imperative. God commands the husband to make up his mind that he will rejoice in his wife. Can rejoicing be commanded? Apparently it can because God clearly commanded us to rejoice. That thought runs contrary to the modern opinion that fidelity is boring. Wicked, unregenerate men cannot even imagine rejoicing in being "stuck" with the same woman for life. That is not their idea of a good time.

Selfish people who think that a good time is had only when personal pleasure is satisfied miss the picture God draws of the wife. God pictures the wife, the pleasing well of refreshment, as graceful, fascinating animals. Her husband is to see her as a lovely deer or a graceful doe. That is how Solomon saw his beautiful first bride. He raved, "Behold, you are beautiful, my love, behold, you are beautiful! Your eyes are doves behind your veil. Your hair is like a flock of goats leaping down the slopes of Gilead. Your teeth are like a flock of shorn ewes that have come up from the washing, all of which bear twins, and not one among them has lost its young" (Song of Solomon 4:1–2 ESV). Solomon's raving about the Shulamite reveals how husbands are responsible to think that the cistern is half full instead of half empty. It is a choice. Make the right one!

Second, a husband is more likely to have a happy cistern if he is satisfied with her (v. 19). God's design anticipates physical, emotional satisfaction from a proper relationship between the husband and wife. He designed woman as she is to appeal to man as he is. It is man's responsibility to direct and nurture his natural desires within the proper boundaries. The result of this directing of desires is that the husband should be intoxicated with his wife. This word *intoxicated* in verse 19 actually describes the staggering of a person under the influence of strong drink. It is the word picture found in Isaiah's description of the so-called leaders of Israel who were delirious with their sins: "These also reel with wine and stagger with strong drink; the priest and the prophet reel with strong drink, they are swallowed by wine, they stagger with strong drink, they reel in vision, they stumble in giving judgment" (Isaiah 28:7 ESV). To be intoxicated by strong drink is not good. For a husband to be swept away with love and satisfaction for his wife is a wonderful thing. God encourages the husband to put himself under such an influence of his wife.

This is a matter of decision not a matter of reaction. Love, true love, determines to make a sacrifice in order to benefit the object of love. Therefore, the husband must decide that he will be satisfied with his own wife and that he will rejoice in her.

WHY BE INTOXICATED WITH A FORBIDDEN WOMAN (vv. 20-23)?

Having set down God's standard for a husband to be satisfied with his wife, Solomon looked at the alternative—which is not good. Husbands must exercise great care in the matter of fulfilling their desires because God observes every man's way (vv. 20–21). Husbands must exercise care because the God Who observes says that some women are forbidden (v. 20). A forbidden woman cannot be a good thing. This fact begs Solomon's question, "Why should a man be intoxicated with such a woman?" The question is arresting. To ask "Why be intoxicated with a forbidden woman?" is equivalent to asking, "How foolish can a man be to yield to the baser instincts, the lusts of the flesh?"

This probing question is posed by a man who learned from his own experience how foolish this action is. No one knows for certain at what point in life Solomon learned his lesson or at what point he wrote these words. However, the evidence seems to indicate that most of Solomon's wives were "strange" women. The historian of Israel recorded the sad truth that "King Solomon loved many foreign women, along with the daughter of Pharaoh: Moabite, Ammonite, Edomite, Sidonian, and Hittite women" (1 Kings 11:1 ESV). "Foreign women" is another way of saying "forbidden women." These are the same kind of women whom the Israelite men married when they came back from Babylon. Some of them were deeply troubled by what they had done. "And Shecaniah the son of Jehiel, of the sons of Elam, addressed Ezra: 'We have broken faith with our God and have married foreign women from the peoples of the land, but even now there is hope for Israel in spite of this'" (Ezra 10:2 ESV). The women were foreign, strange, and forbidden, because they were not part of Israel. They were not born among the covenant people. Although women like this were not similar to the people of God or similar to Solomon, he nevertheless took about 999 of them to himself. If nothing else, the once-wise king proved the fallacy of "evangelistic dating," which claims, "I will date this woman with the purpose of leading her to Christ." It seldom works out to such a pleasant end.

Modern husbands must be alert to the fact that they are surrounded by strange and forbidden women. A strange or forbidden woman is every woman with whom a husband is (or could be) unfaithful. Every woman who is not your wife, who offers the satisfaction of natural desires (whether real or perceived), is off limits. The boundaries are clear and simple. But the boundaries cut across the grain of natural desire and the world's philosophy.

One very good motivation for avoiding forbidden women or exercising care around such women is that God knows when a man embraces a forbidden bosom (v. 21). The greatest "fence" to help us control our desires should be the little song we learned as children: "Oh be careful little eyes what you see. . . . For the Father up above is looking down in love." That is precisely what Solomon asserted. Our ways are before God's eyes. God knows our habits, which can be translated quite literally to refer to our "wagon tracks." Our ways are clear to God and He weighs them in His scale. In the final analysis the decision that really matters is what God thinks, not what the world thinks.

A second good reason for avoiding the temptation to be satisfied by a forbidden woman is the fact that the wage of sin is still death (vv. 22–23). Solomon warned his son that iniquity is enslaving (v. 22). It is very easy for husbands to slide into sin and humanly impossible to get out. The warning is so critical because if a man does not allow himself to be captured by his wife, he runs the risk of being captured by the strange woman. Once a husband is captured by a forbidden woman, he is enslaved by his iniquity. Only God is able to release the foolish wanderer from the trap—and that often involves great pain. Adrian Rogers is credited with saying, "Sin will take you farther than you want to go, keep you longer than you want to stay, and cost you more than you want to pay." Solomon called the payment death!

Indeed, lack of self-discipline regarding these natural desires results in death (v. 23). Adultery begins in folly, continues in folly, and ends in folly. Far better to exercise discipline and set up the fences to keep the natural desires corralled. Failure to discipline self results in spiritual death, separation from God, and, at best, a dulling of our relationship with Him. Sometimes such lack of discipline has even resulted in physical death. Is a few minutes of pleasure really worth the price?

God created man to find woman attractive in form and being. Therefore, it is natural for a man to notice an attractive woman. What he does after noticing her will determine if he carries out God's teaching in this text. The wise man, who is wise because he obeys God's instruction, turns his eyes away from the woman and refuses to think about her. He knows that God has warned that if he gazes on such a beautiful woman his thoughts will lead to lust. When lust is conceived, it leads the man to be dissatisfied with his wife. Dissatisfaction with his wife leads a man to infidelity in thought first, which almost always leads to sinful action. The result is death—broken fellowship with God at best, physical death at worst. Any way we cut it, the result is obviously painful. Is it really worth the cost to drink water from the wrong place? Never!

How quickly would the discouraging statistics of the 2000 census change if men in this culture determined that they will obey God's instruction in this text? Suddenly fornication and adultery would lose popularity. God's people, Christian men and husbands, must blaze the trail to a saner society. We must stand in the center of God's will in this matter even if the entire society rejects it. In the end the world will know that God is always right, His instruction is always true.

PUT IT TO WORK

1. At what age does a man lose a natural attraction toward women?

2. Do you know any forbidden women?

3. What guards do you have in place to lessen temptation toward infidelity?

4. Is your wife confident of your desire for her?

5. Do you have a friend who helps keep you accountable in this area?

Blessed is everyone who fears the LORD, who walks in his ways! You shall eat the fruit of the labor of your hands; you shall be blessed, and it shall be well with you. Your wife will be like a fruitful vine within your house; your children will be like olive shoots around your table. Behold, thus shall the man be blessed who fears the LORD. The LORD bless you from Zion! May you see the prosperity of Jerusalem all the days of your life! May you see your children's children! Peace be upon Israel. (Psalm 128:1–6 ESV)

This is a psalm of ascents. Probably Solomon wrote it to be sung by devout Jewish pilgrims as they traveled up to Jerusalem to keep the festivals. God's law required all males to go to Jerusalem three times each year. God told the Israelites, "Three times in a year shall all thy males appear before the Lord thy God in the place which he shall choose; in the feast of unleavened bread, and in the feast of weeks, and in the feast of tabernacles: and they shall not appear before the Lord empty" (Deuteronomy 16:16). There are several psalms that served as songs for the groups of people to sing as they approached the city. This is one of those songs.

It is important for the reader to keep in mind as he reads a psalm like this that the psalm is in the genre of wisdom literature. Wisdom literature lays down general truths for life, not precise, unalterable, universal truths like the law genre does. The general rule is that everyone who works diligently and respects the Lord will automatically be happy, eat the fruit of his labor, have a gracious, loving, industrious wife who rears wonderful children to take over the family business and who lives to see all of his grandchildren. That is not a universal law. Sometimes it doesn't happen like that. Sometimes righteous men get sick. Sometimes they are persecuted. Sometimes they are victims of violent crime. Sometimes their families are not perfect in spite of the fact that the leader of the home has followed God's plan.

But the pleasant scenario described in this psalm is more likely for a man who fears God than for one who loves self and ignores God. America is a nation of people who love themselves and curse God. Such a nation is dreaming if they think they deserve to reap the fruit described in this psalm. Many middle-aged, and older, people can remember a time in this society when the typical family was characterized by Ward, June, Wally, and Theodore ("Beaver") Cleaver. Back in the good old days when *Leave It to Beaver* kinds of families were common, parents were respectable. They worked hard, tried to live moral lives, and the husbands and wives demonstrated respect and esteem for each other. The children grew up showing honor and respect for their parents and other authorities. In that age, a guy like Eddie Haskell was the bad guy.

As I mentioned in the introduction, I grew up in a *Leave It to Beaver* kind of home. I was taught to respect my parents' authority and all other authorities in life. If I chose not to do that, I was painfully reminded that due respect was very important. When my sisters and I came home from school, our mother was waiting for us. Her habit of being there was a very simple practice that instilled a lot of security in us little kids. Mom never believed that it was important for her to pursue a career, become successful, or compete with men on corporate ladders. To her, success was managing a family in such a way that everyone in the unit could find peace and tranquility.

Things are not like that anymore. Even Christian families are not much like the ideological Cleaver family. Indeed, the typical American family is quite different. As far as Hollywood is concerned, the typical American family today should be like the Osbournes. *The Osbournes*, which ran from 2002 through 2005, depicted a dysfunctional family characterized by foul language and wickedness at every turn. Name the vice and this family either practiced it or approved of those who did.

The sad truth is that in many ways, the typical family in America today has far too many Osbourne traits and far too few Cleaver traits. What happened? How did we come to this sad state of affairs? How is it that

Christian families in America are glued to their televisions to watch Sharon Osbourne pass judgment on who America's next idol should be? The whole scenario is far removed from the picture we see in this psalm. Here, Solomon taught that the man who fears the Lord and walks in his ways will have a wife and family that bring him much joy and comfort. Does your family manifest to all who care to watch that God's hand of blessing is on it?

Derek Kidner described the flow of this psalm well when he observed, "The quiet blessing of an ordered life are traced from the center outwards in this psalm, as the eye travels from the godly man to his family and finally to Israel."[1]

GOD'S BLESSING IS DISCOVERED WITHIN THE CONTEXT OF A RIGHT RELATIONSHIP (Psalm 128:1-2)

The equation for a blessed family is this: "Everyone who fears the Lord, who walks in his ways" will be blessed. In other words, right respect for God is required first (v. 1). The word *bless* speaks of happiness. It flows seamlessly from the previous psalm (127), which teaches that the man with a full quiver is a happy man. Here God promises happiness to the person who fears Him.

Fear of God is a common theme throughout Scripture, yet the very sound of the words cuts against the grain of human nature. Most people naturally believe that fear is a bad thing. To most people fear pictures the humble submission of a quaking inferior to a superior being or thing. That kind of response is always contrary to the sinful desires of the flesh. The flesh prefers to be in control. Fear acknowledges that the mighty thing or mighty being is in control. Fear of God goes back to presinful Eden. Before he failed God, and brought sin into God's creation, Adam demonstrated a deep respect for God. That was good fear. However, after Adam sinned against God, he was afraid of Him. He rightly feared that God could respond in judgment to his offense against God. That was elementary fear.

Fear of God, as used in this verse, speaks of a right relationship with Him. It acknowledges that God is Creator and, therefore, rightfully the mighty Sovereign over all things. It acknowledges that God is powerful enough and justified to cast every part of creation into eternal destruction. This fear acknowledges that each person deserves punishment because of sin.

The man who fears God lives like it.	Most important, mature fear acknowledges that "I" deserve eternal condemnation. It realizes that God shows infinite kindness and mercy by forgiving sin and giving eternal life. Therefore, the person who trusts God concludes that fear of God is a reverence for His majesty, jealousy for His honor,

gratitude for His mercies, dread of His displeasure, desire for His approval, and longing for His fellowship now and in eternity.

The person who fears God lives like it. Notice that Solomon said that God's blessing is for the one who fears God and is walking in His ways. He who talks of fearing God but lives like those who do not does not. Fear is rooted in a person's heart, in the secret part of the inner-most being. Other people can observe if that fear exists because a person's heart is revealed through the words and actions he chooses. Because God created us so that we reveal the secrets of our hearts through actions, right respect for God is generally obvious. Eventually, therefore, the truth about a person's heart is known by all. The man who fears God lives like it.

For that man, God gives a great promise that "it shall be well" (v. 2). That is a general result, not a universal law. It is a great promise in light of the fact that "a well life" is the natural desire of nearly all people. The desired result of a right relationship with God is a happy, stress-free life. Most Christians are in favor of that kind of life!

In practical terms, this text acknowledges that the Old Testament Israelite who feared God looked forward to a good crop and the health to enjoy it, a very practical expression of God's hand of blessing. What could be more tangible? This was not the same as a pagan sacrificing to a mythical god he thought was in charge of rain or sunshine in hopes that the god would be kind enough to produce a good crop. Rather, the Israelites based their hopes on the promises that God had already made to their forefathers. God taught that there was a tangible connection between faithfulness to the covenant and bountiful crops. When did God cease keeping those promises? Can the modern believer say that because God is not working directly with the nation of Israel today that the promised blessing for obedience is void? It is not wise to dismiss such promises from God as ancient and inapplicable. Is it not still true that we can define happiness in terms of responsibility? Is happiness still found in having something to do, and having the health and strength with which to do it? Isn't part of happiness found in partaking in the results or the fruit of our labor?

But life is not always so pleasant even for those who fear God! Sometimes God gives peace and a genuine joy even in the midst of difficulty. The possibility of a God-fearing man not having the joy of eating the fruit of his labor was very real in Israel. It still is. Sometimes failure to enjoy the fruits of labor was the result of war or famine or disease or drought. Sometimes the people did not experience happiness with their harvest because God's curse rested on them when they broke His covenant. Judgment like this didn't really surprise anyone. God warned Israel early in the nation's existence that if they disregarded Him, "I will do this to you: I will visit you with panic, with wasting disease and fever that consume the eyes and make the heart ache. And you shall sow your seed in vain, for your enemies shall eat it" (Leviticus 26:16 ESV). When God leveled judgment against His people, the blessing disappeared. Amos and the people in his day understood that connection. God explained that He withdrew His blessings from them: "Forasmuch therefore as your treading is upon the poor, and ye take from him burdens of wheat: ye have built houses of hewn stone, but ye shall not dwell in them; ye have planted pleasant vineyards, but ye shall not drink wine of them" (Amos 5:11).

These are evidences of not fearing God. That brings us back to the original argument: The general rule of life is that the man who fears God is blessed. It is possible that such a man can be secure and have joy even in the difficult times. Robert Leighton concluded,

> Secure of other things, he can say—'If my God be pleased, no matter who is displeased; no matter who despise me, if he account me his. Though all forsake me, though my dearest friends grow estranged, if he reject me not, that is my only fear; and for that I am not perplexed, I know he will not.' A believer hath no fear but of the displeasure of heaven, the anger of God to fall upon him.[2]

GOD'S BLESSING IS OBVIOUS IN THE WIFE AND CHILDREN (vv. 3-4)

According to Psalm 128:3, one can also expect to see the evidence of God's blessing in the home. Here is the picture of a God-fearing, hard-working man who reaps God's blessings in the field and in the home. The psalm draws a pleasant Currier and Ives kind of picture. Is the picture of the industrious farmer busy in the field with mother and the children content in the home the only suitable expression of God's will? No. Paul did not fit this description, but he was happy. The prophetess Anna did not have a husband or a home, but she was very happy in her relationship with God. Many who are celibate for the kingdom's sake are blessed. However, in principle this is a fair picture of God's blessing on the home.

As God prepared to send His people into the Promised Land, He listed four areas in particular in which He would bless them for their obedience. According to Deuteronomy 28:1–14, God promised to bless the obedient Israelites in 1) agriculture, 2) finances, 3) family, and 4) national security. Psalm 128:3 teaches the principle that a man whose wife is focused on her home and family is blessed by God. God described her as a fruitful vine inside the house. One common translation of this phrase is that the wife will be like a vine "on the sides of the house." However, the word translated "inside" speaks of the remotest parts, the recesses of a house. Rather than referring to the outside of a house, it speaks of a place that is innermost. Furthermore, Israelites were not known for growing fruitful vines up the side of a house. Most cultures aren't.

Conversely, one finds here a picture that paints God's blessing as a wife who loves to be productive in her home. That is not to say that she should feel captive to her home. God's plan does not allow a husband to treat his wife like property. This picture does not encourage the practice of the ancient Egyptians, who denied their wives shoes so they would not be tempted to go out. Nor is it like the Scythian bridegrooms, who brought their wives to their home in a chariot. Then they removed and burned the chariot's axle tree as a symbol of the wife's responsibility to stay in the home.

God's plan for blessing is a wife who gains a sense of accomplishment by what she does to benefit the rest of the family. While the husband is the head of the home, the wife is the manager. She is responsible to see that things are organized and that tranquility reigns. She, more than anyone else in the family, creates an atmosphere of peace and security. The husband and children enjoy the benefit of her much labor and call it God's blessing. This labor takes much time and effort. Common sense dictates that it is difficult for a wife to work full-time outside the home and be productive in the home at the same time. It is practically impossible for a wife to pursue a separate career and fulfill this duty also. Many Christian wives have become frustrated by trying to live according to the world's standard and trying to fulfill this plan also. Some wives do not realize that

God characterized an ungodly woman as one who does not like to be at home. Solomon concluded that such a woman "is loud and stubborn; her feet abide not in her house" (Proverbs 7:11).

God used the picture of a fruitful vine to illustrate the wife because it smacks of being productive. A wife who is productive in the home is an indication of God's blessing. Notice that God did not liken her to thorns or briers, nor even to oaks or to other fruits and trees. He pictured her as a fruitful vine. The grapevine was one of the chief symbols of valuable productivity in Israel. Likewise, the vinelike woman exerts wisdom, creativity, and just plain hard work in order to make life more pleasant for her family.

However, there is more to the picture. While it is true that an actual grapevine is productive, it is also dependent. A productive vine grows on a trellis or arbor, not along the ground. Kudzu grows well on the ground but is not productive. The husband must provide the latticework of support upon which the wife can be productive. Even the best of wives find it difficult to be a blessing when they have no support from their husbands. Furthermore, the vine is fragile wood. Men never made great sailing ships from vines but from oak and hickory. God did not compare the wife to a sturdy redwood or oak. Men are supposed to be like that. A God-fearing husband must be the sturdy support of the family. He must maintain the spiritual, physical, and emotional foundation of the family. The man who would be blessed by God must be diligent to provide the setting where the wife can be productive.

> A wife who is productive in the home is an indication of God's blessing.

Another indication of God's blessing on the family is that the children promise a continuing relationship with God. They are like olive shoots springing up around the parent tree. The shoot of any tree is made of the same stuff as the tree. So what do our children's lives reveal about the root at home? Many years ago I challenged a young husband and wife to set a better example of godliness before their children. They angrily retorted that they went to church often enough for their kids to learn to love God. In reality the parents chose not to fear God and walk in His ways. Predictably, the children all grew up to live lives engrossed in almost every sin imaginable. They now have children of their own, and the whole lot of them has abandoned church and any pretense of Christianity. How do the parents who have created this monster respond? They describe their sinful children and grandchildren by saying, "Oh, they are such nice kids." Do they really believe that?

Such blessing is God's general rule (v. 4). The fear of the Lord is the foundation to godly happiness. Godly fear is the right relationship that results in right living. The world does not have a right respect for God and, therefore, should not expect His blessing on the family. Strangely enough, many talk as though they don't want God's blessing. Many people think that a godly family is backward and boring. The world often despises the riches of God's blessing. Be that as it may, God's blessings still bring happiness to the families who fear God.

GOD'S BLESSING EXTENDS TO THE NATION MADE UP OF BLESSED FAMILIES (vv. 5-6)

A true son of Abraham, that is, a good Israelite, desired God's blessing for the nation. As God promised, Abraham's lineage is as numerous as the stars today. However, not everyone who was born an Israelite was concerned that the nation would serve God. They too were people like us, and they too were tempted to be self-centered. But genuine Israelites understood that God was glorified when the nation was successful. Therefore, they prayed for the peace of Jerusalem (Zion). Devout people of God believed that each family should live in a way that would contribute to the prosperity of the nation.

They also believed that the opportunity to observe and train posterity was an important blessing to the true Israelite. They taught their children, then they taught their grandchildren. They understood that when a man had the opportunity to see his grandchildren, it testified to the longevity of his life.

What was true for ancient Israelites is still true in principle today. Typically, any nation is a corporate expression of the individual families that make up that nation. That is why thinking Christians today are not anticipating the blessing of God on America. The nation is socially challenged because the families that make up the nation are far from God. This culture does not believe God or trust His principles. Therefore, this culture does not know how to live in peace and enjoy God's mercy. This is not the kind of culture that would pray for God to bless His people. Paul encouraged Gentile Christians in his day to live according to the principle in this text. He taught that we should fear God, walk in His ways, and hope for God's blessing on us and on the nation. He told the Christians in Galatia, "And as many as walk according to this rule, peace be on them, and mercy, and upon the Israel of God" (Galatians 6:16).

We do not anticipate God's blessing on the nation because the families of this nation are not blessed by God. Indeed, many Christians actually fear for their grandchildren. Christians appreciate and enjoy the blessing of grandchildren knowing that "grandchildren are the crown of the aged, and the glory of children is their fathers" (Proverbs 17:6 ESV). Because we care for them, we fear what they will face in a society that does not fear God, does not walk in His way, and, therefore, has sacrificed His blessings on the nation and the family.

The task of turning the nation around is impossible. However, each child of God is responsible to see that he or she lives in a way that will allow the blessing of God to flow to his or her family. Husbands must fear God and walk in His way. Wives should seek to be productive in their homes. Children need to determine that they will continue their parent's legacy of fearing God and walking in His way. People who live like that can expect to have the joy of God.

PUT IT TO WORK

1. Does your family enjoy God's blessing?

2. Do you prefer to have God's blessing for your family or do you prefer to have the world's pleasures for your family?

3. What are you, the husband, doing to provide a support for the wife to be a good manager in the home?

4. Wife, how does your family know that your focus is on the home?

5. Grandparents, are you actively teaching your grandchildren to fear God?

PRINCIPLE 6
A wife is like an oasis in the middle of the desert called life.

Go, eat your bread in joy, and drink your wine with a merry heart, for God has already approved what you do. Let your garments be always white. Let not oil be lacking on your head. Enjoy life with the wife whom you love, all the days of your vain life that he has given you under the sun, because that is your portion in life and in your toil at which you toil under the sun. Whatever your hand finds to do, do it with your might, for there is no work or thought or knowledge or wisdom in Sheol, to which you are going. (Ecclesiastes 9:7–10 ESV)

Life is just a dirt sandwich—every day another bite. Life is a party— every day a new blast. Which one of those ideas best expresses your view of life? The pessimist sees life as a series of strange and unfortunate events. The optimist sees life through rose-colored glasses. Neither view is accurate.

It is wrong and dangerous for God's people to view life like Eeyore, the slow-moving, slow-talking, drooping-head donkey friend of Winnie the Pooh. His view of life is expressed in his short but famous line, "Oh bother." If you live with an Eeyore disposition, probably some people will try to avoid you while others will be infected by your spirit and affirm the truth that misery loves company.

On the other hand it is also wrong and dangerous for God's people to face life with the carefree, yea, careless attitude of Tigger, the exuberant tiger friend of Pooh. He is impulsive, energetic, and boisterous. He is the kind of friend who responds without thinking or answers the question before he hears it because being serious doesn't matter. Life is a blast for Tigger. That spirit is also infectious and can lead people to dangerous conclusions or can put a person in difficult circumstances that a little wisdom would have helped them avoid.

The proper attitude of life is somewhere between these extremes. The book of Ecclesiastes presents this kind of balance. On the one hand, it appears that Ecclesiastes is an Eeyore-kind of writing. One cannot escape that attitude as the writing declares in the opening words: "'Absolutely pointless!' says the spokesman. 'Absolutely pointless! Everything is pointless.' What do people gain from all their hard work under the sun?" (Ecclesiastes 1:2–3 GWV). The cry "All is vanity" rings with repetition throughout the writing. The verses in this text repeat the frustrating conclusion by acknowledging our vain life, our endless toil in this vain life, and finally the grave to which we go. Is that all there is to look forward to in this life? Gladly, no!

The first two verses of the text encourage people to eat, drink, and be merry. These verses declare that God has approved of His creatures having a good time in life. Indeed, it is good to wear garments of joy and appreciate some of the finer things in life.

Then which do we do? How should we view life? Is it a dirt sandwich, or is it a daily blast? Much of life is empty and meaningless because of sin's influence. When Adam and Eve strolled through the Garden of Eden enjoying perfect fellowship with God in the cool of the day, they never would have dreamed of saying that life is empty. However, the moment they disobeyed God and ate of the forbidden tree, life became a field of thorns and weeds. God promised that disobedience would result in dying, and now every person lives a dying life. The influence of sin in this world makes for an empty, meaningless life.

Conversely, the influence of God in this world makes life worth living. Scattered throughout this book about vain life are various statements that remind the reader that God is in control. For example, God gives wisdom, knowledge, and joy to one person, but He gives gathering and collecting to the sinner (2:26). God has given the business of being busy to mankind (3:10). "Whatever God does endures forever" (3:14). God will judge the wicked and the righteous (3:17). In all, there are at least thirty-six references to God's sovereign control in this book.

Therefore, Solomon concluded that the right thing for God's people to do is to have awesome respect for Him and keep His commandments (12:13). This was the conclusion of the wise man, who spent much of his life experimenting with all that life has to offer. He tried human wisdom (1:12–18), pleasure (2:1–3), building monuments to himself (2:4–6), possessions (2:6–8), hard work (2:18–24), and honor (5:8–9) only to discover that all of them end up at emptiness in a world tainted by sin.

Solomon learned that it is wisest to live life within the boundaries God has ordained. He learned that God has given His creatures many blessings to enjoy, and a wise man will enjoy what God has given. One of the great blessings that God gives to many men is a wife. She is God's reward. Therefore, a wise husband learns to enjoy life with the wife he loves because this is God's reward to him in a life that can easily become meaningless.

GOD EXPECTS HIS PEOPLE TO LIVE PROFITABLE LIVES (Ecclesiastes 9:7-8, 10)

God approves of His people's enjoying the fruits of their labors (vv. 7–8). He desires that they have merry hearts (v. 7). He equates having a merry heart with the opportunity and ability to eat the fruits of one's labors. This is a principle found throughout the Bible. Cultures that honor this basic principle of life are often successful, and cultures that ignore it are typically in upheaval or are filled with angry citizens. Good governments encourage the labor and reward system. Bad governments discourage this principle by taking the rewards away from the diligent and giving them to the derelicts.

God's plan is for us to rejoice in the profits He provides from our labors. Therefore, His people should eat and be happy. They should drink wine and be merry. Of course that statement often throws up a red flag in the minds of many Christians. It is true that drinking wine was a sign of reward, joy, and happiness in the Bible. Especially in the Old Testament, and in the contextual understanding of this text, the drinking of wine with a merry heart demonstrated the drinker's acknowledgment that God had blessed the vineyard. God had provided bounty and drinking the wine proved it. However, the privilege of rejoicing in that way also comes with such serious warnings in the Old Testament (especially in Proverbs) that it tempers the practice. In the minds of many Christians, it is better to avoid this particular expression of joy because of the many warnings in God's Word that wine and strong drink are dangerous.

God also approves of His people's having a happy view of life (v. 8). This verse says that God's plan is for His people to always have white garments. White garments are symbolic of happiness and joy as opposed to black garments that indicated sadness experienced by the mourners who wore them. It is interesting that the Bible contrasts colors of clothing with contrasting attitudes. God prefers His people to recognize His blessing and rejoice over it.

> God's plan is for us to rejoice in the profits He provides from our labors.

The same idea is expressed in the principle of the person whose head is anointed with oil. That would be similar to wearing perfume or, in the case of a man, cologne. Common laborers, prisoners, or warriors did not have it. Heroes, bridegrooms, or people who were honored had oil on their heads. So Solomon concluded, "Oil and perfume make the heart glad, and the sweetness of a friend comes from his earnest counsel" (Proverbs 27:9). God desires for His people to enjoy the bounty He gives. He wants them to rejoice in the gift but not to the point that they forget the giver of the gift.

While God delights in the joy and merry hearts of His people, He also admonishes them to be diligent in life (v. 10). It is nice to have fun, but life is not all about fun. The culture that must be entertained will have a short history. It is God's desire for people who rejoice in life to be diligent about it also. This command requires God's people to put their hearts into the tasks they undertake. Discipline and determination often give otherwise menial tasks meaning and a sense of accomplishment. The old saying "Anything worth doing is worth doing well" is still true.

The person who honestly considers the expected results of life will be compelled to be diligent in life's pursuits. God expects people to live in light of the common end for everyone, which is the grave. Solomon argued in verse 10 that folks ought to do the best they can right now because in the grave they can do nothing. It is a grim reminder that while a person is able to rejoice in God's blessing, he can never escape the fact that it all comes to an end some time.

GOD EXPECTS THE HUSBAND TO ENJOY HIS WIFE THROUGHOUT LIFE (v. 9)

Solomon concluded that God expects the husband to enjoy his wife because He has given the wife to him in this life as a reward. In fact, the teaching here is that for a husband not to enjoy his wife would be an expression of ingratitude to God. Considering the depressing description of life in this verse, one wonders what kind of person would not be thankful to God for even the smallest gift. Solomon said that life is empty toil; in other words, we all live a vain life. Solomon, of all people, should have known this from experience. He was the guy who tried essentially everything life has to offer and came away realizing that there is no satisfaction in all that life offers.

Having experimented in every area of life, Solomon discovered that, in the end, life is empty. That discovery is expressed repeatedly in the Hebrew word translated "vanity," which means wind, vapor, or breath. Solomon said that life is vain! It is an empty breath. Even though a life span might be eighty years, it seems like a vapor because it passes so quickly. David learned that "man is like a breath; his days are like a passing shadow" (Psalm 144:4 ESV). Because that is true, an elderly person looks back on all that he or she has accomplished and concludes that it is like vapor. It is gone in a moment.

How long are the best of people remembered after they pass away? A news article recently mentioned the growing problem of lack of cemetery space in some cities. I wonder if anyone knows or cares about the majority of monuments in the typical cemetery. Probably when we pass away our families will remember us for the rest of their lives. But by the time a second generation has been born, there is no one left to remember or care. By the time a person has been dead only fifty years, he is virtually unknown. All the money the wealthy man left behind was distributed and spent in a matter of a few years. An author's books are no longer in print. The house the man built through his own labor and sweat is either occupied by someone who never knew him or, worse, has been replaced by a shopping center. The grandchildren, unaware of the toil and tears that went into building the business, have sold it to strangers without a second thought. What is the longevity of the typical person's accomplishments? This is a good reminder for us to invest in eternal rewards. It is good to remember to rejoice in God's blessings because life is short.

Life is short. But even worse is that, while it endures, it is a life of toil. The average American will spend approximately ninety thousand hours of life working a job if one assumes that a person works about forty-five years (from age twenty to sixty-five), for about forty hours each week, for fifty weeks each year (assuming a two-week vacation annually), which amounts to two thousand hours each year. Does that seem incomprehensible? Consider that God's Word says that these ninety thousand hours are toil and labor. It doesn't sound like much fun, does it? It sounds like ninety thousand hours punching in each morning at 8:00, working all day, and punching out at 5:00. It goes on Monday through Friday, week after week, month after month, year after year. Talk about monotonous! No wonder the typical worker lives for the weekend when he or she can do something different.

The endless cycle goes on like this until retirement. Finally the big day comes and the tired laborer retires. But once he retires, he discovers that he is bored because there is nothing to do. Well, he just needs to hang in there a couple of years and things will change. After being retired for just a few years, his days will be consumed with visits to doctors and pharmacists.

Not surprisingly the Hebrew word for *toil* speaks not only of endless labor but trouble, grievance, misery, or mischief. In light of such a stark reality, how can we not conclude with the preacher, "Vanity of vanities, saith the Preacher, vanity of vanities; all is vanity" (Ecclesiastes 1:2). Is that a pessimistic view of life that God-fearing people should dismiss with all haste? No. It is a realistic view of life. Where is the cause to rejoice? Who can see through the clouds of pessimism to the blessing of God?

Into this setting of emptiness and pointlessness God gives one of His great rewards. There are two possible interpretations of the first phrase in Ecclesiastes 9:9: "Live joyfully with the wife whom thou lovest all the days of the life of thy vanity, which he hath given thee under the sun." It is possible that the text says that God gives the husband his wife in the man's vain life. It is more likely that the text says that God gives the man the days that make up his vain life. Be that as it may, later in the verse it is very clear that God gives the wife as a portion in this life of toil. The word *portion* speaks of a share, a possession, or an award. The word is used to speak of an inheritance in the context where Jacob's wives understood that they had no inheritance or reward from their father. When Jacob recommended that they leave Laban, "Rachel and Leah answered and said unto him, Is there yet any portion or inheritance for us in our father's house?" (Genesis 31:14). In a similar way, God promised through Moses that the tribe of Levi would receive no portion of land in the Promised Land because they were God's special servants.

"Wherefore Levi hath no part nor inheritance with his brethren; the Lord is his inheritance, according as the Lord thy God promised him" (Deuteronomy 10:9).

In light of these meanings and uses, it is clear that the wife is God's reward to the husband in an otherwise meaningless life. How many husbands view their wives as God's reward or inheritance? A 1981 movie called *Going Ape* told the story of a young fellow who inherited five million dollars from his father who owned a circus. The catch was that the guy also inherited three orangutans he was responsible to care for. Very quickly he discovered that the five million dollars was no blessing. That is not the kind of reward God gives when He gives the husband a wife. She is not a liability, a project, or a thorn in the flesh. Is it possible that a husband could ever think that of a wife? It is as possible as the wife occasionally thinking the same thing about the husband. How can a husband avoid coming to such natural conclusions?

Because God gives the wife as a reward in an otherwise bleak life, He requires the husband to love and enjoy her. To say *requires* is not overstepping the meaning of the verb. God commands the husband to enjoy his wife. It is interesting that the Hebrew word would be translated "enjoy" when it typically means to look at intently and to perceive. Actually the word has broad and varied meanings such as understand, feel, and enjoy. Here the verb in the verse has to carry the meaning of enjoy to fit with the two verses that precede it. Yet it is a command. How can God command a husband to enjoy another person? Actually, the implication is that because God commands husbands to enjoy their wives, husbands ought to be able to do it. God never commands something He does not give grace to do.

The amazing truth is that when husbands set about to do what God requires (which in the case might seem impossible), they soon discover that God's plan works. Conversely, if a man does not want to obey God, he will never know if the principle works. If a husband does not want to enjoy his wife, he doesn't have to. Generally when a husband makes that wrong choice in this matter, it is not long before life does appear to him to be a dirt sandwich. But in God's plan for the husband and wife, life can be a blast.

Longevity is a necessary element for revealing how this principle works. This truth leads a person to give what appears to be strange advice. "Stick with the marriage at least until you learn to enjoy your wife. Then once you have learned to enjoy her, you can leave her if you still want to." That wacky advice shows how a right attitude can turn a bad conclusion into a good life.

God not only requires husbands to enjoy their wives but He also expects husbands to love their wives. Unlike the previous verb, this verb is not a command. This verb acts more like a description of life. Love for his wife should characterize the husband's life. Typically a young man starts out in this "wife-loving path" by being infatuated with her. He thinks love is something he feels. But real love is much deeper than the giddy stuff one knows in the early years of marriage. Soon the husband outgrows the infatuation, and he learns how to truly care for his wife. He is learning genuine love as he discovers how to make her benefit his first interest. Finally, in mature love, the man not only desires to do what is best for her but has learned how to love her like he loves himself.

At that stage a husband finally understands the nature of God's reward. As a mature man the husband has learned that life really offers nothing but labor and emptiness. But he has also learned along the way that his wife gives vain life meaning because she is God's reward to him.

Life tainted by sin is not pleasant or rewarding. It is monotonous labor until we finally arrive at the grave. But in that unavoidable setting of life ruined by sin, God gives many blessings in which we do well to rejoice. Among the greatest of those blessings is the wife. The husband must enjoy the wife he is learning to love because she is God's reward in an otherwise meaningless life.

PUT IT TO WORK

1. Do you really trust God's plan?

2. What do you pursue in an effort to find joy in life?

3. Is your wife a gift from God?

4. Why did God give your wife to you?

5. What steps can you take to learn how to rejoice in the wife God has given you?

The wisest of women builds her house, but folly with her own hands tears it down. (Proverbs 14:1 ESV)

O nce when my wife, Pat, and I were speaking at a family conference in another city, one of the women in attendance told Pat about a conversation she had had with one of her peers. In the conversation, this woman had mentioned that she was a stay-at-home mom. The other woman responded, "Don't you feel guilty for not contributing to the welfare of your family?" That is an interesting spin on a topic that is not debated often enough in this age. The modern age expects wives and mothers to be engaged in the typical rush, rage, and competition of the work world. When they meet a woman who, even though she might work outside the home, has her desires set on the family, they think she is odd. This is a day when the statement "I am a housewife" is likely to be met with a response like "Oh, that's too bad." The implication of that response is "What's the matter? Are you too insecure, uneducated, and intellectually dull to compete in the real world?" Or, "Are you too lazy to go at it with the movers and shakers of the work world?" Often the questioner wonders why a wife is unwilling to make money so that her family can have the finer things of life.

Actually, being a housewife requires a lot of work. What does the world think a housewife does? The typical dictionary tells us that a housewife is a wife who manages a household while her husband earns the family income or that a housewife is a woman who manages her own household as her main occupation. That definition is partly true. A housewife may very well hold responsibilities outside the home, but her true focus is on managing her family well. The chief goal of wise "wifery" is good management of her home.

The past generation, the one I am a part of, saw an unprecedented flood of women entering the job market. Standing against the flow of popularity were women like Phyllis McGinley, a poet and writer from Utah. Her book, *Sixpence in Her Shoe* (1964), was written as a direct response to Betty Friedan's best-selling book, *The Feminine Mystique* (1963), which proposed the idea that an intelligent, educated woman could never find true happiness by staying home. *Sixpence* stated an alternate philosophy, one that McGinley's own life had been based on: that educated women could fit happily into the framework of the home. McGinley wrote: "To be a housewife is a difficult, a wrenching, sometimes an ungrateful job if it is looked on only as a job. Regarded as a profession, it is the noblest as it is the most ancient of the catalogue. Let none persuade us differently or the world is lost indeed."

Not all women agree with McGinley's focus on building or managing the home. Marilyn Monroe said, "I have too many fantasies to be a housewife. I guess I am a fantasy." Some people thought that she was more like a nightmare. The good news is that the feminists' dream of the 1970s and 1980s has sort of hit the brick wall of reality. Thus, someone wrote,

> As women head into the 1990's, are they really so burned out from 'having it all' (i.e., doing it all), so thoroughly exhausted from putting in a full day at work and then another full evening at home, that they dream nostalgically of the 1950's? Can they really be aching for the dull but dependable days when going to meetings meant the PTA or the Scouts, when business travel meant the car pool, when a budgetary crisis meant the furnace had broken?[1]

A few years ago an ad for *Good Housekeeping* read, "My mother was convinced the center of the world was 36 Maplewood Drive. Her idea of a wonderful time was Sunday dinner. She bought UNICEF cards, but what really mattered were the Girl Scouts . . . I'm beginning to think my mother really knew what she was doing."[2]

So do we hear a shout of joy rising from the ranks of husbands? Not necessarily. Having a wife whose focus is on her home is a wonderful blessing—if she has a godward focus first. Solomon wrote, "A virtuous woman is a crown to her husband: but she that maketh ashamed is as rottenness in his bones" (Proverbs 12:4). It is possible for a wife to actually think a lot about her home, but to think the wrong kind of thoughts. That is not helpful. In this text Solomon concluded, "The wisest of women builds her house, but folly with her own hands tears it down" (Proverbs 14:1 ESV). There is a choice. A wife must decide if she will be wise or, if she chooses not to be wise, she will be foolish. The results of the two decisions are as opposite as the decisions themselves.

THE WISE WOMAN BUILDS HER HOME (Proverbs 14:1a)

There is a worldly wisdom that a person might possess to a certain extent by birth. However, if a wife is going to be wise in the building of her home, she must first attain the wisdom of God before she can put it to use. The Hebrew word translated "wisdom" in this verse is the most common word for the word *wisdom* in the English versions of the Bible. Of the 151 times we see the English word wisdom, 141 times it is this Hebrew word. The word means to consider, discern, or perceive. It speaks of ability or even skill in doing things. For example, God gave wisdom to craftsmen so they would know how to build the tabernacle and the other items that were connected with worship according to the Mosaic law. God told Moses, "You shall speak to all the skillful, whom I have filled with a spirit of skill, that they make Aaron's garments to consecrate him for my priesthood" (Exodus 28:3 ESV). The "skillful" are the wise. Several times in the larger context of this instruction, God reminded Moses and the people that He had granted wisdom to men so that they could do His ordained craftsmanship and work.

More important, this word speaks of the ability to apply the principles of God's wisdom to the everyday circumstances of life. This is the wisdom God granted to Solomon when he asked God to help him lead the nation of Israel. "And God gave Solomon wisdom and understanding exceeding much, and largeness of heart, even as the sand that is on the sea shore" (1 Kings 4:29). Solomon understood how to discern God's will from God's Word and how to make it work in real life.

Where can a wife find this wisdom or how does she attain it? At the beginning of this collection of wisdom statements, Solomon explained that the purpose of the Proverbs is "to know wisdom and instruction; to perceive the words of understanding" (Proverbs 1:2). This wonderful news indicates that the wife can find much wisdom by simply reading, meditating on, and memorizing the Proverbs. Doesn't it seem reasonable that this same rule would apply to all God's Word? Of course it does. What did Solomon mean when he wrote, "For the Lord giveth wisdom: out of his mouth cometh knowledge and understanding" (Proverbs 2:6). He certainly did not mean that God speaks audibly to wives so that they will know His wisdom. However, we can be sure that God speaks clearly through His Word. Therefore, a woman can gain wisdom by reading the Bible and listening to God speak through its words, the chief source of wisdom.

A right reading and understanding of the Bible helps women discover that they need to have a right relationship with God. The Bible calls this right relationship "the fear of the Lord." When a sincere wife and mother reads the Bible, she learns to fear God's retribution because she acknowledges her offenses against God. The Bible clearly demonstrates how each person, man and woman alike, is an offense to God because of sin. The Bible explains that the penalty for that offense is everlasting punishment. The woman who truly grasps this concept will fear God's right and ability to punish sin. However, fear of the Lord does not stop there. The wise woman has learned from the Bible that God has provided the covering for her sin through the sacrifice of Christ. She has learned that if she will but accept the reality of Christ's sacrifice for her own sins, through faith, she will be reconciled with God. The woman who applies that truth to herself learns to hold an awesome respect and love for God. This woman loves God so much that she fears displeasing Him. That is mature fear of the Lord. That kind of fear is what Solomon was talking about when he wrote, "The fear of the Lord is the beginning of knowledge: but fools despise wisdom and instruction" (Proverbs 1:7) and "the fear of the Lord is the beginning of wisdom: and the knowledge of the holy is understanding" (Proverbs 9:10). The first step in gaining wisdom in order to build a home is the establishment of a right relationship with God. By maintaining fear of God, the woman is able to gain more and more wisdom so that she is able to build a strong home.

> The first step in gaining wisdom in order to build a home is the establishment of a right relationship with God.

However, the simple possession of wisdom does not guarantee success in home building. What would happen if a wife and mother gained wisdom from the Bible but never put it to work in real life? The wise woman applies wisdom. Of course, one could argue that if a woman truly gained

God's wisdom, she would certainly put it to work. That is part of wisdom. Indeed, the wise woman does put the principles of wisdom to work in relation to her family. What does that look like? I could cite many examples of wisdom principles from the Bible and show how those principles should apply in real life. But just for example, consider the principle of the wife's respect for her husband. Paul taught the Corinthian Christians, "The head of every man is Christ, the head of a wife is her husband, and the head of Christ is God" (1 Corinthians 11:3 ESV). In order to apply that principle of wisdom, the wife must understand that her husband is her head. However, in common practice, she also will understand that her husband is not always qualified to be in that position because of natural abilities or virtues. Some husbands have little natural ability to lead and even less virtue. Nevertheless, because this is God's plan, the wife respects her husband's position and shows that respect in her attitudes, words, and actions.

Another simple wisdom principle a wife should learn and apply is the principle of submission to her husband. God's plan is "Wives, submit yourselves unto your own husbands, as unto the Lord" (Ephesians 5:22). This means that the wife must learn her husband's desires, plans, and purposes. Then she must arrange her own desires, plans, and purposes according to his. That is how a wise wife builds her home.

Then there is the wisdom principle of expressing love in the rearing of the children. God's Word teaches, "Fathers [the word applies to both parents], do not provoke your children to anger, but bring them up in the discipline and instruction of the LORD" (Ephesians 6:4 ESV). The wise woman understands this truth and applies it by guarding herself against frustrating her children. She aggressively teaches and nourishes them in God's instruction. But she guards against demanding more than they can do.

The woman who has learned this lesson knows from her experience that the principles of wisdom work in right living. She does not cast off the commands of God's Word as old-fashioned or irrelevant. Rather, she learns them, becomes familiar with them, and practices them. She lives like one who fears God.

The result of this kind of woman's gaining and practicing wisdom is that she is wise and she builds her home. That does not mean that the woman actually builds a house, though some women have the wisdom to do that. The meaning here is that the wise woman manages her home in such a way that life in the home is conducive to godliness. This woman is diligent to keep the good things in the home and zealous to keep the bad things out of the home. Because she has wisdom, she is able to recognize the difference between meaningless rules and the principles that flow from a right relationship with God. That explains why the wise woman has good reasons for the way she disciplines her children. She has good reasons for what she and the family are allowed to watch on television. She has reasons rooted in God's wisdom that govern the way she spends money. She has wisdom-based reasons for the boundaries she sets for the children. While the children or even the husband and father might be tempted to resist some of the practical rules of the wise woman, they need to understand that, if her rules flow from God's wisdom, they contribute to the sound establishing of the home.

In light of this truth, we realize that the wise mother is really the chief motivator behind a successful family. While Dad might be the head of the home, no one affects the daily living of the family like the wife and mother who has a hands-on management style. The successful building of a family lies primarily with the woman of the house. She must attain wisdom and use it.

The Bible contains several examples of women who learned and exercised principles of God's wisdom. For example, a man named Sheba rebelled against the king and then took refuge in the ancient city of Abel of Beth-maacah. Joab laid siege to the city and would have destroyed the entire city if a wise woman had not negotiated peace with him (2 Samuel 20:14–22). She understood the cost of harboring a rebel against the king. She understood what it would take to protect her family. Therefore, she convinced the town's residents to hand over Sheba's head to Joab.

Naomi was a wise woman. She took a vested interest in providing a husband for her daughter-in-law Ruth. She not only perceived the need for retaining the family heritage but she also understood the need to provide a righteous husband for Ruth. She did it all without becoming arrogant or pushy. In the end, Naomi helped Ruth and Boaz build a very solid home.

Esther was a wise woman because she perceived the problem the Jews faced, committed it to God, and was willing to be God's instrument in the solution. Wise women are right with God, know God's principles, and put those principles to work for the good of the entire family. Women like this build their homes.

THE FOOLISH WOMAN TEARS DOWN HER HOME (v. 1b)

The foolish woman is foolish because she has not attained wisdom. What does she look like? How does she act? Can she be identified? The fool is defined in various ways in Proverbs. Three different Hebrew words are translated "foolish" in Proverbs. One very common word (*kesil*) speaks of the simpleton, the person who seems to be naturally gullible or a bit dimwitted. One might say that this person is not the brightest light in the harbor. A less common word is the Hebrew word for the man named Nabal (*nawbawl*). The foolish husband of Abigail who owned this name demonstrated well the characteristics of this kind of fool. He was a senseless and vile person. The word used in this verse (Proverbs 14:1) is the most common Hebrew word translated "fool or foolish" (*eveel*), which refers to a quarrelsome person who lacks wisdom. This person is worse than a simpleton but not as bad as the senseless and vile Nabal. Some scholars believe this word comes from the Aramaic word meaning "thick," therefore, giving the sense of someone who is thickheaded or stupid.

In light of the use of this word in the Old Testament, we can rightly conclude that the foolish woman is spiritually deficient. Indeed, by combining the meanings and usage of all the Hebrew words that talk about foolishness, we must conclude that the fool is a person who is morally deficient. Such a person is lacking in sense and is generally corrupt.

Bad as she may be (according to the Bible), the modern culture presents this kind of woman as normal and exemplary. She is displayed on television as the standard for women. She is displayed in magazines as the standard for young women to emulate. This is an accurate demonstration of the fact that what God calls foolish the world praises as wise. Paul warned,

> The foolishness of God is wiser than men, and the weakness of God is stronger than men. For consider your calling, brothers: not many of you were wise according to worldly standards, not many were powerful, not many were of noble birth. But God chose what is foolish in the world to shame the wise; God chose what is weak in the world to shame the strong; God chose what is low and despised in the world, even things that are not, to bring to nothing things that

are, so that no human being might boast in the presence of God. (1 Corinthians 1:25–29 ESV)

The foolish woman is the world's hero and God's fool.

She is morally deficient because she is spiritually deficient. She is spiritually deficient because she does not have a right relationship with God. She might know a great number of facts about God. She might claim to have a relationship with God. She might even quote Bible verses about God. But her heart is fixed on herself not on God. She respects her own desires and purposes. She yields to the desires of her flesh not the clear requirements of God's Word.

The foolish woman acts according to foolishness. Herein is the danger because a senseless and corrupt woman will destroy her home. The Hebrew word means that she tears it down, or destroys or overthrows it. She does to her home what Gideon did to the altar of Baal (Judges 6:25). She does to her home what the people did to the altars of God in Elijah's day (1 Kings 19:10). What causes a woman to do such damage to her home? Often there has been no regenerating work of the Holy Spirit—that is, she is not born again. Always there is rebellion against God in the heart of an unsaved woman.

The Bible presents many examples of wise women, and in the same way it presents many examples of foolish women. There was Rebekah, the woman who was married to Isaac, one of the patriarchs of God's people. She was in rebellion against God in her heart and, therefore, resisted her husband. She planned against him, deceived him, and destroyed her family to her own hurt. Proverbs 14:2 warns that the person who is devious also despises God. Because of Rebekah's sin, her favorite son, Jacob, had to leave home. As far as we know, she never saw Jacob again after he left. However, foolish Rebecca was left behind to live with Esau and his foreign wives to her own pain for the rest of her life.

> A senseless and corrupt woman will destroy her home.

Jezebel had no fear for the true God. She was a classic fool. She not only wrecked her immediate family and did things that led to her husband's death in rebellion against God but she put her mark on Ahab's family for generations to come. That foolish woman wrecked her home.

One of the posterity of Ahab's family was Athaliah, another foolish woman (2 Kings 11). She was a stepdaughter of Jezebel and a daughter of Ahab.

She killed her own family, except for Joash, in an effort to have her own way. She literally destroyed her family because she was a fool. Why would a woman want to be like that? She, like other women, had a choice. Each woman must decide if she will be wise and build her home or be foolish and wreck it. She can learn and apply the principles of God's Word and by wisdom build her family. Or she can do what comes natural and please the desires of her flesh to the destruction of her family.

PUT IT TO WORK

1. What is your goal for your home?

2. How do you plan to achieve that goal?

3. How much time do you spend each day finding wisdom in the Bible and meditating on it?

4. Which is a greater influence on you, your fear of God or your respect for the world?

5. Ask your family if they are able to see the evidence of God's wisdom in your life.

PRINCIPLE 8
Husbands, guard your spirit!

You cover the LORD's altar with tears, with weeping and groaning because he no longer regards the offering or accepts it with favor from your hand. But you say, "Why does he not?" Because the LORD was witness between you and the wife of your youth, to whom you have been faithless, though she is your companion and your wife by covenant. Did he not make them one, with a portion of the Spirit in their union? And what was the one God seeking? Godly offspring. So guard yourselves in your spirit, and let none of you be faithless to the wife of your youth. "For the man who hates and divorces, says the LORD, the God of Israel, covers his garment with violence, says the LORD of hosts. So guard yourselves in your spirit, and do not be faithless." (Malachi 2:13–16 ESV)

It is often said that the strength of the nation is determined by the strength of the family. By logical conclusion then, the weakness of families results in the weakness of the nation. Israel proved the reality of that cause and effect principle. After the nation of Israel was released from bondage in Babylon, they no longer had to fight for their supremacy among nations. Supremacy was not a possibility for them any longer. They would not, and will not, return to the zenith of David's and Solomon's reigns until the kingdom of Messiah in the last days. For the most part, the restored nation had no enemy breathing down their necks in the fifth and fourth centuries BC. As a result, they wandered in their relationship with God. They began to look, sound, and feel much like their contemporary world. Because they patterned their hearts after their world, their habits and practices looked like the world. Therefore, God promised to judge against the "sorcerers, against the adulterers, against those who swear falsely, against those who oppress the hired worker in his wages, the widow and the fatherless, against those who thrust aside the sojourner, and do not fear me, says the Lord of hosts" (Malachi 3:5 ESV).

One area affected most severely by Israel's worldliness was marriage. The men were guilty of divorcing their wives and marrying pagan women (2:11, 16). One day the chickens came home to roost, as they always do. One day the people of Israel realized that God had wandered off—or so it would appear to their proud eyes—and they no longer enjoyed His blessing. One day they realized that even though they attended the temple regularly, and even though they presented offerings to God, and even though they did all the right religious stuff, God was not on their side anymore. In fact, they wondered why God had stopped loving them. Malachi told them, "'I have loved you,' says the Lord." But [they wondered,] "How have you loved us?" (Malachi 1:2a ESV). Because God loved His chosen people, He rebuked their worldly ways. Specifically, God pointed out that the men had failed in their relationships with their wives because they had failed to guard their spirits in that area.

The foregoing brief history lesson ought to sound like tomorrow's news to us. The statistics are in. The modern generation of Christians has progressively embraced the sins of their world. Christians have become so much like the rest of the world that it is almost impossible to tell them and the world apart. Professing Christians, like their world, also take drugs, commit adultery, tell lies, cheat their employees, despise widows and orphans, and wish the immigrants would go home. God accused Israel of those very sins in Malachi 3:5. Professing Christians think and act like the world because they really do not have awesome respect for God and His Word (3:5b). Christians are hedonistic, fleshly, and materialistic just like the atheistic, polytheistic sinners who make up the majority of the culture. To let the culture lead is to assure certain failure.

It is no wonder then that the divorce rate among professing evangelical Christians has surpassed the divorce rate of the culture. Indeed, the chickens have come home to roost. Incredible pain, endless stress, ongoing court battles, embarrassment, emotional baggage, and sorrow characterize many professing Christian families. While the families keep doing all the right religious stuff, and keep praying verbosely to a distant God, they wonder why He stopped loving them.

To many American Christian husbands, the distant God sends the same message He sent to faltering Israelite husbands. Essentially God said to them, "You have caused a breach in your relationship with Me, because you breached your covenant with your wife." And, "You broke covenant with your wife because you did not guard your spirit" (2:16). Husbands, we must guard our spirits lest one day we discover that we are flooding the altar of the distant God with our tears to no avail.

PEOPLE AT ODDS WITH GOD TEND TO BE UNFAITHFUL
TOWARD OTHER PEOPLE (Malachi 2:10-12)

The Israelites, especially the men, were guilty of breaking relationships (vv. 10–11). God describes their sin by saying that they were being faithless toward each other. This treachery, or willful breaking of agreements, was so unacceptable because God Himself was their Father, which is not to teach the universal fatherhood of God. Some people are still "of their father the devil," like the first-century Jews were according to Jesus' assessment. But the Israelite men in Malachi's day had a common bond in God. God the Father had called the nation of Israel into existence through Abraham. He created the nation just as surely as He created each person in the nation. This is the same Father figure mentioned in 1:6, where God reminded the rebellious Israelites that sons are expected to honor their fathers. Certainly the heavenly Father should receive respect from His children.

God rightly stands as the Father figure to Israel. It is not a position He usurps or demands but a position that is rightly His since He birthed the nation. Many years before God spoke through Malachi, Isaiah encouraged the nation by saying, "But now thus saith the Lord that created thee, O Jacob, and he that formed thee, O Israel, Fear not: for I have redeemed thee, I have called thee by thy name; thou art mine" (Isaiah 43:1). How could those people not understand that God was their Father by right of giving them birth?

Because each member of the nation shared the common relationship with God, they each had a responsibility toward each other. The people of God are rightly called "brothers." Since each one was part of the same covenant with God, each citizen was responsible to obey the stipulations of God's covenant. Each one was responsible for his actions and attitudes toward other members of the covenant. That was God's plan. That kind of response is precisely what common logic demands.

> Because He adopts us into His family, He is definitely our Father, and we are certainly responsible to answer to Him.

Instead of being faithful to each other, the people of Israel, in particular the men, dealt treacherously with each other. The word translated "treacherously" or "faithless" means that the people broke faith with each other. They were not dependable to keep their agreements or the promises they made toward each other. The word *treacherous* hints at disguise, deceit, or underhanded dealings. Why did the people do that? The people needed to remember that the restored nation of Israel (which was much smaller and less significant than Israel under David and Solomon) had been established on the covenant of God in the beginning. When that covenant became unimportant to them, they became unfaithful toward God. When they became unfaithful toward God, they became unfaithful toward each other. Their faithlessness was rooted in "dishonoring or treating as common" the covenant of God. They were guilty of profaning the covenant. It affected every social, business, or familial relationship. The society was in shambles because of the people's wrong view of the covenant God made with them.

Though Christians are not Israelites, God can justifiably level similar accusations against us. God calls His people today into the body of Christ through the covenant of His blood. Because He adopts us into His family, He is definitely our Father, and we are certainly responsible to answer to Him. Therefore, Christians are responsible to each member of the same family. However, it is too common for Christians to be faithless in their promises and agreements just like the ancient Israelites were. As a result, many Christians do not keep their word in business. Too many of them do not keep their covenant in church membership. The result of such faithlessness might very well be a temptation for other Christians to feel like Job, who complained, "My brethren have dealt deceitfully as a [seasonal] brook, and as the stream of [seasonal] brooks they pass away" (Job 6:15). It is not easy to live with people who have taught their peers to doubt them and second-guess their decisions.

The Israelites' were treacherous toward each other because they were faithless toward God first (v. 11). This was the root problem. God expected the priests to teach the people His law and the principles of that law.

Then God expected the people to obey the principles the priests taught. Apparently no one, priests or people, was doing what God expected. In particular, it appears that the priests also failed to teach God's principles regarding marriage, and the results were devastating. It is obvious that the priests were guilty because in 1:6 God blamed them for setting the standard of despising His name for the rest of the people.

Apparently the priests did not teach, or at least did not emphasize, purity of marriage among the people of God alone. Mixed marriages resulted in the pollution of God's sanctuary. The men disregarded God's will, desire, and law and married foreign women. Why did they do that? Because the women were beautiful! What greater reason does a man need for disobeying God? So what did God have against foreign women? Interracial marriage was not the issue here. Interreligious marriage was the problem. These foreign women served false gods. God called the worship of foreign gods an abomination, and, therefore, marriage to such women was also an abomination in God's catalog. An abomination is a ghastly sin and offense against the heavenly Father.

God said that marriages like this, marriages that disregarded His uniqueness and His holiness, resulted in profaning His sanctuary. Though the men who were involved in these mixed marriages did not themselves go into the temple and profane the Lord's sanctuary, the fact that priests who served God tolerated their sins repulsed Him. How does God view the treachery of modern Christians? Is God still repulsed by Christians' unfaithfulness?

God promised serious consequences because of the Israelites' sins (v. 12). He declared that He would separate the perpetrators from the assembly. This was His law from the beginning. God prescribed "cutting off" of people who ignored His covenant. Leviticus 18:1–29 speaks pointedly about moral purity; the need for Israelite men to abstain from foreign women is implied in a couple of verses in that text. Generally, being "cut off" meant death.

God promised this serious consequence for the abomination of faithlessness in spite of the perpetrators' outward rituals. These men regularly offered prayers through the priests. They appeared to be quite serious about religion, but their outward religious activity disguised a heart that was faithless toward God and faithless toward God's people. God is not impressed with our external expressions of religion because these things can be done out of a faithless heart.

HUSBANDS AT ODDS WITH GOD TEND TO BE FAITHLESS TOWARD THEIR WIVES (vv. 13-16)

The Israelites did not understand the sin that caused a breach between them and God (vv. 13–14). They certainly realized that a breach existed (v. 13). This is Malachi's underlying argument. The people questioned if God loved them. They thought that God had abandoned them. They appeared to grieve over the broken relationship. Most people who read this story and observe the tears of these brokenhearted men flooding God's altar would assume that these guys really wanted to be right with God, which is interesting in light of the fact that typically only the priests approached the altar. This might be a symbolic statement indicating that the men flooded the altar through the work of priests. That is, the men wept and the priests offered their offerings. Many Christian husbands sorrow when the consequences of sin come to bear in their lives. Sometimes it is the first time they have seriously engaged in prayer. But nothing seems to happen. The problem doesn't disappear. The shame still hovers over them. "What is wrong?" they wonder. "Where is God? Why did He forsake me? I don't deserve this," they conclude. They are wrong on every count.

The treacherous, faithless, abominable Israelite men did not understand that the breach between them and God was caused by marital problems (v. 14). They prayed profusely, but it seemed as though God did not answer. They were right! God really did not answer their prayers because they had broken their marriage vows. When each of these men married the wife of his youth, he made a vow to God to love her and care for her. These men almost certainly engaged in an actual covenant publicly. Witnesses observed what they promised. Can you imagine anything so serious? Of course we can. A similar scenario takes places dozens of times annually in the typical American church.

So too, Christian husbands make a similar covenant with the woman they marry, in the presence of God, in the presence of many witnesses. Typically, the pastor asks something like, "Groom, will you have Bride to be your wife, to live together after God's ordinances in the holy estate of matrimony? Will you love her, comfort her, honor and keep her in sickness and in health, and forsaking all others keep yourself only unto her so long as you both shall live?" In all the weddings I have performed, the groom, at this point says, "Yes." So far, not one groom has said, "No," or asked for time to think about the questions. Getting an affirmative answer from the husband to be, the pastor continues by asking the groom to repeat something like the following: "I, Groom, take you, Bride, to be my wedded wife, to have and to hold from this day forward, for better for worse, for richer for poorer, in sickness and in health, to love and to cherish, till death us do part, according to God's holy ordinance; and thereto I promise you my loyalty."

How sad to see that, like the Israelite men, modern husbands break the covenant they made in the presence of God and peers when marriage becomes inconvenient. God's indictment for such sin is fitting:

> She whom you thus wronged was the companion of those earlier and brighter days, when in the bloom of her young beauty she left her father's house and shared your early struggles, and rejoiced in your later success; who walked arm in arm with you along the pilgrimage of life, cheering you in its trials by her gentle ministry; and now, when the bloom of her youth has faded and the friends of her youth have gone, when father and mother whom she left for you are in the grave, then you cruelly cast her off as a worn-out, worthless thing, and insult her holiest affections by putting an idolater and a heathen in her place.[1]

God promises not to listen to the prayers of such men, even today. Peter warned, "Likewise, ye husbands, dwell with them according to knowledge, giving honour unto the wife, as unto the weaker vessel, and as being heirs together of the grace of life; that your prayers be not hindered" (1 Peter 3:7). God is very serious about the husband's faithfulness to his wife.

God's plan does not allow for unfaithfulness under any circumstances (vv. 15–16). In a brief review of His plan, God pointed out in verse 15 that He ordains unity in order to produce godliness (v. 15). His original plan was to make a one man/one woman unit. The pronoun *them* refers to Adam and Eve, whom God ordained to be one flesh. Malachi pointed out that God made them one with only a portion of the Spirit. He had enough Spirit in creation to make

God is very serious about the husband's faithfulness to his wife.

an entire harem for Adam. But that would result in confusion, conflict, jealousy, envy, hatred, and other such sins and sorrows. Only foolish men would ever think that multiple wives should get along just fine. Women know that this is a ridiculous idea.

God's plan reveals His wisdom in that the one man/one woman unit is more likely to produce offspring that will bring about God's glory. If there is any doubt about this principle, consider the evidence of the generation produced by dysfunctional families. Our culture has quickly gone from one that once respected God, God's Word, God's people, and God's work to one that laughs at God-ness and teeters on the brink of anarchy.

This is why God hates unfaithfulness (v. 16). The Hebrew words make for a very difficult translation in verse 16. The English Standard Version translation is very accurate word for word, but it does not flow with the continuity of the text. A better translation is "'For I hate divorce,' says the LORD, the God of Israel, 'and him who covers his garment with wrong,' says the LORD of hosts. 'So take heed to your spirit, that you do not deal treacherously'" (Malachi 2:16 NASB). The warning in this verse could not be clearer. God hates divorce. That conclusion ought to be obvious from God's clearly stated standard from the beginning. His plan for Adam and Eve was "So they are no longer two but one flesh. What therefore God has joined together, let not man separate" (Matthew 19:6 ESV). How could God make His will any plainer?

God hates the breaking up of a marriage so much that He likens divorce to covering the "garment" with violence. That is a strange picture, but it probably stems from the practice of a would-be groom spreading the corner of his garment over the bride to be. This act symbolized the desire for conjugal rights or symbolized the would-be groom's claiming of the woman as his wife. That is exactly what the story of Ruth and Boaz reveals. It is similar to the Christian view that the bed is the point or place of consummating the marriage. In the Christian culture, to defile the marriage bed is to treat the foundation of the marriage with violence. God despises anyone who boldly dares to attack His will in this matter.

So what should a man do to keep from committing this abomination? God gives a simple solution to the problem: husbands are required to be vigilant and put up a guard. The word *guard* means to pay attention to, take care of, guard or protect. The object to be guarded is our spirit. That word literally speaks of breath or wind. It is the power or life of the person.

The spirit is the unique feature of human life such as mental capacity, emotions (joy, anger, or temper), personality, and will. The spirit is the real person. When it leaves, the body is dead. Some say it is synonymous with soul, or the same as heart. That seems clear from God's desire for His people to "love the Lord your God with all your heart and with all your soul and with all your might" (Deuteronomy 6:5). God repeats this requirement ten times in the Scriptures. He really wants His people to love Him with their whole being. He really wants husbands to protect that being. To guard the spirit with diligence is not an option—it is a requirement.

Practically, the solution or antidote to faithlessness requires that husbands get their thoughts about other women under control. The same requirement goes for how the husband feels about his wife, how he responds to his wife, and what he desires for his wife. The consequences of not doing this are devastating. It breaks fellowship with others, it breaks fellowship between the husband and his wife, and it breaks fellowship with God, Who refuses to answer the treacherous man's prayers. It is far better for husbands to follow God's advice and put up the fences around their spirits.

PUT IT TO WORK

1. What kind of thoughts do you entertain about women other than your wife?

2. Do you think those thoughts are harmless as long as you don't act on them?

3. Does it matter to you that God knows your thoughts?

4. Does God consider a treacherous thought to be as bad as a treacherous action?

5. Does God answer your prayers?

He who finds a wife finds a good thing and obtains favor from the LORD. (Proverbs 18:22 ESV)

W hat is a wife worth? King Lemuel's mother taught him that an excellent wife is worth more than precious jewels. The modern culture probably doesn't agree. According to a fictitious letter written to Dear Abby, there are other things more valuable than a wife to some men. The letter said,

> Dear Abby,
>
> I've never written to you before, but I really need your advice on what could be a crucial decision. I've suspected for some time now that my wife has been cheating on me. The usual signs . . . phone rings but if I answer, the caller hangs up. My wife has been going out with the girls a lot recently although when I ask their names she always says, "Just some friends from work, you don't know them." I always stay awake to look out for her taxi coming home, but she always walks down the drive. Anyway, I have never approached the subject with my wife. I think deep down I just didn't want to know the truth, but last night she went out again and I decided to really check on her. I decided I was going to park my Harley Davidson motorcycle next to the garage and then hide behind it so I could get a good view of the whole street when she came home. It was at that moment, crouching behind my Harley, that I noticed that the valve covers on my engine seemed to be

leaking a little oil. Is this something I can fix myself or should I take it back to the dealer?

Are there really some men who value their toys more than they value their wife? If so, they do not understand or do not acknowledge the value God places on the wife He gave them. When a husband does not hold his wife in proper esteem in his heart, his devaluation of her will be obvious in his actions and responses. That devaluation often causes the wife to share his low view of herself. As a result, the whole family is turned on its head regarding the value of the wife and mother. The children don't respect Mom because Dad does not evaluate her properly. Therefore, Mom ends up with a low self-image, which can lead to depression, which causes greater problems for the family. Who wants to live in that kind of family? Many women do live that way even if they would prefer not to.

Would it not be better for everyone in the family to value the position of the wife as does God? What does God think of the wife? How important, how valuable is she according to God's standard? An interesting comparison of two proverbs reveals just how important the wife is in God's scheme. In Proverbs 8:35 Wisdom says, "For whoso findeth me findeth life, and shall obtain favour of the Lord." The Bible clearly states that this God-given wisdom is the chief thing. It is so valuable that God encourages us to seek it above all else.

In comparison, it appears that God said the same thing regarding the wife. Our text says, "Whoso findeth a wife findeth a good thing, and obtaineth favour of the Lord" (Proverbs 18:22). To find a wife is to obtain favor from God just like finding wisdom is to obtain favor from God. Obviously, God thinks very highly of the wife. Then is it not important for the husband to also think highly of her? Yes. It is also important for the wife to remember that God considers her to be the evidence of His favor to the husband. That view will bolster a wife's self-esteem immensely. While the world's overemphasis on self is sinful, it is also wrong for wives to think of themselves more lowly than does God. A wife does not honor God if she sees herself as a lowly loser when God clearly states that she is the evidence of His blessing to her husband.

TO FIND A WIFE IS TO FIND GOD'S FAVOR

Solomon concluded that when a man finds a wife he has found a good thing. Since these words are in the Bible, one must assume that this is

God's assessment of the situation. The word translated "find" lays down an important principle in the process. This kind of finding presupposes that seeking took place first. This is not a picture of a husband accidentally finding a wife. Rarely does this Hebrew word mean "befall" or "happen upon." The guy in this picture does not stumble across this treasure and declare, "Eureka, I found it!"

However, it is interesting that when the scholars translated the Old Testament into Greek during the third through first centuries BC (the Septuagint), they translated the word for *find* with the Greek word *hure*. That is the root word for *hurisko*, which is precisely the English word "Eureka," which means "I found it." However, even *hurisko* means to find while searching. For example, in the New Testament we read that the wise men searched diligently for the Christ child and were elated when their search was successful (Matthew 2:8–11). Jesus taught that His work is like that of the shepherd who goes out and searches for the one lost sheep (Matthew 18:13). In both of these illustrations, a diligent search is implied. The finding was the result of diligent searching.

But it is true that the word can also mean to stumble across an object or truth accidentally. One would be wiser to conclude that such fortunate stumbling is apparently by accident because there are no accidents with God. When the authorities demanded a tax from Jesus and His followers, Jesus told Peter to go to the Sea of Galilee, throw in a hook at random, pull in the first fish caught on the hook, open its mouth, and there he would find a coin that would be sufficient to pay taxes. Peter wasn't searching for a coin in a fish's mouth. That would be a futile search indeed! That he found a coin in the fish, just as Jesus promised, was a miracle. *Hurisco*, he found it!

In this text in Proverbs, Solomon painted a picture of a man who was diligently seeking something in particular. The Hebrew word is used consistently to describe the searching/finding process. God encouraged His people to do this: "But if from thence thou shalt seek the Lord thy God, thou shalt find him, if thou seek him with all thy heart and with all thy soul" (Deuteronomy 4:29). God promised His people during Jeremiah's day, "And ye shall seek me, and find me, when ye shall search for me with all your heart" (Jeremiah 29:13). God also warned people in Isaiah's day to "seek ye the Lord while he may be found, call ye upon him while he is near" (Isaiah 55:6). When God calls people to Himself, He commands them to search for Him diligently, and He promises that He will be found.

In this text, the man who searches for a God-honoring, God-ordained wife will be like a man on a treasure hunt. The searching man who finds the thing searched for has gained the goal. The word *find* also means to attain. It speaks of reaching a goal. That is what a treasure hunter does. In this case, the goal is a wife. The same Hebrew word is used in Proverbs 16:31, where Solomon concluded, "Gray hair is a crown of glory; it is gained in a righteous life" (ESV). That is not to conclude that one attains gray hair because he lives a righteous life. A lot of people who are very unrighteous attain gray hair. In fact, there are usually only two choices in the matter: either our hair turns gray or it turns loose. In this verse the person attains the crown of glory through a righteous life. He searched for it and found it.

The same is true for the man who searches for a wife. He does not gain gray hair or even a crown of glory. What does the man gain as the result of his search for a wife? When God created the universe, He did everything well. But having created the man, God was not quite finished. "Then the LORD God said, 'It is not good that the man should be alone; I will make him a helper fit for him'" (Genesis 2:18 ESV). God's plan for making a helper for the man was to take one of his ribs and form a helper from it. "And the rib that the LORD God had taken from the man he made into a woman and brought her to the man. Then the man said, 'This at last is bone of my bones and flesh of my flesh; she shall be called Woman, because she was taken out of Man.' Therefore a man shall leave his father and his mother and hold fast to his wife, and they shall become one flesh" (Genesis 2:22–24 ESV).

After that creative act God pronounced everything "good." Therefore, Solomon concluded that when a man finds a wife, it is a good thing. In a sense, it means that the wife concept completes God's plan for man. But there is more to it than that in this text. Generally, the word translated "good" means to be pleasing, delightful, or delicious. In this text, the word speaks of other aspects of goodness such as beauty, desirability, or pleasantness. In an abstract sense, the concept of wife is "good" because she fulfills God's plan.

> Solomon concluded that when a man finds a wife, it is a good thing.

Not all wives fill this qualification. It is true that "a virtuous woman is a crown to her husband" but on the other hand, "she that maketh ashamed is as rottenness in his bones" (Proverbs 12:4). It is not good when "a foolish son is the calamity of his father: and the contentions of a wife are a continual dropping." But it is good when "house and riches are the inheritance of fathers: and a prudent wife is from the Lord" (Proverbs 19:13–14). Too many husbands have learned that "it is better to dwell in a corner of the housetop, than with a brawling woman in a wide house" (Proverbs 21:9). Therefore, it is obvious that not all wives are good even though they complete God's plan. Let's not forget that sin wrecked the ideal plan.

The wife that is good has that intrinsic quality of being desirable, pleasant, delightful, and pleasing. To say she is "expensive" (as the word can fairly be translated) would be a fair assessment of her value, not an indication of her cost. The word *good* speaks of "superior quality or relative worth." That is what a man blessed by God finds when he searches for a wife.

It is not entirely up to the man to come to this good end. To find a wife is to obtain God's favor. God's favor is the blessing. The good wife is evidence of God's goodwill and favor, or, to put it another way, she is evidence of God's will. God grants this special blessing to the searching man simply because He is kind. As Jeremiah concluded, "[His mercies] are new every morning" (Lamentations 3:23). At times God does let His blessings dribble out a little at a time. However, the husband who has found a wife obtains an outpouring of God's blessing. The word for "obtain" in Proverbs comes across as "gushing out" in Isaiah, which says, "If you pour yourself out for the hungry and satisfy the desire of the afflicted, then shall your light rise in the darkness and your gloom be as the noonday" (Isaiah 58:10 ESV). God is not stingy when He allows us to obtain His blessing.

God provides the blessing of a good wife in the same way He provides the blessing of wisdom—both are gifts. Earlier Solomon had concluded, "For the Lord giveth wisdom: out of his mouth cometh knowledge and understanding" (Proverbs 2:6). In similar fashion he said, "Happy is the man that findeth wisdom, and the man that getteth understanding" (Proverbs 3:13). In this text Solomon used the same words when he concluded, "He who finds a wife finds a good thing and obtains favor from the LORD" (Proverbs 18:22 ESV). The wonderful find is of the Lord. It is His doing, His favor.

WISE HUSBANDS AND WIVES RECOGNIZE GOD'S BLESSING

A wise husband realizes that his wife is God's gift. He has searched diligently and God has blessed. If the man is truly wise, he will search with wisdom. Sometimes it seems that many husbands actually do discover their wives by accident. How does that happen? Well, there is a young man walking through a mall or across campus. He sees this beautiful young woman, and instantly he is smitten with love (at least he would call it love). He contacts her; they date; he proposes; she accepts; they say, "I do." Now what? Now he needs to learn what love really is because he has committed himself to her for life. Wouldn't the relationship be stronger at that point if he had pursued the woman with wisdom?

Wisdom requires a careful searching. In practical terms, the wise search means that the man should write down what he desires in a wife. While the exercise might seem foolish, it does allow him to see if any of his desires are foolish or not God-honoring. The practice also helps the man eliminate anyone who does not measure up to God's will for him.

Second, if he is exercising wisdom in his search, the man will look in the right places. If I want to buy a Coca-Cola, I am not going to go into a bar to place my order. I can probably find a Coke in the bar, but people generally don't go to the bar to drink soft drinks. People usually go to 7–11 or McDonald's if they want a soft drink. So too, a wise man will not go to a bar or club or rock concert to find a wife who wants to be a missionary as he claims he wants to be. If a man wants a Christian wife, he should look in places where one would expect to find Christian women. If a man wants a wife to go to the mission field with him, he needs to look in a place where missionaries are trained. Furthermore, the wise man will search according to his criteria. What good is accomplished by making up a list of desirable traits and then ignoring the list?

Third, the most important practice in the search process is prayer. The man must diligently pray over his criteria and about his search. More than anything else, he must desire God's will.

Then one day, after having identified God's will, praying about God's will, and pursuing God's will, when he finds his treasure, the man will rejoice greatly. One time I watched a documentary film about the men who found the *Titanic*. They had invested all the money they could gather, plus the money of sponsors who underwrote their search. The project required millions of dollars and years of hard searching. When the underwater cameras finally affirmed that the rusty object below was indeed the object of their search, they were quite happy. Indeed, one would have been surprised to see the treasure hunters standing on the deck of the ship

The husband who finds a wife should rejoice in God's leading and God's blessing.

with somber faces. Of course they were happy! They were shouting and jumping and rejoicing because they had finally found what they had dedicated their lives to search for. So the husband who finds a wife should rejoice in God's leading and God's blessing.

Some of the joy in finding a wife should be in the fact that the man knows that he has obtained God's gift. He realizes that God brought about His will. He searched, but God directed. That confidence makes for stronger marriages.

A small warning is in order here. Not everyone who searches finds. Sometimes a category three guy wants a category one wife, and his search is frustrated. Maybe he is a Shimei, but he wants to marry an Esther. That probably won't happen. Or maybe he is an Alexander the coppersmith but wants to marry a Priscilla. Thinking too highly of oneself is an effective way to scuttle good results. At other times, failure results because a guy is looking in the wrong place for the right thing. However, there are also times when a search for a wife comes up empty because it is not God's will for the man to marry. In such situations, the search fails because God has greater plans for the person that requires full dedication. Paul unfolded this situation in 1 Corinthians 7:32–34.

A wise wife understands that she is the evidence of God's blessing to her husband. It is important for a woman to be fixed in this understanding so that when she has a bad day her confidence will not be shaken. And bad days do happen! At certain times of the month she might feel inferior or depressed or useless. During those days, the wise wife must remember that God gave her to her husband to show the man His favor. Then there will be days when the wife will do something foolish. On those days, she might wonder if she is a burden to her husband instead of a blessing. If she dwells on her failure and forgets that God gave her to her husband as a favor, she will harm the relationship. The wise wife must always understand that God gave her to her husband as an indication of how much favor He bestows because He loves the man.

Her understanding helps her fulfill God's role as the suitable helper for her husband. She needs to remind herself daily that she is the evidence of God's blessing to her husband. Remembering God's plan gives her confidence to carry out her role as the helper that is fitting, the home manager, the encourager. God gives a good wife to a man in order to show favor.

The good wife needs to constantly remind herself of God's plan. Apparently God sees the wife as a quality, superior, "expensive" kind of person or he would not have given her to her husband.

Solomon's God-inspired idea is not quite the same as the ideas one hears espoused on television these days. Human wisdom is convinced that happiness in marriage is either a mirage or might be found in multiple relationships. God's plan is so much easier and safer. The husband who possesses God's wisdom because he has awesome respect for God understands that his wife is a gift from God.

Likewise the wise wife understands that God gave her to her husband as a demonstration of His kindness. That kind of relationship will enjoy the very happiness the world clamors for but never finds.

PUT IT TO WORK

1. How did you find your wife?

2. After you said "I do" to your wife, what was God's will for you regarding her?

3. Wife, why did God let your husband find you?

4. Husband, what can you do to reinforce God's teaching so that your wife understands that she is a treasure?

5. What can you do, as a couple, to help other couples learn this important truth?

PRINCIPLE 10
God intends for the husband to be the point man.

I want you to understand that the head of every man is Christ, the head of a wife is her husband, and the head of Christ is God. (1 Corinthians 11:3 ESV)

For the husband is the head of the wife even as Christ is the head of the church, his body, and is himself its Savior. (Ephesians 5:23 ESV)

The title "point man" refers to a soldier who is assigned to a position some distance ahead of a patrol as a lookout. In cavalry terminology, the men scouting ahead of the main force were said to be "riding point." The concept seems to have been introduced to the American military at West Point by Professor Dennis H. Mahan, who taught most of the top officers on both sides in the Civil War. His *Elementary Treatise on Advanced-Guard, Out-Post and Detachment Service of Troops* (1861) was standard instruction in the middle nineteenth century.[1]

Point man was the most dangerous position in the platoon. John M. Zehnder, Army SP/4, was killed in Vietnam on September 28, 1967, serving in such a capacity. He was awarded the Bronze Medal with one Oak Leaf Cluster and the Purple Heart posthumously. The award said in part,

> While on a search and destroy mission, Specialist Zehnder was walking point for his platoon when they were suddenly pinned down by a heavy volume of enemy automatic weapons fire. . . . Realizing the need for instant retaliation he

started crawling to the nearest enemy position and when he was within a few meters of it he assaulted the position by firing his weapon and throwing hand grenades into it. . . . He succeeded in knocking out the position and broke up the assault. . . . Then observing a wounded man lying in an exposed position and with complete disregard for his own safety he ran through the withering hail of enemy fire in an effort to reach his wounded comrade when he was mortally wounded.[2]

That is what a point man does.

Vietnam veteran Jerry Lyons recalled:

We operated in the Mekong Delta area during most of my tour. One of the major contributors to our unit's casualties was the VC [Viet Cong] booby trap. They were well-concealed anti-personnel explosives, often detonated by an unsuspecting GI on patrol who snagged a trip wire attached to a grenade, claymore mine, or artillery round. I eventually volunteered to be my squad's Point Man so I could have more control over the pace of movement on operations. . . . I became somewhat competent in this job, but not without some close calls. On Christmas day 1968, I stepped on a grenade that was set into the mud for an unsuspecting American to kick by accident. The pin was pulled so the handle should have flown off and set the fuse when I kicked it. Thank God for dry weather. The mud was dried and the handle didn't move. I was fortunately able to observe and learn from the best Point Man around. His name is Tyrus Becker. As I remember, before he went home, Becker went on to instruct at and possibly started-up the Brigade Booby Trap School. He was that good. He taught me things that I know kept us out of trouble. He spotted a trip wire caught on my flack jacket zipper one morning in the Pineapple Grove, Southwest of Saigon, while on a company-sized operation. I hadn't noticed the thin monofilament fishing line caught on my flack jacket until he told me to freeze. The booby-trapped artillery round at the other end would have done major harm to more than just me, had he not seen it. I would learn to see these things as he did. My survival would depend on it."[3]

That is what point men are like. Steve Farrar picked up this idea and built on it in his book, *Point Man: How a Man Can Lead His Family.* This book encourages and equips Christian men to lead their families successfully through hazards and ambushes like divorce, promiscuity, suicide, and drug addiction. That is a good description of real life. In the war against the family, God is looking for faithful point men. Indeed, God ordained that the husband/father is in that position. Many Christian husbands hear that God appointed them to be the head of their homes and rejoice with glee, not realizing what the position requires. Husband, your job is not to make decisions and command the other family members to toe your line and do your bidding. That is the description of a fool, not a leader. The real leader is the point man. God's job for husbands is to lead their families through the enemy's minefield. It is his duty to discover and point out booby traps that the enemy plants to destroy his family. He does it because he loves them.

God gave three examples of his authority structure (1 Corinthians 11:3).

First, in God's plan for leadership, Christ is the head of every man. Some people would argue that this must be true, while others would argue that it is not true at all. It is certainly true that Christ is the head of the church. Or it might be safer to conclude that Christ is supposed to be the head of the church. God's plan is for Christ to be the leader, or governor, of the church. This must be the case because God the Father "put all things under his feet, and gave him to be the head over all things to the church" (Ephesians 1:22). Christ not only inherited this position as head of the church from the heavenly Father but He also won it. Paul reminded the Ephesian Christians that "the husband is the head of the wife, even as Christ is the head of the church: and he is the saviour of the body" (Ephesians 5:23).

Because of His perfect life, and the sacrifice of His life for the church, Christ rightly deserves to be the head. Paul argued that "He is the head of the body, the church: who is the beginning, the firstborn from the dead; that in all things he might have the preeminence" (Colossians 1:18). The fact that Jesus Christ is the beginning, and the firstborn from the dead, cements His right to be the head of the church.

> God's job for husbands is to lead their families through the enemy's minefield.

Unlike earthly human husbands, Christ won and deserves to have the position as not only the head of the church but the head of every person. In reality, Christ is the head of every person. Sadly, most people don't understand the relationship. Christians are supposed to understand this as well as acknowledge Christ's headship in their lives. That is one of the things that makes them different from unbelievers. Unbelievers reject the concept and reality of Christ's headship. However, one day everyone will admit that Christ is his head. Christ, God the Son, willingly laid aside much of His glory for a time and came to earth to give His life as a ransom for sinners. "Wherefore God also hath highly exalted him, and given him a name which is above every name: that at the name of Jesus every knee should bow, of things in heaven, and things in earth, and things under the earth; and that every tongue should confess that Jesus Christ is Lord, to the glory of God the Father" (Philippians 2:9–11). That will happen because Christ is the head of every person.

The picture of Revelation 20:11–15 is a fearful sight. In those verses John described the great white throne judgment. There we learn that in the end of the ages Christ, Who really is the head of all people, will judge those who rejected His headship. He will condemn them for eternity. He is your head! Believe it and accept it.

Second, God illustrated His plan by saying that the husband is the head of the wife. The most accurate application of the principle in this text has to do with the man/woman relationships in the local assembly. The context of the example is the argument for orderliness in public meetings. In order to avoid chaos in the meetings, God ordained that in the church, the man must be the head. Because that is true, women are supposed to learn quietly and in submission to the male leadership (1 Timothy 2:11–12). That is not exactly a popular opinion today.

While the example in this text applies to the local church setting, the same principle applies to the husband/wife relationship both here and in Ephesians 5:23. Notice that even within the local assembly context God requires of wives, "if they will learn any thing, let them ask their husbands at home: for it is a shame for women to speak in the church"

(1 Corinthians 14:35). God's plan calls for the husband to be such a head to his wife that she will be able to learn from him. Ephesians 5:23 further clarifies the application to the husband/wife relationship. That passage will come under observation a little later in this chapter.

Third, God illustrated His plan by saying that God is the head of Christ. This example might be difficult to comprehend. Is it not true that God the Father and God the Son are eternally equal? Yes. Then how can one be the head of the other? The incarnate God (God the Son, Jesus Christ) submitted to the headship of God the Father. It is true that God is one. But He manifests Himself in three separate persons: God the Father, God the Son, and God the Holy Spirit. All three persons are equal; yet, all three have separate functions on occasion.

Therefore, God the Son proved often during His incarnation, His earthly ministry, that God the Father was His head. One day when the disciples returned from Sychar, where they had gone to get food, Jesus told them, "My meat is to do the will of him that sent me, and to finish his work" (John 4:34). The statement confused the disciples about food, but not about headship. On another occasion God the Son told the critics who doubted Him, "I can do nothing on my own. As I hear, I judge, and my judgment is just, because I seek not my own will but the will of him who sent me" (John 5:30 ESV). Of course the ultimate expression of God the Son yielding to the headship of God the Father was in the Garden of Gethsemane, where He prayed, "Father, if thou be willing, remove this cup from me: nevertheless not my will, but thine, be done" (Luke 22:42). A greater illustration of submission to headship will never be found.

Is God the Father the head of God the Son? Obviously yes. Is Christ the head of every person? Yes, even though everyone does not admit it yet. Is the husband the head of the wife? Since the other two examples are true, this must be also.

GOD APPLIED THE PRINCIPLE OF AUTHORITY TO THE HOME (Ephesians 5:23)

Unlike the divine standard, the husband's position as head is not due to a superior nature. No husband deserves to be the head of his wife. God the Father deserves to be the head of Christ, and God the Son deserves to be the head of every person, because They are perfect in every way. When it comes to the headship of the husband, the same standard does not apply at all. Since Adam's sin, no husband has been even close to perfect. We each are tainted with the sinful nature because of Adam's fall. Since we have the sin nature, we each also have obvious flaws in character. Would a husband be so foolish as to attempt to make himself look better than his wife and, therefore, conclude that he ought to be the head?

God did not ordain that husbands should be the head because they are superior in any way. That fact is obvious from the words found a little further into this argument about husbands and wives in church. God said through Paul, "Nevertheless neither is the man without the woman, neither the woman without the man, in the Lord. For as the woman is of the man, even so is the man also by the woman; but all things of God" (1 Corinthians 11:11–12). God deserves to be man's head, but man does not deserve to be woman's head. We are equal—equally needy of spiritual life and maturity.

If husband and wife are equal, why did God ordain that the husband would be the leader? The husband must serve as head in order to facilitate orderliness. God, Who created the world in orderly fashion, does all things orderly. That includes family issues. Sin-tainted creatures must have leadership. Someone must be responsible to point the family in the right direction. Someone must be responsible to take the blame when family members go the wrong direction.

The buck must stop on someone's desk. God ordained that the husband should take that responsibility. It is really not a position of ease and prestige anymore than being a point man is the position for which soldiers typically compete.

Like the divine standard, the husband must exercise his headship through love. A tyrant is not a leader. For a time it may appear that the heavy-handed husband has everything and everyone in perfect order. *The Sound of Music* was based on a true story. Sometimes true stories are enhanced to make good movies. In this case Captain von Trapp was a real person. Not much is known about the real von Trapp's character, but in the movie his character impresses the viewer with the idea that he ran his family with perfect order. Captain von Trapp was in charge. Was he the consummate leader? No. He was more like a tyrant who stifled the hearts and souls of his family.

Some Christian husbands believe that it is best to emulate von Trapp and rule with an iron fist. They demand that their wives clean the house, prepare meals, do the laundry, teach the children, and keep everything in spotless order—after they have worked a job most of the day. "Why shouldn't I expect as much," they argue. "God is orderly, isn't He?" More than anything, God proves that a leader must lead with love not tyrannical demands. If the tyrant's wife does not fulfill his desires to the tee, he considers her to be unscriptural, ungodly, and unsubmissive. This causes a breach in their relationship, which exacerbates the problem until an almost unresolvable dislike is rooted in the wife and children.

What causes a man to behave like that—and call it leadership? Sometimes a man like that has a very unrealistic view of life. He has developed the foolish assumption that life really can be lived according to his dreams, or like he saw in a movie or read in a book. "Little House on the Prairie" was never, in real life, like the books or the movies portray. The average American really would not have liked to live then and there. Isn't it funny that people who lived in the good old days always thought it would have been better to have lived in the good old days?

Sometimes a husband leads without love because he has an unrealistic view of himself. He fails to see his own weaknesses or shortcomings and, therefore, expects his wife and family to live according to a standard he thinks only he achieves. Men like that generally love themselves instead of their families. They make lousy leaders. Often, in such cases, tyranny is an unconscious effort to mask their own inadequacies.

At other times, Christian husbands convince themselves that God's plan is to run the family like the military. They demand absolute submission to authority. In that setting, there are no negotiations just as there are no negotiations between a private and a general. Subordinates do as they are told without asking questions. Actually, that attitude does not work well even in the military. Husbands like that need to wake up to the wonderful reality that they are not generals, their wives are not sergeants, and their children are not privates. They are all God's children. God saddled the husband with the responsibility to lead them in love.

The sad truth is that the tyrant's failure is often revealed years later when it is too late to effect any changes. Because he does not love, there is continual tension in the home. At best, that results in husbands and wives tolerating each other, with the wife looking forward to the day when the tyrant dies. It is not unusual in such settings that when the children grow up, the wife leaves. Also not unusual is the fact that the kids grow up rejecting the Christianity the tyrant father claimed to have.

A real leader is willing to sacrifice. Like the point man who is willing to lay down his life in order to save those who follow him, so is the Christian husband. How can a husband claim to be willing to lay down his life for his family when he won't even lay down his opinion for them? A real leader has wisdom to listen to the needs, desires, and opinions of his followers.

Real heads of the family are like Christ, the head of the church, Who did lay down His life for His disciples in every age. He Who was perfect in every way, sacrificed His life for bumbling, faltering followers. No husband even approaches Christ's perfection in this life. Yet some pretend that their conclusions are always right, which is to claim perfection. Some errantly think that if a wife disagrees, she is ungodly. Real love sacrifices pride and personal opinions for the good of the wife. The chief characteristic of the point man must be love. The husband who really leads must love the Lord his God with all his heart, soul, mind, and strength. And he must love his neighbor as himself. The husband's nearest neighbor is his wife and then his children. A good point man follows the example of the greatest point man, Jesus Christ.

PUT IT TO WORK

1. Husband, why did God determine that it is best for you to be the head of your wife?

2. How have you shown your family that you love them in the past month?

3. How does Christ lead His people through the minefields of life?

4. What should a husband do if he wants to understand Christ's leadership better?

5. Why do some husbands think that listening to their families is a sign of weakness?

An excellent wife who can find? She is far more precious than jewels.
(Proverbs 31:10 ESV)

A few years ago, I was talking to a young man in the church parking lot when his sister came bursting out of the building, jumped into the car, and sped away. He just shook his head and said, "She'll never be a P31W." That was the first time I had heard the phrase and I, like some of you, wondered what he was talking about. He explained that among his peers, P31W was the code name for all that is contained in this text from Proverbs 31. A P31W is a woman who measures up, at least to some extent, to God's standard for wives according to these verses.

Some people conclude that this text, which begins in verse 10, starts with a rhetorical question: "Who can find an excellent wife?" They say that the implied answer is "No one." According to this view, the wife described in this text does not exist—never has—never will! However, such a conclusion causes a person to wonder why God put the standard in His Bible if it is unattainable. Why God would conclude this section by saying that these are the traits of a woman who fears the Lord (v. 30), if the principles just stated are impossible to attain?

While it is true that the standard is high, it is also true that God gave the principles in order to define His standard for wives who have a right relationship with Him. Is the standard attainable in real life? Possibly not in totality, but probably in part. This standard is like the standard for the Christian life. Christians strive to be like Christ, knowing that in some part they will always need to improve. Necessary improvement notwith-standing, true believers do not abandon the entire standard of Christ because it is too difficult to achieve. It is always the goal.

No doubt many wives feel that the standard in this text is unreasonable or even harsh. Surely, they conclude, these requirements are the product of a man's imagination—an uncaring man's imagination. Surely this is the standard of a man who has lofty goals for his wife, but no earthly idea what it is like to be a woman. Actually, the case can be made that these are the recommendations of a woman who was inspired by God regarding these conclusions. It appears that the words of verses 10–31 are the continuation of the motherly advice taught by King Lemuel's mother. Some ancient translations of the Old Testament place these words apart from the foregoing teaching of Lemuel's mother. However, most modern translations have the words where they are in the English Standard Version text, indicating that they are a continuation of motherly advice.

Is the standard high? No one should argue that they are not. Are the requirements unattainable altogether? No, not since God recommends them to God-fearing wives. Should a wife set this standard as her goal? Yes. Should she become distraught if she falters while trying to achieve the goal? Never.

THE GENERAL CHARACTERISTICS OF AN EXCELLENT WIFE (Proverbs 31:10-12)

As you might expect, the excellent wife is valuable (v. 10). That conclusion must be drawn in light of the evidence laid down about this kind of woman. She is excellent because she is rare. How rare the woman is might be indicated by the fact that the Hebrew word translated "excellent" refers to strength, power, wealth, or might. Those are not the typical traits one would expect in a godly woman. Excellent men might look like that, but not virtuous wives. However, the word also speaks of something that is worthy or a person who is virtuous or a person who achieves high moral standards. Therefore, excellence might be seen more accurately as an achievement in life instead of a trait a woman possesses from birth. The excellent wife is not born excellent; she becomes excellent.

"Who can find such a woman?" the writer wonders. The question does not imply that such a wife does not exist, but it does imply rarity. In a museum in Charlotte, North Carolina, I saw a 1993 Cobra-R Mustang. Ford produced only 107 of these cars. This particular car had been driven a total of seven miles. To say that it is rare is an understatement. Who can find such a car? It is rare, but it can be found. When a man finds it, he also discovers that it is very valuable. So is the excellent wife.

Because this kind of wife is rare, she is more valuable than jewels. She cannot be bought; she is not for sale. No amount of rare gems will equal her value to her husband. Because she is excellent, she is not so foolish as to sell herself to the highest bidder. Lesser women do that, but not the excellent wife. Her husband would never exchange her for any amount of money. What makes her so valuable? Why does her husband hold her in such high evaluation?

The excellent wife is rare because she is beneficial to her husband. The excellent wife is rare and excellent because she is beneficial to her husband (vv. 11–12). Is that to conclude that most wives are not beneficial to their husbands? Most wives do not benefit their husbands the way this woman does. First, her husband finds her to be trustworthy (v. 11). In his soul, he trusts her. The deep inward nature of this trust means that he does not trust her simply because someone told him that he should. Nor does he trust her because she demands it. Rather his very being has the strongest confidence in her. He just knows that she will respond correctly in every circumstance.

In practical terms, that means that the husband of the excellent wife trusts her around men. He knows that she will conduct herself properly. He is confident that she will not flirt or try to gain the attention of other men. But the "other men" issue is not the only area where this kind of woman proves trustworthy. Another area of life that seems to foster lack of trust in the modern age is money. The husband of the excellent wife is completely confident that he can trust her with money. He does not hesitate to hand her the checkbook or the credit card and tell her to go to the store and have a good time. He knows that when he invites her to buy whatever she wants, she will be wise and discreet.

This is obviously not an imposed trust. It flows from within the man's soul. What causes him to trust her so deeply? The husband of the excellent wife has learned from experience that he will benefit from her character (vv. 11b–12). Her lifestyle causes him to have no lack of gain. The man knows that this wife will bring gain, increase, or prosperity. Of course, the human mind turns to money and financial gain at the mention of such a trait. However, the excellent wife does not just cause her husband to prosper financially—though that is the chief thought here. Rather, she also brings to her husband emotional, spiritual gain. The big picture of her life reveals that the excellent wife does her husband good, not harm. What must a wife be like who establishes that kind of reputation?

THE SPECIFIC HABITS OF THE EXCELLENT WIFE (vv. 13-27)

In verses 13–27 is a list of at least thirteen different practices that characterize the excellent wife. For the sake of clarity, these characteristics can be divided into three categories. However, they are completely artificial, which allows for some overlapping.

First, there are three practices that prove that the excellent wife is diligent. The text states that this kind of woman works with her hands (vv. 13, 19). This is obvious as the woman goes out of the home and searches for basic necessities such as wool and flax (v. 13). Having gathered these items, or in the process of gathering them, this woman willingly works with her hands. The word willingly indicates that she is glad to do it. No one has to twist her arm to get her to exert real physical labor. She is not afraid to engage in what many modern women consider to be below them.

Second, this wife shows diligence as she expends extra effort in order to be frugal (v. 14). She brings food from afar, which means that she puts forth the extra effort to get a good deal on food. In modern settings, this wife is the proficient coupon clipper. She knows she does not have time to get food every day so she plans ahead, clips the coupons, goes to the store where they allow triple couponing, and saves a good chunk of money in the process.

Third, the excellent wife is diligent because she exercises regularly. Really? That's in the Bible? Sure. On the one hand, God said through Paul's letter to Timothy that physical exercise is somewhat profitable (1 Timothy 4:8). On the other hand, verse 17 of this text clearly states that the wise woman dresses herself with strength and makes her arm strong. There is no better way to interpret the verse than to say that she exercises. This kind of woman understands how important exercise is to good health. That connection is indisputable in this modern age of medicine. She also understands the importance of looking nice for her husband. It is rather unfair for a young woman to work out incessantly in order to keep in shape so that she can win her husband's attention with her nice appearance and then let herself go once she has snared him. Therefore, the excellent wife continues to exercise and stay fit. She does not do this in order to attract the attention of other men. She is interested only in her husband's attention, and as a result his heart safely trusts in her.

It doesn't take too many days of regular exercise for the would-be excellent wife to realize that exercise takes discipline and determination. She must be diligent. A lazy or slothful woman will not benefit her husband or family. She will be like an albatross around their necks. Lack of diligence can be the result of sickness. However, more often it is the result of wrong thinking. The excellent wife knows it is good to be diligent and sets her heart to that end.

The second group of practices proves that the excellent wife focuses on others before being concerned for herself. According to verse 15, this woman cares deeply for her household. Each morning she gets up early, while it is still dark, in order to get food ready for her family. Notice in this verse that there are also household servants in the larger context of the family. Why would a woman with household servants (maidens) even get up early in the morning? We would expect her to stay in bed and have the servants bring her breakfast. But this excellent wife not only gets out of bed, she even gives portions to her servants. That might mean that she gives a portion of food to those who would be expected to serve her, or it can mean that she distributes to them their portions, that is, their responsibilities for the day. Either way, why is the woman so diligent that she gets out of bed while it is dark in order to attend to her duties? She does so because she cares for others.

Because the excellent wife is concerned for others, she refuses to be lazy (v. 27). The ways of her home are important to her. This wife could sit by idly taking care of herself alone, but she knows that her home would suffer. Therefore, she chooses to be a diligent, proactive manager of her home. A manager like that will know the family members' schedules. She knows where the children and husband are and what they are doing. She stays one step ahead of circumstances and causes things to happen instead of reacting when something unexpected happens.

The excellent wife also manifests concern for others by caring for people who are outside her family (v. 20). She opens her hand to the poor and reaches out her hand to the needy. The open hand indicates generosity.

This kind of wife is able to discern when a person is poor (afflicted, humble, wretched) or when a person is just foolish. She is able to discern true need. She understands that the truly needy are people in want, and she also understands that there are times when the needy only appear to be needy. Sometimes people are in want because they are lawbreakers or lazy. The excellent wife is familiar with Paul's warning to Christians about work and obeys the principle. Paul warned the Thessalonian believers, "For even when we were with you, this we commanded you, that if any would not work, neither should he eat" (2 Thessalonians 3:10).

This woman promotes her husband (v. 23). Her husband is known as a leader among the people. He is the kind of fellow whom one would find sitting among the elders and leaders in the city gate. Some of this is due to his wife's reputation of benefiting him. She is never his competition but always his ally.

The excellent wife reveals her concern for others in the way she communicates encouragement (v. 26). She speaks wisdom. That wisdom begins with God's principles, as Proverbs 14:1 teaches, and works out in common sense practices. The rare wife teaches with kindness, not pride, arrogance, or a "know-it-all" attitude. In many ways the excellent wife is "others" focused. She will be hospitable, kind, compassionate, and encouraging. She knows that this takes time and energy, but she is willing to do it.

> The excellent wife reveals her concern for others in the way she communicates encouragement.

Finally, there are five traits that indicate that the excellent wife exercises wisdom in life. First, she is wise to take care of herself (v. 22). While it is good and necessary for a wife to look beyond herself to help her family and people outside her family, at the same time it is right and good for her to take care of herself (v. 22). One way she does this is to make tapestries or bed coverings for herself. She also clothes herself with fine linen and purple. These words teach that the excellent wife pays attention to her clothing so that she does not look frumpy or embarrass her family by being unkempt.

Second, the excellent wife is perceptive (vv. 16, 18a). She is able to see a potential business opportunity, map out how it will work, and then make it work (v. 16). She knows when her work is valuable and when it is not and needs a change of direction (v. 18a).

Third, she is creative (vv. 16, 24). She looks at a raw field, sees the potential, plans a vineyard, plants the vines, takes care of it, and then harvests a vineyard (v. 16). That takes creativity and initiative. She also runs a manufacturing business where she makes the merchandise and then takes it out and markets it (v. 24).

Fourth, this kind of wife exercises wisdom in that she is always prepared (vv. 21, 18*b*). She looks ahead to the coming winter and makes sure that her family will be prepared by getting warm clothing together for them (v. 21). The seasonal change does not take her by surprise. Also, she reveals her preparedness in the middle of the night, when she must get up to take care of the children. She never steps on toys that were left on the floor because the night-light is on. Why is the night-light on? Because the excellent wife made sure that the lamp had oil and that the wick was lit. Her light does not go out at night (v. 18*b*).

Fifth, the excellent wife is confident (v. 25). Because of her moral strength, she has a sense of dignity. This quality helps her face the future with confidence. The excellent wife exercises practical wisdom in a way that makes people place confidence in her.

THE PLEASING CONSEQUENCES OF THE EXCELLENT WIFE'S HABITS (vv. 28-31)

One of the most refreshing consequences of all the hard work, discipline, and love the excellent wife expends is that her family praises her (vv. 28–29). Her children rise up and call her blessed. When the text says that they rise up, it means that they show her respect. However, the children of the excellent wife go beyond showing respect. They also publicly acknowledge her efforts and her character. What causes children to respond like that? The excellent wife has won their confidence and respect by her godly life. This is quite different from wives and mothers who attempt to beat their children into submission. A tyrant can demand obedience, but an excellent wife wins honor and respect by the way she orders her life.

Another consequence of the excellent wife's life is that her husband also praises her (vv. 28*b*, 29). Literally, the text says that her husband says, "Hallelujah!" (v. 28*b*). Really. The English word is virtually a transliteration of both the Hebrew and Greek words. Typically when we say, "Hallelujah," we use the word to boast of God. The husband of the excellent wife boasts about God first, and then about his wife. He concludes about her,

"Many women have done excellently, but you surpass them all" (Proverbs 31:29). Those words make for good boasting. God would have husbands do that.

The excellent wife is what she is because she simply lives out a right relationship with God (v. 30). Her relationship with God helps her avoid common pitfalls in life. One of those pitfalls is found in charm. The excellent wife understands that charm can be put on like makeup and actually hide the real person. Charm is not necessarily authentic. Another potential problem is beauty. This woman understands that beauty is vain. It is already passing away. It too can be put on, hiding the real person. Notice that nowhere in this text is beauty listed as a trait of the excellent wife. Yet a woman's beauty is often the chief attraction to men.

Most important of all is the fact that this woman has a right relationship with God that results in praise. She does what she does because she has awesome respect for God. She is humble before God, and God allows her to be exalted. In the end, the excellent wife will reap what she has sown (v. 31). She will reap the fruit she has planted.

The works of her hands will become as obvious as if they are declared in the public gate. If the wife has been selfish and careless in her family relationships, those fruits will be declared later in life and she will be embarrassed. Far better for the wife to fear God and live a life that honors Him. The fruit of her hand will exalt her in days to come.

It is unlikely that any wife will meet all these qualifications, but the wife who seeks to be excellent should strive for them. Nevertheless, she should not make this standard a list of laws to be checked off or left blank each day. Those efforts will become a depressing burden. Rather, this standard should be used as a measuring stick to measure "fear the Lord." A right relationship with God is the foundation for the excellent wife. To some extent, she can gauge her walk with God by her desired lifestyle. If her life is characterized much like the standard the world suggests, she is out of fellowship with God. If her life is characterized more by these principles, she is more likely to be in fellowship with God. The woman who succeeds in keeping many of these standards through sheer grit and determination will ultimately be a very miserable woman. The woman who is characterized by doing things like this because of her relationship with God will be happy, blessed, and worthy of praise.

PUT IT TO WORK

1. How much does your husband trust you?

2. Is there anything you can do to encourage your husband to trust you more?

3. Based on your life so far, what will the works of your hands say about you in the end?

4. Do you really fear the Lord or are you content to try to keep traditions?

5. What can you do to gain greater respect for God?

PRINCIPLE 12
Tell the truth in a helpful way.

Therefore, having put away falsehood, let each one of you speak the truth with his neighbor, for we are members one of another. Be angry and do not sin; do not let the sun go down on your anger, and give no opportunity to the devil. . . . Let no corrupting talk come out of your mouths, but only such as is good for building up, as fits the occasion, that it may give grace to those who hear. And do not grieve the Holy Spirit of God, by whom you were sealed for the day of redemption. Let all bitterness and wrath and anger and clamor and slander be put away from you, along with all malice. Be kind to one another, tenderhearted, forgiving one another, as God in Christ forgave you. (Ephesians 4:25–27, 29–32 ESV)

In a study done a few years ago, a group of industrial engineers were asked how to improve productivity. Communication concerns drew the strongest response to any question on the survey. More than 88 percent of the engineers strongly agreed that the lack of communication and cooperation among different components of a business leads to reduced productivity.

CEOs have also recognized the importance of communication. In one study, an employee-benefits consulting firm found that 97 percent of the CEOs surveyed believe that communicating with employees positively affects job satisfaction. Furthermore, the survey found that 79 percent think that communication benefits the bottom line. Ironically, only 22 percent of the CEOs surveyed admitted that they communicate with employees on at least a weekly basis.

Communication is an important element of successful businesses. It is also important for the local church. One of our greatest challenges at our church is accurate and thorough communication. Often someone in the chain of command gets skipped, or we wrongly assume that everyone or at least someone knows the latest plan. The problem is exacerbated by the fact that some people think they need to know every detail, while other people really don't care about details. Trying to figure out how, when, where, and why to communicate plans and details is a bit challenging. Just letting the proper people know the proper things in a proper manner is a big enough obstacle alone.

If communication is important for businesses and churches, it must be important for families too. In fact, communication is one of the most important elements for successful families and yet one of the most commonly neglected. It's the kind of thing that takes work. It doesn't happen of its own volition. It appears that communication in the typical American family amounts to the husband yelling at the wife, the wife in turn yelling at the children, the children in turn yelling at the dog, and the dog barking at the neighbors. It's called the trickle-down theory. Surely there must be a better way to interact.

The better way is described in Paul's letter to the Christians who lived in Ephesus. In the first three chapters of the letter, Paul described the wonderful reality of salvation in Christ. Beginning with the first verse of chapter 4, Paul explained in certain details how a person who is truly born again ought to live. The last eight verses of the chapter contain several characteristics describing Christian communication (with one verse about stealing stuck in the middle). This instruction is invaluable for setting the standard for communicating in a marriage.

A marriage is in trouble when the only things the husband and wife communicate about are money and what to watch on television. And even then they end up yelling at each other. God has a better way. God's plan for communicating requires us to tell the truth (especially when we are angry), to communicate grace, to avoid harmful words, and to be kind and forgiving.

TELL THE TRUTH—EVEN WHEN YOU'RE ANGRY (Ephesians 4:25-27)
According to verse 25 one of the important characteristics of being one of the redeemed is truth telling. The verse states a negative approach and

a positive approach. Negatively, the people whom God redeemed from sin should put away falsehood and keep telling the truth. Lying is the root issue in this thought. People of this postmodern age, in keeping with postmodern ways of thinking, will retort, "What is lying to you is not necessarily lying to me." That way of thinking betrays the fact that the postmodern citizen is his own authority—alone! However, the very words of this text clearly explain what constitutes lying. The Greek word gives us the English word *pseudo*. Something that is pseudo looks like truth but is not. The word is often attached as a prefix to a compound word in order to describe an action, attitude, or object that looks like the real thing but is not really the real thing. From that fact someone fairly deduces that, in many cases, a lie is an attempt to cover what is really true. As such, a lie takes many forms. Lies might be half-truths, exaggerations, or outright false statements. They are found in regular conversations, expense accounts, taxes, and claims regarding the amount of time worked.

Christians are supposed to have put such habits aside. God's people are to lay aside the practice of lying like a laborer lays aside a dirty garment after work. The concept is pictured by the person who lays aside a garment in order not to be hindered in the work. A very ugly illustration of that is found in Acts 7:58, where the people who stoned Stephen to death laid their garments at Saul's feet. They didn't want garments impeding their grizzly progress. Lying impedes progress on the road to heaven.

Therefore, laying aside lying like a dirty garment is just a part of the overall new practice of converted people. Just a few verses earlier in this letter Paul said, "But that is not the way you learned Christ!—assuming that you have heard about him and were taught in him, as the truth is in Jesus, to put off your old self, which belongs to your former manner of life and is corrupt through deceitful desires, and to be renewed in the spirit of your minds" (Ephesians 4:20–23 ESV). Putting away lying is a decision the individual makes. Putting away lying is the character of converted people because changed people act like . . . changed people.

The positive approach requires that changed people tell the truth to their neighbor. Like the lawyer mentioned in Luke 10:25, you might ask, "Who is my neighbor?" Our neighbors include everyone with whom we have any kind of relationship. My neighbor is found at work, in the neighborhood of course, in the store, and at church. Paul argued that Christians must not lie, but keep on telling the truth to the neighbors because we are all members of the same body. That truth applies directly to Christians who are members of the body of Christ and secondarily to everyone because we all depend on each other. Some cultures have demonstrated the horrible results of lying. In those cultures it seems that no one trusts anyone and as a result families suffer, business suffers, and even the economy suffers.

In a more specific way, this same truth applies to the husband and wife relationship. A husband's wife or a wife's husband is his or her nearest neighbor. A husband and his wife are more intimately members one of another than is true in any other human relationship. Because husbands and wives depend on each other so much, they must trust each other. A successful relationship depends on trust, and trust is built on truth. There is no alternative for telling the truth in a marriage.

But what if the truth makes the spouse angry? That's okay because the text instructs God's people to get angry, but not to the point of sinning (vv. 26–27). Do humans really need a command to get angry? It seems obvious that getting perturbed is a common experience of human nature (v. 26). However the word Paul used here speaks of a deep-seated anger, a settled conclusion, as opposed to an outburst or losing one's temper. Whenever anger jumps up, it is a good indication that there is a problem—and not necessarily with the one who is angry. Often the expression of anger is sinful because it is an expression of unrighteousness. More often than not anger is an expression of selfishness. Selfishness is the root problem when a person responds angrily to circumstances or people who thwart personal desires.

> Because husbands and wives depend on each other so much, they must trust each other.

Anger can also be a matter of righteous indignation. When that is the case, anger is actually useful. In a sense, anger is a God-given emotion that serves like a red flag to indicate that something is wrong and needs attention. In that sense, it is the emotion Jesus experienced when He needed to address a problem. For example, Mark recorded that Jesus was angry because the religious people were so hardhearted and hypocritical (Mark 3:5). Did that mean that Jesus lost His temper? Not even close. Anger is certainly the emotion that drove Jesus to cleanse the temple on two different occasions (Luke 19:45; John 2:13). In a similar way, Jesus taught that it is possible for a person to be angry with his brother for just cause (Matthew 5:22). In fact, the verb form in this verse requires that the phrase be translated "keep on being made angry." It is a command to deal with this common emotion.

While it is possible for anger to be used in a productive or useful manner, it is also possible to sin in anger if the emotion is not used productively (v. 27). This is a warning for God's people to guard against letting anger fester. The Christian husband or wife should never let the sun go down on his or her wrath. Christian spouses must always be aware that unresolved anger leads to bitterness, which leads to all kinds of trouble. Therefore, God's people must keep short accounts, especially with their nearest neighbor, their spouse.

Wisdom requires that we deal with things as soon as possible because not to deal with the problem leads to sin. It gives place to the Devil, and Satan's influence does not have good results in any circumstances. To open the door, or to give a foothold to Satan, is a very dangerous thing to do. Yet the statement sounds so theological that someone must wonder how the problem appears in real life. What does it look like? One example might be that, for the fiftieth time, your wife has done the same thing that bothers you. Instead of taking care of the problem when the red flag of anger waves, you become sullen and keep dwelling on how much her habits bother you. She asks, "What's wrong?" You say, "Nothing, I'm just tired." You just lied. You are supposed to put away falsehood and tell the truth, especially when the problem causes anger.

It is generally better to be honest and deal with the problem—unless of course we are willing to live with the problem. Not all problems in a marriage need resolving through confrontation or negotiation. Some problems can be easily resolved through patient acceptance. For example, if a wife is not a gifted cook, the husband will probably not resolve the problem by telling her that she is not a good cook each time she serves a meal. Does she serve lousy meals? Yes. Is the man being truthful by telling her that she is a lousy cook? Yes. But not all truth needs to be stated. If it is possible to live with a problem through love and patience, that is a wise position to take.

However, if husband and wife are going to solve a conflict, they must do so by telling the truth and working out the problem according to the standard stated in verses 29–32. Sometimes the best way to deal with the anger is to honestly assess the problem. If after honest assessment we discover that the problem is not really an important issue at all, we must determine not to get angry about it anymore. Stopping the angry response is a viable solution to the problem. Sometimes honest assessment helps a couple realize that the perplexing problem is unsolvable. Snoring is like that most of the time. Instead of getting angry about an unresolvable issue, it is wiser to get over it. Sometimes a couple discovers that the thing that stirs up the anger is an issue on which one or both can make a personal sacrifice. Once the couple draws that conclusion, the problem doesn't matter and they can stop being angry. Anger requires that we tell the truth to ourselves first, and then to the person (spouse) who appears to be causing the anger.

TELL THE TRUTH IN A HELPFUL MANNER (vv. 29-32)

It is one thing to blurt out the truth and quite another to speak truthful words that are helpful (v. 29). Christian husbands and wives must cease from speaking corrupting words. The word translated "corrupting" refers to something that is rotten, like bad fruit. Jesus taught that bad trees produce rotten fruit (Matthew 7:17). The fruit from such trees is not useful and might even be harmful. Words can be like that. Thus, Paul said that each person is responsible to stop letting such words travel out of their mouths.

So, someone might conclude that if he simply told the truth all the time, he would never have to worry about letting rotten words travel out of his mouth. That is not necessarily true. Sometimes even the truth is more harmful than it is good. How can that be? While it is important not to lie, it is not always necessary to say everything that is known, and it is especially not necessary to always say what we think. Wisdom requires that love cover idiosyncrasies, shortcomings, and failures. Peter challenged Christians, "And above all things have fervent charity among yourselves: for charity shall cover the multitude of sins" (1 Peter 4:8). How does that work? In all honesty, your husband is not the handsomest man in the world, or even in the hollow for that matter. It is also true that he is not the brightest light in the harbor. However, what good could possibly come from telling him that he is stupid and ugly? Is it true? Yes, for the most part. Do those words help? Not even a little bit.

Instead of letting rotten words travel from our mouths, we should speak words that offer grace. The goal should always be to use words that are of benefit to our spouse. Acknowledging that goal forces us to ask, "Why do I want to talk about . . . ?" Or it makes us wonder, before we speak,

"In what way will it build her up?" Will your wife be a better wife, better mother, or better Christian for hearing what you have to say? If our words are going to build up, we must communicate in such a way that the result is like building a house, strengthening a wall, or building up muscle. That is what Paul meant when he wrote, "So then let us pursue what makes for peace and for mutual upbuilding" (Romans 14:19).

To speak words that result in building up the hearer is to communicate grace. Grace is undeserved favor. Our words to our spouses should demonstrate a kindness of heart that is predisposed to help.

Unfortunately, words are often flung out like barbs in order to belittle the spouse. Why? It is often an attempt to tear down the spouse in order to make self look better. The goal must always be to communicate with useful and profitable words.

Positively, God-honoring spouses will speak words that please God (vv. 30–32). Angry words, words that flow out of deep-seated anger, or words that are driven by passionate anger, do not please God. Words like that grieve the Holy Spirit (v. 30). In other words, it is possible to speak words to the nearest neighbor that cause the Holy Spirit to sorrow. Most people probably give little thought to the possibility that they might say something that grieves God. But how can a Christian really want to make the Person sad Who guarantees his eternal salvation?

Words spoken out of a bad heart do that very thing. Therefore, God taught in verse 31 that His people must determine that they will have bad words lifted up and carried away from their minds and lips. The verb in this phrase means that someone or something removes such words. The teaching plainly requires that the individual must determine to yield to the Holy Spirit so that He will make this change in habits. The individual must stop speaking wrong words, but this can be accomplished only through the ministry of the Holy Spirit.

What kinds of words are wrong words? Paul listed six different kinds of words, or motivations behind words, that disqualify them from the Christian's repertoire. First are words that flow from bitterness. Bitterness is deep-seated resentment caused by envy toward another. Second, words that are driven by wrath are disqualified. Wrath is not like anger. It is passionate, boiling over. Wrath happens when a person loses his temper. Third, words of anger must also be removed. This word describes

the kind of anger that is deep-seated. It becomes especially deep-seated when the person refuses to deal with it. Fourth, words of clamor are forbidden. Clamor means yelling and screaming. Fifth, words of slander are words that speak blasphemy. They are words that talk down about someone in an effort to defame the person. Finally, words of malice convey hostility and hatefulness with the desire to hurt the hearer with words. The rule for Christians regarding such words is simple. Do not talk like this—period!

Bad words are not helpful because they are not useful. God-like forgiveness is helpful (v. 32). Therefore, God told His people to be in the continual process of becoming kind to each other. To be kind is to rise above natural human responses. It means that we will take the high road instead of groveling with the masses. In addition to becoming kind, God requires His people to be becoming tenderhearted toward each other. The word means to be compassionate. Compassion is a tenderness that flows from the depths of the heart. Kindness and tenderheartedness are going to require a unique heart. A typical human heart can accomplish such tasks only through incredible discipline. And then it is usually not lasting.

Finally, God's people must forgive each other. When spouses forgive, almost all problems are solvable. In some cases, this word means to hand over into custody. That is a great description of forgiveness. It looks like this: Someone sins against you, which causes pain. The pain becomes a burden, which the offended person is now forced to carry. Then the offender repents of his action or attitude and comes and confesses the sin to the person he offended. You, being the offended one, hand over the burden to the person who caused it. You cannot carry the burden of offense anymore because you gave it away. Forgiveness is a lot like canceling the debt, which is another meaning of the Greek word. This is what God did for sinners through Christ. Forgiving is an ongoing thing. Hopefully, things are not so bad between a spouse and his nearest neighbor that he will need to forgive every day. But if daily forgiveness is required, it must be offered.

This kind of communication makes for strong families. In fact, this kind of communication will solve a large majority of all family problems. This standard is the truth. It is God's standard. Tell the truth in a way that will benefit your nearest neighbor.

PUT IT TO WORK

1. Do you tell your spouse how you really feel about things?

2. Do you feel compelled to tell your spouse unnecessary things that you know will hurt him or her?

3. How can you give your spouse advice without sounding condescending?

4. How do you keep the conversation going with your spouse?

5. Do you think that raising your voice is the best way to get your point across when talking to your spouse?

> **But I want** you to understand that the head of every man is Christ, the head of a wife is her husband, and the head of Christ is God. . . . For a man ought not to cover his head, since he is the image and glory of God, but woman is the glory of man. For man was not made from woman, but woman from man. Neither was man created for woman, but woman for man. (1 Corinthians 11:3, 7–9 ESV)

Men and women are different. That is not a profound conclusion. Everyone knows it. Little children understand this reality. Too often the parents of little children act as though they are trying to change the reality. Men and women not only look differently and function differently biologically but they think and feel differently. As a result, some things in life are characterized as masculine and some are characterized as feminine. Someone concluded that if women ruled the world, even traditionally masculine things like bowling alleys would immediately take on a feminine appearance. And almost everyone admits that car dealerships would suddenly emphasize car color instead of make or model if women ruled the world.

The foundational motivation for the various modern feminist movements is a desire to eradicate the natural (God's design) differences between men and women. The women involved in these movements claim that they want for themselves all the so-called benefits that men have enjoyed for years. Therefore, they seek to erase as many differences as possible. They have had some success. A couple of generations ago young women did not play the same sports boys played. Now there are even professional women's basketball and soccer teams. Is that unbiblical? Probably not. But seeing how deeply women are involved in what was once a "man's" domain does indicate that the feminists are succeeding, to some extent, to erase boundaries that differentiate.

The business arena is another area where these differences are disappearing. There was a time when a woman would almost never be found in a corporate board meeting, unless of course she was a secretary taking notes. Now it is not uncommon for the chairperson of the meeting to be a woman. The fences to that part of the man's world have also been broken down in many areas. Is that ungodly? Probably not.

One of the most obvious areas where feminists have made progress in breaking down walls of distinction is in clothing. Not too many years ago a person could tell the difference between a man and a woman at a distance of one hundred yards. Now it can be difficult to tell the difference when the person is standing a few feet away. A few months ago my wife and I heard a clerk address a customer as "Ma'am, I mean sir, uh . . . Ma'am?" Is this a problem? This is indeed a problem.

God really did create the man and the woman to be different. The process He used to bring the very first man and first woman into existence was different. The purpose He gave them in life was different. The positions and authority levels He gave them were different. When did God change all that? At what point did God issue a disclaimer in which He declared that all the original differences were declared null and void?

Some scientists even acknowledge the God-ordained differences between men and women. A recent news article revealed that researchers have discovered that evolution made the backs of women different from the backs of men. This was necessary so that women are able to adapt while carrying babies. The researchers concluded that if men carried babies, they would fall over because their backs are incapable of adjusting to the extra weight carried out front. Now, according to this news article, "evolution" is personified. It has the power to create men and women differently!

Men and women are different. We are different because God the Creator made us that way. In fact, thousands of years after God made the original distinctions between men and women, He reaffirmed those differences in the letter He inspired Paul to write to the Corinthian Christians. The

Corinthian culture was a lot like our modern culture. Those ancient Christians had to deal with many of the issues of sin, license, and liberty—as they are opposed to righteousness—that we struggle with. Even feminism reared its head in the first-century Roman Empire, which caused Christians to step back and consider the ramifications of such movements.

God, through Paul, established His authority structure in the third verse of this text. God said that the head of every man is Christ. Christians should be quick to agree with that. God also said that the head of Christ is God. How can we disagree with that? God also said that the head of the wife is the husband. A lot of folks disagree with that conclusion, but their cries of "foul" fall on deaf ears. This is God's plan—period!

In the context of that statement, God showed the Corinthian Christians how He expected the wife to show respect to her head (her husband) in the meetings of the Christian assembly. God really did make a difference between the husband and the wife. For the wife to acknowledge that difference in her appearance and deportment is to honor God's plan. For her to attempt to erase that difference is to imply that God was somehow mistaken in His plan. A wife can, and should, demonstrate respect for her husband in the meetings of the local church.

GOD'S PLAN FOR FIRST-CENTURY CORINTHIAN CHRISTIANS

Women, not men, were to have their heads covered while praying and prophesying (vv. 4–6). In fact, in the Corinthian culture, a husband would dishonor his head if he covered his head while ministering (v. 4). The kind of ministering is stated in the words *praying* and *prophesying*. That is not to say that a man is ungodly if he is stuck in a tree wearing a baseball cap and he prays for the Lord to get him down. The context in this argument is public ministry, which would take place in the context of the local church gathered in someone's house.

Praying is talking to God about people. Prophesying is talking to people about God. That being true, prophecy might take the form of preaching, which is declaring God's message to many people. Or it might take the form of admonishing or edifying an individual by communicating the principles of God's Word to him or her.

In that ancient culture, if a man engaged in these kinds of things with something on his head, he was guilty of dishonoring his head. That statement helps point out the significance of the uses of the word *head* in this text. The same word might refer to the actual head, the place where a person puts his ball cap. If so, how could he put to shame or disgrace his cranium by wearing a head covering? However, *head* is also the same Greek word found in the previous verse, where it speaks of Jesus Christ. That being true, it is clear that the man can dishonor, or put to shame, his direct authority, Jesus Christ, by covering his literal head. How could this happen?

Christ is the head of the man. That fact was established in verse three. In the first century Roman culture, for a man to cover his head while engaged in worship symbolically sent a clear message. For a man to pray with his head covered (in normal circumstance, unlike a soldier wearing a helmet) was to declare that someone present was his authority. The head covering in Paul's culture demonstrated submission to the higher authority. That was the issue. Christ is the man's authority. If the man prayed with a hat on, he dishonored Christ by symbolizing that someone in the meeting was a greater authority than Christ. That is a difficult principle for us to understand because we do not live in a culture where the head covering means such a thing.

Unlike their husbands, wives dishonored their head if they uncovered their head while ministering (vv. 5–6). Again this principle is set within the context of ministering (v. 5). Here we see the possibility of the wife praying (talking to God) or prophesying (talking to people about God) within the context of the gathered church. But, isn't the woman supposed to be quiet at church? Why would she be praying or prophesying? Paul made that point abundantly clear later in this letter when he said, "Let your women keep silence in the churches: for it is not permitted unto them to speak; but they are commanded to be under obedience, as also saith the law. And if they will learn any thing, let them ask their husbands at home: for it is a shame for women to speak in the church" (1 Corinthians 14:34–35). In that text, the argument is regarding peace and orderliness in the meetings (14:33). So the argument is, rather than have a wife blurt out in public, questioning her husband, she must wait until she gets home to ask him her question. If we remember that the church met in homes, it is clear how easily a wife asking her husband questions would disrupt the meeting. If the wife did not remain silent, it is very likely that she might humiliate her husband.

Rather than speak out, Paul said, she should fulfill God's law about this matter. What does God's law say about this? For the Jewish thinker, God's law is contained in the first five books of the Bible. Genesis 3 contains God's curse against Eve and Adam because of their sin. "Unto the woman he said, I will greatly multiply thy sorrow and thy conception; in sorrow thou shalt bring forth children; and thy desire shall be to thy husband, and he shall rule over thee" (v. 16). Women do have pain in childbirth, and women do struggle with the desire to take the leadership in the home, but God's plan is that the wife should not exercise authority over the husband. That the wife should not usurp her husband's authority is His law.

Furthermore, this dilemma is answered when we realize that God also taught that the woman is not to exercise authority over the man in the public assembly. Paul told Timothy, "Let the woman learn in silence with all subjection. But I suffer not a woman to teach, nor to usurp authority over the man, but to be in silence" (1 Timothy 2:11–12). Does that mean that it is impossible or unlawful for a wife to pray to God in a public assembly? Of course not. Can a wife encourage or teach another woman or children in a public assembly? Sure.

> That the wife should not usurp her husband's authority is His law.

While the first-century Christian woman in the Roman culture prayed and encouraged others, she needed to be sure her head was covered. The issue is a symbol of respect (vv. 5–6). The veil (literally the statement here is "having down from head") was a common head covering for many years in that culture. Ancient sculptures help us understand that the peplos was worn at least in the second century BC. A sculpture of Caesar Augustus's wife, Livia, reveals that on the occasion commemorated by the sculpture, sometime near AD 29, she wore a veil. There seems to be good evidence that the peplos was still common among women of the Roman Empire in first century AD. The women of that age did not always wear the long flowing head-to-toe veils. For example, one sculpture of a typical older woman in AD 65–70 shows her with no head covering.

The women who lived in those ancient cultures wore veils in order to show respect for their fathers or husbands. When a woman was in public wearing a veil, she indicated that she was untouchable. Everyone knew that the veil signaled that she belonged to someone.

More than that, the veil taught that only the woman's head knew what was under the veil. She did not display her treasures for all the men in the world to see. Conversely, the rule of the day was that, once the woman in that culture removed the veil, she was fair game for other men.

Women in many Middle Eastern cultures still wear the yashmak for the same purpose. In the Middle East, the long veil is still a symbol of respect for authority. It is a veil that covers from head to toe and prohibits another man from seeing what the husband sees. It is the woman's way of reminding other men that she is reserved solely for her husband.

This concept of demonstrating respect toward the husband's authority came into question at times. There were occasions in the ancient Roman culture when feminism took hold. When women exerted themselves at such times, they threw off the signs of man's authority, which certainly included putting aside the veil. This might have been the problem that precipitated Paul's instruction to the church. Were some women tempted to discard the old symbols of submission? What did it say about them if they did?

Paul reminded the women in the church at Corinth that they were supposed to show respect to their husbands by covering their heads (vv. 7–16). Moving on to verse 7, Paul argued that, in a similar way, husbands are supposed to reflect the glory of their head. God created the man in His image from the dust of the earth. He was a unique creation in order to reflect God's glory. In similar (yet different) fashion, wives are supposed to reflect the glory of their heads (vv. 7*b*–16). Who is the wife's head? The husband. Paul reminded the readers that God created the woman for the man (vv. 7*b*, 9). She is a helper that is suitable for him. She came from the man, not from the dust of the ground (v. 8). She is unique according to God's design just like God designed Adam to be unique. But the wife is not inferior to man (vv. 11–12).

One way a wife is able to reflect the glory of her head is for her to be careful not to appear to reflect the glory to herself. Paul warned the women of his day not to dress in a way that caused undue attention. They were to remember that the angels show utmost respect and honor to God (v. 10*b*). Nature itself teaches that it is wrong for either the man or the woman to appear in such a way that it draws attention to them and distracts from glorifying God in worship (vv. 14–15). Such principles should have made it easy for the wives of the church in Corinth to show respect for their husbands. But what about modern Christian wives?

GOD'S PLAN FOR TWENTY-FIRST-CENTURY CHRISTIANS

Christian women should still display a respect for God and man in the church. Do they know what to do? Maybe someone needs to teach them how to show respect. Indeed, the man of the modern church needs to lead the way by showing respect for his Head—Jesus Christ. How? Sometimes we can do this through symbols. Every culture has symbols or demonstrations of respect. For example, we rise when a dignitary enters a room. That shows respect. In the military, a soldier salutes a fellow soldier who is wearing a symbol of superior rank on his or her shirt or hat.

In our culture, men can also demonstrate respect for their Head, Jesus Christ. They love Him and demonstrate that love through worship and sacrifice and by honoring His Word. They act respectful toward Christ by not taking His name in vain and by not treating Him or His truth lightly. To men like this, the idea of gathering for public worship of Christ is significant. The man who demonstrates respect for Christ proves that he does not view Sunday as just another day, and that going to church is not a meaningless habit or nuisance. Men who demonstrate respect to their Head have taught this principle to their family. Conversely, the man who has not established this attitude in his own life cannot teach it to his children.

The man who respects his Head has learned how to display the connection between going to church and having an ongoing relationship with Christ. Throughout the week this kind of man demonstrates a respectful relationship with Christ his Head. Then the Lord's Day is that special day each week when he and his family gather with other men who desire to exalt the name of Christ and reflect the glory of their Head. Is this an ideal or is it the norm? Sadly it is probably a dream, the ideal of what we should do.

Men who set the standard for showing respect can help their wives learn how to do the same. If their wives see a demonstration of respect for Christ, they might be more careful not to call undue attention to themselves. Marion Soards concluded, "Genuinely Spirit-filled behavior is not to be subsumed under a self-aggrandizing show of personal freedom."[1] In other words, wives like this meet to worship God, not to put themselves on display. The women of the world love attention, but godly women reflect attention to Christ. Christian women are different.

A Christian wife is careful to demonstrate respect for her husband. She guards against diminishing his glory. She does not respond like this because she is married to the perfect husband. No husband is perfect, and most are barely tolerable. Rather, the wife who seeks to show respect for her husband knows and freely admits that her husband is her God-ordained authority. Therefore, she will avoid embarrassing him, belittling him, or criticizing him in public. This respectful woman always bears in mind that God created her for her husband to be a suitable helper. Life cannot possibly be centered on that kind of person. She concludes that life must be about someone else.

Like their husbands who demonstrate respect for God, good wives have learned from them how to respect God first. They have learned that they must have respect in their hearts before they can ever demonstrate it. The wife who attempts to demonstrate something that does not exist in her heart generally ends up being inconsistent at best. Therefore, the wife must work daily to keep a proper respect for God first, and a proper respect for her husband also. It does require work, but the result is well worth the price. A marriage will work without love as long as there is respect. Of course, love makes the marriage a lot easier.

Christian wives must demonstrate by the way they dress, the way they act, and their overall deportment, that they belong to their husband and that they know that he is their God-ordained head.

PUT IT TO WORK

1. Does your attitude demonstrate that you respect your husband?

2. Do your words demonstrate that you respect your husband?

3. Does your choice in clothing declare that your husband is your authority, or does it say, "Look at me"?

4. Do you respect God first?

5. How do others know that you respect God?

PRINCIPLE 14
The wife should submit to her husband through love.

Wives, submit to your own husbands, as to the LORD. For the husband is the head of the wife even as Christ is the head of the church, his body, and is himself its Savior. Now as the church submits to Christ, so also wives should submit in everything to their husbands. (Ephesians 5:22–24 ESV)

Children obey your parents, "parents teach your children self-discipline," "husbands love your wives," and "wives submit to your husbands." In a nutshell, those are God's general requirements for a successful family. And suddenly we are back to the Ward and June Cleaver or Ozzie and Harriet Nelson models of family living. Those were idyllic days in the fifties and early sixties, but we don't live in those days anymore. Daniel Boone and Davey Crocket were also real people who inspired legends, but there just isn't much call for pioneers and frontiersmen these days. It might be nice to read about the past and, if you're old enough, to reminisce about it. But we can't live there.

This is a new day. Families are different. In fact, many folks are not even sure what a family is. The very definition is up for debate. The idea of the wife submitting to the husband is so passé that it must have gone out of style along with Conestoga wagons.

Feminism has changed the landscape of husband and wife relationships forever in America. The movement began in the late nineteenth century, dealing mainly with the issue of suffrage. That was an outgrowth of the antislavery and abolitionist movements in which women, who were fighting for the rights of the oppressed, discovered that they too were oppressed. At least they decided that they lacked some of the rights they were fighting to win for others. In the mid to late twentieth century (1960s–80s), feminism dealt with the inequality of laws, as well as unofficial inequalities, such as equal pay and equal access to all schools, clubs, and organizations. Essentially, it was an attack against every institution that was perceived to be the exclusive property of men. That part of the movement peaked with the failure of the Equal Rights Amendment to the U.S. Constitution. The foundational principles of feminism are still alive and well, having shaped our culture so that much of their doctrine is accepted as the norm.

Gladly, Christians have the Bible to act as a guide in husband and wife relationships. The Bible is manifestly clear about this matter. For example, the text of Ephesians 5:22–24 leaves no doubt that wives are supposed to submit to their husbands. However, what is clear to a person controlled by the Holy Spirit is not clear to a merely religious person who reads the same Bible.

In an article titled "Papal Preacher: Wives Should Not Obey Husbands," Marian T. Horvat reported, "Husbands love your wives, this is good. Wives, submit to your husbands, this is unacceptable." That was not Ms. Horvat's conclusion but the message of a recent sermon by Capuchin Fr. Raniero Cantalamessa, who commented on this passage from Paul's letter to the Ephesian Christians. According to one report,

> Fr. Cantalamessa had no problem with St. Paul's words recommending husbands to love their wives. . . . The snag for the papal preacher is "that he [St. Paul] also recommends to women that they be submissive to their husbands, and this—in a society strongly (and justly) conscious of the equality of the sexes—seems unacceptable." He goes on to explain that we do not have to read the passage literally, since on the point of the authority of the husband in the marriage, "St. Paul is conditioned in part by the mentality of his age."[1]

Is the Roman church up in arms about such heresy? Not exactly. In his Apostolic Letter Mulieris Dignitatem (August 15, 1988), John Paul II considered that the verse in question, "Wives be subject to your husband," would be rendered effectively null by the previous verse 5:21, "Be subject to one another out of reverence for Christ."

So what does the Bible require? Is the wife supposed to submit to the husband, or are husband, wife, and children on exactly the same plane in the hierarchy? Or did God even establish a hierarchy in the family? The text is plain enough to teach what the true church has taught for centuries. A wife must submit to her husband or the family will be found standing on its head—like many American families are today.

THE REQUIREMENT (Ephesians 5:21-22)

The lesson in this text is built on the previously established fact that people who are filled with the Holy Spirit submit to one another (v. 21). The argument in the verses preceding the Ephesians 5:22–24 passage reveals that people who are filled with the Holy Spirit understand God's will (v. 17). What is God's will? What is God's will in this particular issue? Actually, the overall thrust in the last half of Ephesians is a detailed explanation of what it means for a Christian to live a life worthy of his or her calling. Beginning with 4:1, Paul unfolded many important and practical traits that ought to characterize people who have received God's gracious provision of salvation.

In the first three chapters, Paul explained the marvelous truth of salvation. Christ has lavished His grace upon the people who now make up the church (1:7–8). Christ gave such people eternal life (2:1–2). Christ saves those individuals by grace (2:8–9). These are amazing truths. It is an astonishing thing to be a child of God through faith in Christ. Therefore, the argument goes, the recipients of such grace should live as though they have received grace. That is the argument beginning in 4:1.

Among other things, living the "eternal life through grace" kind of life includes the need for all the members of the body of Christ to submit to their spiritual leaders (4:1–16). Not only that, but everyone must submit to each other (5:21). Also, according to God's plan, children must submit to their parents (6:1–3). Servants must submit to masters, which, according to modern application, means that employees must submit to employers (6:5–9). In similar fashion, the letter to the Roman Christians teaches that Christian citizens must submit to governing authorities (Romans 13:1). But the highest standard of submission comes from James's epistle, which teaches that all Christians must submit to God (James 4:7). Christians ought to be very familiar with the concept of submission.

When Christians actually submit to God and others in the church, it looks a lot like the scene described in 5:15–20. Those people will be known for making the best use of their time because they know it is an evil day (5:15–16). They are people who submit themselves to the influence of the Holy Spirit (5:18). People who are under the influence of the Holy Spirit minister to the spiritual needs of others through psalms, hymns, and spiritual songs (5:19). They are thankful to God for all things (5:20).

Beyond those traits, genuine Christians who are under the influence of the Holy Spirit and, therefore, who understand God's will, concede to others (v. 21). That is essentially the meaning of the word *submit* in this verse. It means that the members of Christ's body do not think that life is all about them. They are the kind of folks who love their neighbors as they love themselves, knowing that their neighbors are in the same local assembly with them. These people yield control to others in the body of Christ. They submit because they have deep reverence for Christ, Who won their salvation through His sacrifice, Who offered His grace to save them, Who gave them life when they were dead in sin. People who are under the influence of the Holy Spirit just cannot get over the wonder of His grace. It affects the very details of their lives.

Then should it not also stand to reason that wives who are influenced by the Holy Spirit will submit to their husbands (v. 22)? Of course they will. This kind of wife concedes to her own husband. She yields leadership to him. She arranges her plans, purposes and desires under her husband's plans, purposes, and desires. A wife cannot do that unless she first knows what her husband thinks, how he feels, and what he desires. That kind of intimate knowledge is not shared on a first date. They are truths that the wife discovers through ongoing, profitable communication. She talks with her husband so that she can learn what he thinks, how he feels, and what he desires. This wife is not satisfied with simply learning about her husband through communication. She is also concerned to act in light of what she knows.

> Genuine Christians who are under the influence of the Holy Spirit concede to others.

This is not a difficult or novel thing for the Christian wife to do. Paul said that she submits to her husband in the same way she submits to the Lord. The phrase "as to the Lord" means that the wife is to submit to her husband in the same way she submits to the Lord. In other words, she is experienced in the practice. Also, the phrase means that she is to submit to her husband as a ministry to the Lord. Is that even possible? How does it work?

THE EXAMPLE (vv. 23-24)

God pointed out through Paul that the husband is the wife's head like Christ is the church's head (v. 23). How did Christ become the head of the church? He is the head of the church by divine appointment. The Greek word translated "head" denotes the literal head of a body, which is responsible for leading the body. When the head is severed from the body, the body dies. That simple illustration helps explain the importance of the head.

However, the term *head* is also used metaphorically in the Bible, as well as in common English conversation, to describe that which is first or supreme. The head is the most important part of the organization, business, city, nation, or almost any group of people in any setting for any purpose. The head is the chief ruler. When a person walks into a business and asks to speak to the head "cock-a-doodle-do," everyone knows that he wants to see the leader.

Christ is the supreme leader of the church by God's design.

Earlier in Ephesians Paul taught that God the Father "put all things under his feet, and gave him to be the head over all things to the church, which is his body, the fulness of him that filleth all in all" (1:22–23). Therefore, "he is the head of the body, the church: who is the beginning, the firstborn from the dead; that in all things he might have the preeminence" (Colossians 1:18). Jesus Christ is not the supreme leader of the church because He won a popular vote. He deserves to be the leader because God the Father appointed Him to that position and because He has commanded respect from His followers through His sacrifice.

The husband is the head of the wife also by divine appointment. He is not her head because he deserves the position. No husband is intrinsically a better person or more qualified for leadership than his wife. No husband is of higher natural standing with God and thus more qualified to be the head. That is what Paul meant when he wrote, "There is neither Jew nor Greek, there is neither bond nor free, there is neither male nor female: for ye are all one in Christ Jesus" (Galatians 3:28). Every husband is prone to failure. Be that as it may, God appointed the husband as leader in order to assure an orderly family. Some kind of leadership is required in every successful operation in life. Whether the organization is a child's treehouse club or a local church, there must be a leader or the operation will flounder.

By God's design, He made Adam and then made a helper who was suitable for him. God says the wife is a helper suitable for the husband, not a good leader for the husband. Modern culture has proven that any attempt to change God's order or plan will stand the family on its head. Modern America is the nation of dysfunctional families. As a culture, we are so confused that many people do not even understand what constitutes a family. Is it any surprise that the society is riddled with crime, sunk down in sin, declining academically, and predictably fast losing its position as the leading nation in the world?

The wife should submit to her husband just as the church submits to Christ (v. 24). Or maybe it would be more accurate to say, "Just as the church is supposed to submit to Christ." According to God's plan, the true church submits to Christ. That submission allows each member of the body to grow into the pattern of its Head, Jesus Christ. A previous chapter in Ephesians warned Christians not to be tossed about by false doctrine: "But speaking the truth in love, may grow up into him in all things, which is the head, even Christ" (4:15). The local assembly that is submissive to Christ will take on the very character of Christ as it grows into His pattern.

Human wisdom does not encourage that kind of submission to our Head. Because of that, Paul had to warn the Colossian believers, "Let no one disqualify you, insisting on asceticism and worship of angels, going on in detail about visions, puffed up without reason by his sensuous mind, and not holding fast to the Head, from whom the whole body, nourished and knit together through its joints and ligaments, grows with a growth that is from God" (Colossians 2:18–19 ESV).

Growing into Christ through submission is God's plan for the church. However, according to sinful nature, the visible church often does not submit to Christ. Many people in the visible church (which is not necessarily the true church) deny the authority of His Word. The visible church claims to belong to Christ, but it denies His authority continually. A glaring example of this fault was demonstrated when

Presiding Bishop of the Episcopal Church, Katharine Jefferts Schori, criticized Nigerian Archbishop Peter Akinola's planned move to install Martyn Minns as head of a new denomination for conservative Episcopalians. She said that "such action would violate the ancient customs of the church." The irony of Schori's criticism is that she supported the consecration of gay bishop Gene Robinson and she referred to "Mother Jesus" in a convocation sermon at an Episcopal convention.[2]

Who violates the ancient customs of the church? Sadly, many wives are like the visible church. They do not submit to their head—either Christ or their husband.

THE APPLICATION

The Christian wife must submit to her husband. In practical terms, this means that she must arrange her life according to her husband's life. Then, beyond knowing well her husband's likes, dislikes, plans, purposes, and desires, submission requires that she make everyday decisions in light of what she knows. In other words, submission requires the wife to think about her husband's desires when she shops for groceries. She would never buy a red dress when she is shopping for clothes if she knows that her husband does not like red dresses. It means she even cleans the house with the knowledge of what her husband likes. She is sensitive to her husband's desires when she interacts with others, especially men. She thinks about her husband when she spends money. Submission is rather all-inclusive. It is a lifestyle. Are your decisions motivated by what your husband thinks or do you care what he thinks? Or even worse, is it possible that you do what you do to spite your husband?

The submissive wife will find it necessary to fight her natural tendency to rule over her husband. Because of Eve's original sin, the wife has a natural desire to take her husband's position of leadership. God promised the woman, "I will greatly multiply thy sorrow and thy conception; in sorrow thou shalt bring forth children; and thy desire shall be to thy husband, and he shall rule over thee" (Genesis 3:16). For the wife to have a desire to overthrow the husband's position as head is as natural as weeds growing in the garden. It is going to happen.

Submission is opposed to this desire. The Christian wife must recognize this natural desire burning in her soul. She must identify that natural desire as sin. She must determine to yield that craving to Christ so that she can yield to her husband.

There is an undeniable connection here. Christian wives must submit to Christ if they would ever be successful in yielding to their husbands. The concept of submission should not be a new experience to the Christian wife. She already understands Christ's will and yields herself to it. She is experienced in saying no to any desire that is contrary to Christ's desires for her. She knows submission from experience. But what if a wife does not have that experience? It is entirely possible that a wife's difficulty in submitting to her husband might be caused by her refusal to submit to Christ. If a wife is able to truly submit to Christ, she ought to be able to submit to her husband also.

The standard is clear. God's expectation is obvious. It is not palatable to the world's way of thinking, nor is it embraced by human wisdom. The sinful nature mitigates against the wife's submitting to her husband. But God's plan is unchanged and unchanging. He still receives glory when the wife will do what God has ordained. When the wife controls her desire to be in charge and concedes to her husband's desires, God gets the glory from an orderly family. It is His plan and rightfully His glory.

PUT IT TO WORK

1. In what ways do you submit to Christ?

2. Do you see mutual submission commonly practiced in the local church?

3. How are you teaching your children to submit to God-ordained authority?

4. Are you aware of your husband's plan, purposes, and desires?

5. How would you handle a conflict if your husband's desires were contrary to your own desires?

PRINCIPLE 15
Husbands love your wives like Christ loves the church.

Husbands, love your wives, as Christ loved the church and gave himself up for her, that he might sanctify her, having cleansed her by the washing of water with the word, so that he might present the church to himself in splendor, without spot or wrinkle or any such thing, that she might be holy and without blemish. (Ephesians 5:25–27 ESV)

O ccasionally throughout these many years of ministry, I have been seated across the desk from a husband and wife who were struggling to keep their marriage intact. Things like that happen to Christians in the same way they happen to other folks in the world. At some point in counseling I will say, "If one of you desires to make this marriage work, it can work." Is that really possible? Does it not take two working together in unity toward the same goal to make a marriage work? Ideally, yes. But when the crisis comes, and it appears that everything is falling apart, someone needs to step up to the plate and determine that he or she will do whatever it takes to make the marriage work.

That someone might be the husband. Indeed, if the man is truly the head of the wife (Ephesians 5:23) and the husband is really the head of the home (1 Corinthians 11:3), he needs to take the leadership in this area. Instead of sitting by passively and letting whatever may happen, happen, the head of the home must be proactive. He must determine that he will lead the wife and family to establish a solid home that God will use to bring glory to Himself.

Without argument, the husband who desires a solid, God-honoring family will find it necessary to love his wife. What? That sounds ridiculous. Whoever heard of a husband who does not love his wife? Actually, many husbands do not love their wives. Most husbands are completely subjected to the desires of their flesh, and the desires of the flesh cause the husbands to love themselves. Too often when a handsome young man tells a gullible young woman that he loves her, he really means, "I love me and I want you." Self-love is the natural thing, and unless we take steps to avoid it, we all will fall into the same pit in which the world wallows.

Sometimes (especially around Valentine's Day or anniversaries) husbands think quite seriously about loving their wives. During those special times, they are more prone to verbalize their love than during the normal days. But are we sure even then that we love our wives? I told my wife recently that studying this text drives me to believe that I barely love her at all. Is that shocking? I fear it is bluntly honest. I thank God that He gave me a wife who understands my extreme conclusions. So what would drive a sincere and loving husband to such an astonishing conclusion? The simple standard of love. God said through Paul that husbands are supposed to love their wives just like Christ loved the church. The husband who responds by saying, "I do that!" obviously has not spent much time meditating on this command.

How much does Christ love the church? The husband's answer to that question will determine how much ambition and hard work he is willing to expend to match the standard in his relationship with his wife. How hard are you willing to work to have a good marriage? A Christ-honoring marriage requires an immense amount of self-sacrifice and effort. The results make all the effort and sacrifice well worth the price.

LOVE YOUR WIFE LIKE CHRIST LOVES THE CHURCH (Ephesians 5:25-28)

The standard of this text is higher and more stringent than one can tell at first. How much does Christ love the church? Christ loved the church so much that He died for her (v. 25). In willingly offering Himself up as an eternal sacrifice for sin, Jesus Christ manifested a sacrificial, volitional love that eclipses anything humans know by nature. Christ never demonstrated a fleshly and impure love. Love flowing from the desires of the flesh is the most natural kind of love, though it is not love at all compared to Christ's love. That is the kind of love most people express.

Sometimes Christ demonstrated a *phileo* kind of love toward His dear friends. That is a tender affection someone might show toward family and friends. According to John 20:2, Jesus Christ loved John the apostle with that tender affection. Revelation 3:19 states that Christ loves all His people with at least that kind of affection.

> Christ loves the church so much that He sanctifies her.

However, the vast majority of information in the Bible proves that Christ's love for the church is extreme love. The Greek word for this kind of love, which is familiar to most Christians, is the word *agape*. This distinctly Christlike kind of love is a determined love, not a natural reaction to certain stimuli as is romance. This love chooses to love an object and, therefore, does not require that the chosen object be worthy of love. It is, therefore, a sacrificial love that takes into account the need of the object not the desires of the one loving. This is a demonstrated love, not a secret love that the lover keeps hidden in the depths of the heart. The benefit of the object loved stirs *agape* love. Therefore, the lover must demonstrate this kind of love in some way.

That is the kind of love Christ has for the church. His expression of love is the ultimate standard of love. Everything else that is called love is measured against Christ's love and generally falls short of the standard. This is especially true when you understand that Christ's volitional, sacrificial love caused Him to die for sinners, who are unworthy of any favor. Such love is beyond the scope of natural human responses. John concluded, "Greater love hath no man than this, that a man lay down his life for his friends" (John 15:13). In his first Epistle John declared, "Hereby perceive we the love of God, because he laid down his life for us: and we ought to lay down our lives for the brethren" (3:16). Who among men willingly lays down his life to benefit someone simply because he loves the person? That is very rare. Christ loves the church so much that He willingly died for her.

Furthermore, according to verse 26 in this text, Christ loves the church so much that He sanctifies her. To sanctify her means that Christ sets the church apart from sin and unto God. The tense and voice of this verb (aorist, active) translated "love" indicates that Christ's love was determined for all eternity. It was not that Christ began to love the church at the crucifixion and then ceased loving the church once He had paid the price for sin. Rather, the expression of Christ's love continues as He sanctifies the object of His love. Because Christ loves Christians, He actively sets us apart from sin and unto God. Sanctification means that the person being sanctified is becoming more like God and more useful for His glory. Sanctification means that the person is becoming less like the world that hates Christ and of which he, the Christian, is not really a part. Jesus warned the disciples that "if [they] were of the world, the world would love [them] as its own; but because [they] are not of the world, but [He] chose [them] out of the world, therefore the world hates [them]" (John 15:19). It seems strange that folks who are supposed to be in the process of sanctification hate being separated out of such a world. Why would a person who the world hates try so diligently to stay in fellowship with it?

Christ sanctifies the church through the Word. Sanctification is not a magical blessing that Christ utters in behalf of a new believer and suddenly the person is fully separated from sin and able to live just like Christ. Positional sanctification allows God to see the new believer standing in perfect righteousness. But living out that perfect righteousness requires progressive sanctification. It is a process through which Christ repeatedly, systematically washes away the natural sin of the flesh and the corrupting influence of the world. At salvation Christians are sanctified positionally by the Holy Spirit. That is what Paul meant in the only other place in the Bible where this particular use of the word *wash* occurs. He told Titus that Christ saved us "not by works of righteousness which we have done, but according to his mercy . . . by the washing of regeneration, and renewing of the Holy Ghost" (Titus 3:5). The Christian is washed at the new birth, but we must continue to be washed throughout life. In life we are sanctified progressively through the teaching and application of the Bible. This is the process Jesus referred to when He prayed to the heavenly Father, "Sanctify them through thy truth: thy word is truth" (John 17:17). If a person is part of the church, he or she is being washed by the water of the Word because Christ loves the church.

The result of Christ's sacrificial love is a holy church (v. 27). Christ will present the church to Himself. She will be holy and without blemish. She will reflect the ramifications of Christ's work.

She will reflect the ramifications of Christ's love.

But how is a normal human husband supposed to apply that kind of love in his real relationship with his wife? Someone might ask, "Do you love your wife enough to sacrifice for her?" (v. 25). That question is not a hypothetical question to which a husband might answer, "I would be willing to sacrifice _____" and he fills in the blank. The question has nothing to do with what a husband might think he is willing to sacrifice but has everything to do with what he is already sacrificing for his wife.

"Sacrifice?" the husband wonders. Does God expect him to sacrifice for his wife? Yes. That must require some kind of superhuman love. It doesn't require superhuman love, but it does require a love that is deep-seated, thorough, involving the mind, the will, and the emotions. The emotions of romance will never accomplish this kind of love. God's requirement for love is strict, but it is clear. In spite of the requirement, it seems as though most husbands sacrifice little or nothing for their wives. This conclusion is borne out through much research for stories about this special kind of love. It is very difficult to find a story in the recent news about a husband who virtually risked his life to save his wife. Sadly, it is very easy to find stories about men who abuse their wives, beat them, cheat on them, or even kill them. Recently there was a news story about a guy who offered to trade a $2100 ring he bought for his wife for a ticket to the Super Bowl. Expressions of that kind of self-love are natural and too common.

Some men sacrifice more for their friends or hobbies than they do for their wives. Some husbands might even be willing to sacrifice more for an animal than they would sacrifice for their wives. Wayne Olivo, forty-nine-years old, of Billings, Montana, is a retired police officer. In July, 2001, about 3:00 a.m., he was driving across the Huntley Bridge when he spotted a man and a woman standing beside a van stopped on the bridge. Mr. Olivo pulled over to check if they needed help, at which point he heard the woman cry out, "Don't throw my baby in the river!" Mr. Olivo realized that the man and woman had been arguing over a bundle that was now in the man's possession. Immediately, Mr. Olivo approached the man and managed to wrestle the bundle away from him but was unprepared when the man pulled a small revolver and shot once. The bullet passed through Mr. Olivo's left hand and into the left side of his chest, rendering him unconscious. He awoke sometime later and called 911 from his truck; the man and woman had driven off, leaving the bundle on the ground. In the bundle was a Labrador retriever puppy. In this case, man truly was dog's best friend. Would the man have risked his life if he knew the bundle was a dog and not a child? Who knows? That is not to conclude that Mr. Olivo would not do the same for his wife—if he even has a wife. Probably he would. How many guys would make such a sacrifice if it came to that?

Most husbands would like to think that they are willing to make the ultimate sacrifice for their wives. Recently, a story appeared in the news about an elderly man in California who risked his life to rescue his wheelchair-bound wife from their burning home. That is a wonderful display of love. Real Christlike love drives a husband to respond like that. But do you love your wife enough to sacrifice your time, energy, and pride for her? Seldom do circumstances require a husband to give his life for his spouse. Most of the time wives would probably be delighted if their husbands gave up a little free time to benefit them.

"Do you love your wife enough to sacrifice for her?" is a tough question. Maybe a more difficult question to answer is "Do you love your wife enough to sanctify her?" Actually, that is a more demanding proposal for some men than to ask them to take a bullet for their wife. If the husband really loves his wife like Christ loves the church, he will work to make her more like Christ and less like the world. He will accomplish this sanctification by washing her with the water of the Word. What does that mean? It means that the husband plans time each day, or at least several times a week, when he opens the Bible, reads to his wife, and helps her become more like Christ. This kind of love causes a man to desire that his wife be conformed to the Bible standard. This kind of love requires a significant sacrifice of time. More than that, it requires the sacrifice of pride. Why? What man can read the Word of God for any length of time without being rebuked or corrected? How many husbands are humble enough to acknowledge that they have failed to meet the Bible standard—the same standard their wives just heard them read. The sacrifice of ego is a huge sacrifice. That is why many husbands prefer not to read the Bible to their wives. The sacrifice of ego to humility is costly. But love compels a husband to endure the humility while he sanctifies his wife.

> Some men sacrifice more for their friends or hobbies than they do for their wives.

The text leaves the husband with an important question: "Do you love your wife enough to contribute to her holiness?" (v. 27) The process of washing the wife with the water of the Word sanctifies her. That sanctification process makes her less sinful. Who reaps the most immediate benefit of a wife who is less prone to respond to circumstances in a fleshly way? The husband who helped wash her with the Word. The husband who loves his wife enough to help her become more like Christ actually does himself a big favor.

LOVE YOUR WIFE LIKE YOU LOVE YOURSELF (vv. 28-30)

Again the standard here is Christ. He loves His body (vv. 29b–30). The church is Christ's body. Because the church is the body of Christ, she is the full expression of Christ in this world. Paul pointed out that truth earlier in this letter when he said, "[The church] is his body, the fulness of him that filleth all in all" (Ephesians 1:23). In fact, Jesus Christ is the head of the body. "For the husband is the head of the wife, even as Christ is the head of the church: and he is the saviour of the body" (Ephesians 5:23).

How can real people become part of the spiritual body of Christ? The union is the result of intimate relationship. Faith in Christ makes the believer one with Him. Often Paul mentions the fact that the Christian is "in" Christ. That is another way of describing the deeply intimate relationship members of Christ's body have with the Head of the body. An even more descriptive, more intimate, description of the relationship is discovered in Jesus' conversation with doubters in His day. Christ taught them that faith in Him is tantamount to eating His flesh and drinking His blood. What picture could possibly demonstrate a deeper intimacy? Jesus told the would-be disciples who were not interested in being so closely connected to Him, "Verily, verily, I say unto you, Except ye eat the flesh of the Son of man, and drink his blood, ye have no life in you" (John 6:53). Indeed, the true Christian is actually a part of Christ's body.

Christ cherishes the church, His body. Because He loves us, He nourishes us. The word translated "nourish" means to provide food. Jesus, the church's head, counts it a joy and privilege to feed the individual members spiritual food. It is the joy a mother experiences as she feeds her little baby. It is the joy of a shepherd who loves to feed his sheep. Christ, the head, nourishes the body. And He cherishes it. That means that He gives to His people whatever is necessary because He loves them.

Husbands must love their wives in similar fashion (vv. 28–29a). Verse 29 states an obvious truth. It is patently true that husbands naturally love themselves. Of course, most husbands will shy away from making such an admission. Husbands typically avoid the admission because the words sound so selfish and arrogant. But by nature you and I are selfish and arrogant. It is true that husbands naturally love themselves first and best.

Actually, the text indicates that God expects husbands to be natural, to some extent, in this matter. The man who refuses to care for himself, at least in some fashion, needs help. Sometimes lack of self care is the result of physical or emotional trauma. Nevertheless, the world pities the man who cannot or will not care for himself, and many people try to help such a needy person. Self-preservation is natural. Most people eat well (sometimes), exercise regularly (or at least on occasion), and take care of the external body. Some men even take care of the internal matters. How much time and energy does the typical husband expend caring for himself? One way to get a good idea of the answer to that question might be to fill out the following table:

Event	Time	Event	Time
Sleep		Exercise	
Eating		Hobby	
Pastime		Study	
Making money			

Filling out a chart like this will probably reveal that the husband spends most of his life taking care of himself. That is to be expected. But how much time does the average husband spend taking care of his wife?

As Christ loves the church, so the husband must cherish his wife because she is his body (vv. 28b, 31). The husband cannot escape the fact that his wife is one flesh with him. Notice that God inspired Paul to stick that foundational truth in the text right here: "For this cause shall a man leave his father and mother, and shall be joined unto his wife, and they two shall be one flesh" (Ephesians 5:31). God established this standard for the family at creation. The one-flesh idea helps explain why it is so important for the husband to care for and provide the needs of his wife. What happens when a man takes care of only one-half of his body? We can only imagine.

Because, in God's plan, the wife is one with the husband, the husband must care for her like he cares for himself. That requires that he will need to provide for her physical, emotional, and spiritual needs. Now is a good time to start. It is unlikely that any husband is completely righteous in this matter. That does not mean that you and I should not get busy doing what God requires now.

PUT IT TO WORK

1. Do you really love your wife or do you just have romantic feelings for her?

2. What concrete evidence is there to prove your love for your wife?

3. How much time do you sacrifice for your wife?

4. How are you sanctifying your wife?

5. When was the last time you read the Bible with your wife and prayed with her?

Put on then, as God's chosen ones, holy and beloved, compassion, kindness, humility, meekness, and patience, bearing with one another and, if one has a complaint against another, forgiving each other; as the LORD has forgiven you, so you also must forgive. And above all these put on love, which binds everything together in perfect harmony. And let the peace of Christ rule in your hearts, to which indeed you were called in one body. And be thankful. Let the word of Christ dwell in you richly, teaching and admonishing one another in all wisdom, singing psalms and hymns and spiritual songs, with thankfulness in your hearts to God. And whatever you do, in word or deed, do everything in the name of the LORD Jesus, giving thanks to God the Father through him. Wives, submit to your husbands, as is fitting in the LORD. (Colossians 3:12–18 ESV)

There were times in ancient cultures when wives were considered to be nothing more than a piece of property. In Greek culture the wife was to be secluded and respectful. She lived in separate quarters that only her husband could enter. She was never to appear in public alone, and to find her talking to another man would be grounds for divorce. Unmarried women lived quite a different life in the same culture. They were often unchaste and many of them even worked as religious prostitutes.

Judaism exalted the position of wife compared to Greek culture. However, the wife was still suppressed in the Jewish culture. The young woman was under the authority of her father until she married. Then, after she was married, the woman lived under the authority of her husband. In many respects the Jewish wife was not really a person but a thing. She was not allowed to learn law, and she was not allowed to have any part in the proceedings at the synagogue. She was not allowed to be a teacher and was in the same class as children and slaves.

In Roman culture the wife's chief function was to produce posterity. She had no rights. One lawyer in that age admitted that if a husband caught his wife committing adultery he could kill her on the spot with impunity. But if the wife caught her husband committing adultery, she could not lift a finger against him. A common conclusion of Paul's day was that men had wives in order to have children and they kept mistresses in order to be satisfied. A happy marriage in the Roman Empire was rare.

Maybe one of the greatest changes that Christianity brought into the world was to change the wife's standing. There is no question that Christianity brings good effects wherever it is established. It improves employer and employee relationships. It improves the relationship between citizens and government. It improves the way citizens view and obey laws. It improves the way parents rear children and the way children respond to their parents.

While it is true that certain cultures have inspired moral living, no other doctrine or philosophy has brought about as many good changes as Christianity does in a culture. Why is this? The simple teaching and practice of the Bible change the way people think and act. The Bible acknowledges that human nature is deficient and needs to improve. The Bible points out the exact deficiencies and establishes the appropriate corrective measures. The Bible especially teaches the need for sinners to confess their sins, forsake their sinful ways, and live like Christ. When people live like Christ, the culture will always change for the better.

That explains why a culture that moves further and further from the standard of the Bible will also proportionately develop relational problems between employers and employees, government and citizens, children and parents, and husbands and wives. The Bible sets the standard for all these relationships. When the authority of the Bible is removed, the relationships become difficult to maintain. Recent news has been that the divorce rate in the United States is dropping dramatically. That is good news indeed after years of increasing numbers of failed marriages. The bad news is that the reason there are fewer divorces is that almost half of the couples under the age of forty are living together out of wedlock. Those relationships break up with regularity but are never entered as statistics in the record books.

Why can't husbands and wives get along? Why are there so many fractured relationships? The Bible answers those questions in plain and simple teaching. God commands wives to submit to their husbands as it is fitting. Wives find it difficult to submit to their husbands and blame their husbands for making the task impossible to fulfill. But if husbands and wives alike would simply do what God requires in the verses preceding that command in Colossians 3:18, the whole problem would be solved. Verses 12–17 teach that submission must flow from a right relationship with Christ. When husbands and wives are right with Christ, submission is almost natural. When their relationships with Christ are out of whack, submission is almost impossible.

SUBMISSION FLOWS FROM A RIGHT RELATIONSHIP WITH CHRIST (Colossians 3:12-17)

In the letter he wrote to the Christians in Ephesus, Paul also taught Christian wives to submit to their husbands (5:22). In that case, he explained that submission flows from a heart governed by the Holy Spirit (5:17–21). God taught Christians that the wife is more likely to submit to her husband if both of them are in a right relationship with Christ.

A right relationship with Christ is characterized by the Christian loving the way Christ loves (vv. 12–14). Christ's love for His people affects all the relationships a Christian has with other people (vv. 12–13). How does Christ love? First, Paul pointed out that Christians are God's beloved. As such, they are the recipients of His love. He has poured His love into our hearts. According to Romans, believers have hope in Christ, "and hope maketh not ashamed; because the love of God is shed abroad in our hearts by the Holy Ghost which is given unto us" (5:5). The results of God pouring His love into the Christian's heart are amazing.

How does a person actually know that he or she has received the love of God? He demonstrated this love by setting His people apart for His own service and glory. That is the essence of the Greek word that is translated "holy" in the English versions. Holy people are chosen people. God chose each believer to make him or her holy and to receive His love. God chose to love His people and to demonstrate His love to them according to His own good pleasure. No one ever received God's love because he deserved it. Therefore, each Christian wife enjoys the abundance of God's love because He chose to pour it out on her.

Relationships are more likely to work when Christ's people do everything in the name of Christ

Because God chose to pour out His love, each Christian (wife and otherwise) ought to put on, like putting on an article of clothing, several traits that testify to the loving choice of God. First, the believer should put on compassion. To have compassion is to love others from the depths of the heart. Second, the person whom God has chosen must cloth himself with kindness. This is moral goodness, integrity, or gentleness. The third article of clothing is humility. Humble people think very honestly about themselves. They think the right thing or draw the right conclusions about themselves. The right conclusion agrees with what God says in the Bible about the individual. The fourth necessary trait is meekness, which is simply strength under control. A man or wife might have the ability to yell, scream, cajole, or even punch his or her spouse in order to get his or her way. But the Christian chooses not to do this because he or she has strength under control. Finally, God expects His chosen ones to put on patience. Patience is steadfastness while enduring others. It is never the same as stubbornness.

Once the chosen child of God puts on this proper clothing, he or she is more likely to accomplish the kinds of things listed in verse 13. Proper spiritual clothing enables Christians to tolerate each other. It helps Christians deal with differences in a calm manner. Ultimately, they can forgive each other. Without these Christlike traits family "wars" will be common.

As Christ's people work out the details of His love in their lives, they discover that His love holds every relationship together (v. 14). How does a person work out that love? What does that love look like in real life? Very simply, the people of Christ must cloth themselves with self-sacrificing love. Self-sacrificing goes a long way toward binding together that which tends to fly apart otherwise.

Furthermore, relationships are more likely to work when Christ's people do everything in the name of Christ (vv. 15–17). The person who does everything in the name of Christ must be saturated with Christ's character (vv. 15–16). That means that he or she will keep letting Christ's peace umpire (v. 15). The peace of Christ is peace that He alone gives. People who live in fellowship with Christ enjoy having His peace make the rules for how they live in their hearts. This is God's plan for the ones He calls. When the believer actually experiences Christ's peace ruling, he or she is very thankful for God's plan.

Also, the person who hopes to do everything in the name of Christ must let the Bible take up residence within him (v. 16). It is the recipient's responsibility to let the Bible reside within him abundantly. The only way for that to happen is for the person to read the Bible, hear the Bible read and taught, and study the Bible. Beyond that Christians also keep teaching and warning each other with the principles and text of the Bible. One way to do that is to sing the truths of God's Word with thanksgiving.

God's chosen people are not only saturated with Christ's character but, because they are saturated with it, they practice it. That is the lesson in verse 17. Christ's people must do and say everything with thanksgiving, and they must also do and say everything in the name of Christ. This means that the Christian will think and act in light of Who Christ is. Our thoughts and actions will declare that Jesus of Nazareth is indeed the Holy God. It means that we will think and act in light of the work Christ has done in our behalf. He is our Savior from sin. It means that we will think and act in light of who we are in relation to Christ. Christians are God's children, His representatives.

In real life this means that the wife who lives life in light of her relationship with Jesus Christ will discover that submission to a God-ordained authority is not impossible. Generally, it will not even be difficult. Submission becomes a strain when it cuts across the grain of self-will. In fact, a person never knows submission until the authority requires something unfavorable. The wife who is thankful all the time that Christ has chosen her for His glory will not resist submitting to her husband. Of course, the husband who is always thankful that Christ has chosen him, and lives out the truths of Christ's Word, will make it very easy for his wife to submit to him.

SUBMISSION MUST BE FITTING (v. 18)

God certainly approves of the principle of submission. He showed that submission is fitting in His plan by illustrating the principle. First, He illustrated submission by making the church subject to Christ. That statement is very clear in the Ephesian letter, where Paul taught, "Now as the church submits to Christ, so also wives should submit in everything to their husbands" (5:24). Second, God illustrated the principle of submission when He planned for Christ to be subject to the Father. That idea could not be clearer than it was when Jesus prayed in the Garden of Gethsemane for the Father to remove the coming cup of sorrow and grief at the crucifixion. He prayed, "Father, if thou be willing, remove this cup from me: nevertheless not my will, but thine, be done" (Luke 22:42). He was most obviously submissive to the Father's will.

There are many other examples where submission is necessary in order to maintain order. In the context of this lesson it is obvious that God plans for the employee to submit to the employer (v. 22). He plans for the children to submit to the parents (v. 20). In other passages in the New Testament it is clear that God plans for citizens to be subject to the government (1 Peter 2:13) and for the members of the body of Christ to submit to spiritual leaders (Hebrews 13:17). How could God have made the principle any clearer?

God illustrated how submission of the wife to the husband is fitting. He also commands the practice. God did not command the wife to submit to the husband because the husband is superior to the wife in some special way. In their relationship with God there is no difference between a man and a woman (Galatians 3:28). It is true that, in the beginning, God made the woman from man. But neither husband nor wife are independent of each other (1 Corinthians 11:11).

God does not consider it fitting for the wife to submit to the husband because she is not equal with him, but He requires the practice in order to bring about His own glory. God is an orderly God. There is no question about that as one views the work of His hands in creation. God demonstrated how orderly He is in creation. He continues to demonstrate His orderliness in the way He runs the world. Consider the orderly fashion by which one season continues to follow another. Therefore, it is not surprising that it is also God's will for the family to be orderly for His glory. That is what God meant in the message He gave to Malachi. The prophet asked, "Did he not make them one, with a portion of the Spirit in their union? And what was the one God seeking? Godly offspring. So guard yourselves in your spirit, and let none of you be faithless to the wife of your youth" (2:15 ESV).

This orderliness is best achieved when the wife submits to the husband. God issues the command according to His plan. Would anyone doubt the certainty of His command? Just to make sure that no wife would miss His plan God commanded the principle at least five times in the New Testament. He requires, "Wives, submit yourselves unto your own husbands, as unto the

Lord" (Ephesians 5:22). The verse from Colossians says the same thing: "Wives, submit yourselves unto your own husbands, as it is fit in the Lord" (3:18). Peter concurred: "For after this manner in the old time the holy women also, who trusted in God, adorned themselves, being in subjection unto their own husbands" (1 Peter 3:5). Paul explained to the Romans that "a married woman is bound by law to her husband while he lives, but if her husband dies she is released from the law of marriage" (7:2 ESV). He said essentially the same thing to the Corinthians: "The wife is bound by the law as long as her husband liveth; but if her husband be dead, she is at liberty to be married to whom she will; only in the Lord" (1 Corinthians 7:39).

> Orderliness is best achieved when the wife submits to the husband.

The command is clear. The expectation is obvious. A sinful world rejects God's requirement out of hand, but that is not an option for wives whom Christ has chosen and who, belonging to Him, desire to serve Him. Wives must submit to their husbands because the practice is obviously fitting according to God's revealed will.

But mere submission does not necessarily please God. God must approve the practice. It is possible that a husband might ask a wife to do what God forbids. This is due partly to the fact that a sinful husband will not be able to understand what is fitting to God. He does not have the Holy Spirit residing in his heart and directing his conscience.

He does not understand the principles of God's Word. Paul warned that "the natural person does not accept the things of the Spirit of God, for they are folly to him, and he is not able to understand them because they are spiritually discerned" (1 Corinthians 2:14 ESV). Scripture principle does not make sense nor bear any weight for the unspiritual person.

Therefore, the unredeemed husband typically makes decisions based on the desire of His flesh. Sadly, his flesh is opposed to God. His flesh is subject to satanic influence. His flesh demands that which God forbids. To respond to the desires of his flesh is the expected norm. It is what he and his friends talk about at work. It is the way his world expects him to respond.

Because the sinful husband has no ability to control the flesh and because he cannot understand the Scripture, conflicts arise. Sometimes an uncaring husband will request his wife to do something that God clearly forbids (i.e., lying, cheating, stealing, or sexual impurity). Sometimes an unspiritual husband will demand that his wife stop doing what honors God (i.e., reading the Bible, praying, attending church). But this is not just a problem experienced between a Christian woman and her unsaved husband. Even a redeemed husband is capable of expecting his wife to do something that God does not deem fitting. A Christian out of God's will is capable of any sin. The great problem with sin is that it likes company. Eve illustrated this truth well. Be that as it may, the Christian wife cannot, must not, ever engage in anything that is not fitting according to God's will as He has described it in the Bible. She must be honest and admit when it is a matter of preference and not a matter of God's will.

Finally, the wife must be submissive to God first if she hopes to be submissive to her husband as it is fitting. She learns how to submit to her husband by submitting to God first. Then, if, or when legitimate conflict arises she must appeal to her higher authority. She must be able to appeal to God like Peter did when the religious authorities told them to stop preaching about Christ. "But Peter and John answered . . . them, Whether it be right in the sight of God to hearken unto you more than unto God, judge ye" (Acts 4:19). He offered the same response a little later when the authorities threatened them again saying, "We ought to obey God rather than men" (Acts 5:29).

For the wife to submit to her husband as it is fitting in the Lord is not to do something supernatural. It would be supernatural if she had to depend on her own flesh and desires to pull off the feat. But the Christian wife is God's chosen vessel. She already lives in a way that subdues her flesh and is alive to Christ. By living out the character of Christ it is possible for her to successfully submit to her husband in a way that is fitting to the Lord.

PUT IT TO WORK

1. How much time do you spend reading the Bible?
2. Does the peace of Christ umpire your heart?
3. Have your forgiven others the way Christ has forgiven you?
4. Have you learned how to submit to Christ?
5. What does your husband require of you that is not fitting in the Lord?

PRINCIPLE 17
Husbands must not be bitter toward their wives.

Husbands, love your wives, and do not be harsh with them. (Colossians 3:19 ESV)

Wives, if you think living with your Christian husband is a challenge, try to imagine what it would be like to live with him if he were not regenerated. Such a proposal speaks volumes because it implies that there is a difference between the way born-again husbands think and act and the way non-born-again husbands think and act. Is that surprising?

In this letter to the Christians in Colossae, Paul explained that the people whom God chose are unique. God expects Christians to be unlike the people who have not received God's grace through salvation. Therefore, they think differently and act differently. In Colossians 3:12–17 Paul explained that the chosen people are set apart for God's service and glory (holy) because He loves them (v. 12). People like that are supposed to be putting on, like a new garment, things such as compassion, kindness, humility, meekness, patience, bearing with each other, and forgiving each other (vv. 12b–13). God expects His people to put on love and to have hearts ruled by the peace of Christ (v. 14). They are to be thankful people who let the Word of Christ abide in them abundantly. They are characterized by teaching each other and admonishing each other with thankfulness (v. 16). In fact, Christians do all that they do for the glory of Christ (v. 17).

These traits are to be ever increasing, ever more obvious in Christian husbands. A good wife ought to be able to live quite comfortably with a husband like that. However, not all Christian husbands manifest these traits.

Some Christian husbands seem to struggle with getting dressed properly. Their flesh is powerful and refuses to be submissive. Therefore, they yield to the natural desires of the flesh, which is opposed to godliness, and cause conflicts. Those conflicts disrupt the unity of the family. That is why God inspired Paul to tell husbands who are the chosen ones of God to keep on loving their wives and to stop being bitter or harsh with them. To some extent, at some time in their lives, these simple commands apply to all Christian husbands.

KEEP DOING THE RIGHT THING AND STOP DOING THAT WHICH IS NOT FITTING FOR GOD'S CHOSEN ONE

God expects the husbands whom He has chosen for salvation to keep on loving their wives. That statement is simple enough to understand. However, what it requires is not always easy to carry out. For the husband to love his wife means that he must act and think according to sacrificial love—all the time. This supreme love is not at all like romance. Romance is all about feeling. Romance is fickle. Romance is typical love in an unsaved world. The world, the way of thinking and feeling that is influenced by Satan, knows very little of sacrificial love. Their love is self-centered and self-serving. If a husband is taking his cues about love from what he watches on television, he is not even getting close to what God requires.

The kind of love God wants husbands to keep giving to their wives is the same kind of love that God demonstrates to redeemed people. That kind of love causes God to love sinners even though they are His enemies. That kind of love causes God to save sinners from eternal damnation unto abundant life with Him. God's supreme love knows what is best for His people. More than knowing what is best, God's love always does what is best. God demonstrates that love to people, who don't even like Him, in spite of the cost. He demonstrated that love most obviously on the cross when He Himself provided the sacrifice that is necessary to cover sinners' sins. Now, the God Who showed what love looks like requires, "Husbands, love your wives, even as Christ also loved the church, and gave himself for it" (Ephesians 5:25).

It is not enough for husbands to love their wives almost "like Christ loves the church" on her birthday, or anniversary, or Christmas. The verb tense requires that redeemed husbands love their wives all the time. It should become a habit of life. A Christian husband's relationship with his wife should be characterized by this self-sacrificing, "ultimate concern for her well being" kind of love. It is a command, not a suggestion. God is very serious about husbands carrying out His expectations. Since He has commanded love and expects Christian husbands to do it, the believer can probably expect to face this requirement as a test of his works when he stands before the judgment seat of Christ. Paul warned, "For we must all appear before the judgment seat of Christ; that every one may receive the things done in his body, according to that he hath done, whether it be good or bad" (2 Corinthians 5:10). Surely this requirement will be one of the standards of "good" done in the body.

Husbands who do the right thing should find it easier to avoid doing the wrong thing. The instruction also requires Christian husbands to stop being bitter or stop being harsh. Being bitter and harsh is the wrong thing. Sometimes this Greek word Paul uses here *(pikraino)* means harsh and sometimes it means bitter. The meanings are very similar in origin. Originally, the word referred to something pointed or sharp like an arrow. We can easily see, therefore, how the word would come to speak of that which was sharp and penetrated the senses or feelings.

In light of this evolution of use, the ancient world occasionally used the word to speak of sternness, severity, or responding angrily to something or someone. The context of Ephesians 4:31 requires this interpretation. In the larger context, Paul had been warning about proper communication. Then he said, "Let all bitterness, and wrath, and anger, and clamour, and evil speaking, be put away from you, with all malice." Obviously, the word *bitterness* is connected with anger and harsh, hurtful words in this warning.

Therefore, it is right to conclude that God expects Christian husbands to stop being harsh with their wives. He means that they should stop speaking to them in sternness or severity. He means that Christian husbands should stop being angry with their wives.

It is true that chosen people who are putting on the traits of Christ ought not to speak to anyone, especially their spouse, with harsh words. However, the most common interpretation of this Greek word points to bitterness of spirit because early on the word was used to describe a shrill noise, an offensive smell, or something painful or unwelcome to the senses. From this stage the word use developed so that people commonly used it to describe something bitter or sharp to the taste.

The instruction from Paul is that Christian husbands must stop having deep-seated anger against their wives.

The idea of something bitter or unpleasant to the taste is a Bible use of the word. In the Greek translation of the Old Testament, this exact Greek word was used to describe the water the Israelites found at Marah. Moses recorded, "And when they came to Marah, they could not drink of the waters of Marah, for they were bitter: therefore the name of it was called Marah" (Exodus 15:23). The same idea is conveyed in the New Testament when John saw a star fall from heaven into the rivers on earth. "And the name of the star is called Wormwood: and the third part of the waters became wormwood; and many men died of the waters, because they were made bitter" (Revelation 8:11).

Naturally, the same idea of bitterness or distaste extends to the feelings or the spirit of man. It describes the experience of something unpleasant to the soul. It might refer to that which is emotionally painful. Again, the Greek translation of the Old Testament used the word when Naomi answered her friends in Bethlehem when she had returned from Moab. They called her by her name Naomi. "And she said unto them, Call me not Naomi, call me Mara: for the Almighty hath dealt very bitterly with me" (Ruth 1:20). So, too, Solomon concluded in frustration, "And I find something more bitter than death: the woman whose heart is snares and nets, and whose hands are fetters. He who pleases God escapes her, but the sinner is taken by her" (Ecclesiastes 7:26 ESV).

In the New Testament, the most common use of this Greek word is to convey bitterness of spirit or emotional pain. Peter felt that way after he realized that he had sinned in exactly the way Jesus had said he would. "And Peter remembered the saying of Jesus, 'Before the rooster crows, you will deny me three times.' And he went out and wept bitterly" (Matthew 26:75 ESV). It was the condition of Simon the magician's heart. Peter assessed him well when he admonished, "For I perceive that thou art in the gall of bitterness, and in the bond of iniquity" (Acts 8:23).

In light of the clear meaning of the word, the instruction from Paul is that Christian husbands must stop having deep-seated anger against their wives. "Why?" some husbands ask. In all honesty they might say, "I like it" or "I can't help it because she makes me so angry." Be that as it may, God said, "Stop it." In fact, God said, "Stop it" for good reasons.

WRONG PRACTICES HAVE SERIOUS CONSEQUENCES

Bitterness brings with it some serious personal consequences. History and research prove that there are physical, mental, and emotional consequences to harboring bitterness. The physical consequences typically include things such as headaches, ulcers, sleeplessness, and even heart attacks. That is not to conclude rashly that everyone who has a headache, ulcer, or heart attack is bitter. Rather, these are typical physical ailments that accompany deep-seated, unresolved anger.

There are also emotional consequences to bitterness. Things such as anxiety, fear, tension, and depression are common companions to the sin.

Bitterness also drags along mental consequences too. Some of these are negative thinking, hypercritical attitudes, or anger and resentment when things don't go our way.

As with any sin, the sin of bitterness carries spiritual consequences. Some of those consequences can be the inability to love God, the inability to love others, and the inability to forgive others. Many of these spiritual problems stem from the fact that a bitter person finds it natural and easy to have an unhealthy focus on self. Is it not true that an unhealthy focus on self was really the root cause of the first sin Satan committed?

The consequences of bitterness do not just disappear one day. It is not like having the flu, where one day the victim wakes up and feels better. Rather, bitterness is a downward spiral. It does not just go away. Though the cliché sounds nice, time does not heal all wounds. Bitterness chains the victims to the very thing, experience, loss, or person from which they wish to be free. Until we deal with the bitterness, we cannot escape from the loss. The bitter person seeks, hopes for, even prays for vengeance against the supposed perpetrator but hurts himself the most. The sin keeps getting worse and hurts not only the bitter person but everyone it touches.

As a result, there are also corporate consequences to the sin of bitterness. Relationships are broken because bitterness spreads and infects others who come in contact with it. Because it is true that misery loves company, people who are influenced by the bitter person can also become angry and hypercritical. Or it is possible that people will seek to avoid the bitter person because they are offended by his bitter, complaining, critical spirit. Often relationships are destroyed for life because a husband chooses to see himself as a victim and becomes bitter.

A worse result is that many are defiled. That is why God warned Christians, "Looking diligently lest any man fail of the grace of God; lest any root of bitterness springing up trouble you, and thereby many be defiled" (Hebrews 12:15). Far too many Christians have experienced this "deadly root" springing up in someone they know. Businesses have failed because of unresolved bitterness. Churches have split or been ineffective for years because of this. Families have been splintered unresolvably because of bitterness. Who illustrates the problem better than Esau? Immediately after warning Christians to watch out for the root of bitterness, the author to the Hebrews described Esau. Was he not bitter? Of course he was because Jacob stole his birthright and stole his father's blessing. As a result, he not only wanted to kill the perpetrator, but the next verse in the text says that he became a fornicator (Hebrews 12:16). The original story reveals that he married foreign women on purpose to hurt his mother (Genesis 26:34–35).

Innocent people have been caught up in such personal battles many times since Esau's day. They have taken sides and broken relationships for life because the bitter person attempts to influence others that he or she is right, that he or she was the victim. Bitterness destroys the victim and damages many other relationships in the process.

GOD COMMANDS HIS CHOSEN ONES TO GET OVER IT

The first step in getting out of the pit of bitterness is to identify it. Often the problem is connected with perceived loss. It appears that something or someone we love has been taken away; and because we are unable, or unwilling, to deal with the accompanying anger, bitterness sets in. It happens when we refuse to give up the fight when it appears that someone has wronged us. It overtakes us when we refuse to take a loss, vowing in the secret place of our heart to get even one day. Often it flows from the sense of loss in a bad business deal, a lost position, a divorce, a romantic breakup, the loss of innocence through abuse, or even the loss of self-esteem through an embarrassing situation.

When a person loses something or someone significant, he often experiences common thoughts and emotions during the time he grieves over the loss. Most people experience denial at times of loss. They say, "This can't be happening to me. I will wake up and it will go away!" We are prone to have shock and numbness during which time we really cannot function. Then there is guilt and we begin to think, "I did something wrong. I'm being punished. This is my fault!" Depression comes along especially when a death occurs. At that time, we might conclude, "Life is now meaningless. I can't cope!" Then there is the hypothetical reasoning when the offended person says, "If only." People can "if only" themselves into bitterness by reliving the circumstances and wishing they had done something differently. These feelings are a normal part of grieving over loss. But in the end, the offended person must let go of the process. He must get over it.

But the flesh does not like to be confronted with an inability to control circumstances. As a result, the husband can let bitterness set in without even realizing what has happened. To avoid this he needs to be honest with the traits that help identify real bitterness. Generally, it is manifested in anger and he might wonder, or even say out loud, "How dare that person mess up my life!" Sometimes the result is a loss of temper, a bursting of anger, which in a way is better. Bitterness is the result of deep-seated, unresolved anger. It is secret, subtle planning, conniving. Worse, it is hard to admit. And yet, it must be identified, confessed, and dealt with.

What does it look like? Generally speaking, we manifest bitterness when we are oversensitive to a verbal remark, action, or lack of action. It shows itself as ongoing hurt feelings, repulsive feelings toward a person at the thought or sight of him or her. It is revealed when the offended person insists on retaining wounds and frequently talks about them. It is commonly expressed by the alienation of a person or by verbal slander against the person. Ironically, bitterness is often revealed as the offended one becomes like the one person he despises.

Having identified the problem, Christian husbands must take steps to extricate themselves from it. The first step of extrication is to confess bitterness for what it is. To confess is to say the same thing. He must acknowledge that God hates bitterness. He must admit that it is disobedience and an offense against Him. He must agree that bitterness is rebellion against God, indicating that he thinks he is more important than God or anyone else. He must be willing to say that the sin is pride in that he blames others for the way he feels.

Having confessed bitterness as sin, the husband must repent of the sin. That is precisely what God meant when He inspired Paul to write, "Let all bitterness, and wrath, and anger, and clamour, and evil speaking, be put away from you, with all malice" (Ephesians 4:31). To repent is to "put it away from you." Obviously, God knows His people can do this or He would not command it. Therefore, the bitter person must trust God enough to do what He requires. God knows that it is possible for the bitter person to put away bitterness because bitterness is not the result of others' actions toward us. Bitterness is the result of how we choose to respond to those actions. No one or nothing makes another person angry. The individual chooses to be angry. Joseph didn't choose to be angry or bitter. If anyone had the right to be angry and bitter, it was the young man who was ridiculed by his brothers, sold into slavery, falsely accused, and forgotten in prison. Rather than choosing to be angry, he chose to see God's will and plan being worked out in his life for the glory of God. The Greek philosopher, Epictetus, once said, "People are disturbed, not by things, but by the view they have of things." By God's grace and power choose to get out of the pit of bitterness.

Finally, the offended husband must forgive the offender in order to break the chains of bitterness. Immediately after telling Christians in Ephesus to put away bitterness, Paul said, "And be ye kind one to another, tenderhearted, forgiving one another, even as God for Christ's sake hath forgiven you" (Ephesians 4:32). The offender may or may not ever confess sin or ask for forgiveness. Nevertheless, the offended person must complete the transaction in his heart. He must forgive and always have forgiveness lying on the counter when the offender wants to come and get it.

God's will is clear. Husbands must keep on loving their wives and stop being harsh with them or bitter against them. That is the way God expects chosen husbands to demonstrate the love He has poured into their hearts. Do you harbor unresolved anger against your wife? How long will it be before it bursts into open bitterness and many are defiled? Determine that you will call bitterness what it is and extricate yourself from the pit right away.

PUT IT TO WORK

1. What causes you to become angry with your wife?

2. Does your wife know when she offends you?

3. Are you willing to forgive the way Christ has forgiven you?

4. Why do you choose to be angry?

5. Do you think that your wife owes you an apology? Have you talked to her about this?

Likewise also that women should adorn themselves in respectable apparel, with modesty and self-control, not with braided hair and gold or pearls or costly attire, but with what is proper for women who profess godliness—with good works. (1 Timothy 2:9–10 ESV)

I enjoy the wedding season because I enjoy weddings. They provide times of joy and gladness, beauty and madness. Sometimes it seems as though the whole wedding scene is out of control. It is not uncommon for churches to struggle with various issues connected with weddings. For example, recently my wife and I were returning home from a wedding, and while trying to carry on a conversation with her, I was, at the same time, thinking about services coming up the next day. As a result of attempting to multitask, I unthinkingly made a reference to topless wedding dresses. Of course my wife wondered what I was talking about. I explained that I meant to refer to the modern, and very popular, wedding dresses that don't have sleeves. She reminded me that there is quite a bit of difference between sleeveless and topless.

However, the modern trend in dresses is not too far from the unacceptable. Pure young women are forced to become very creative just to find a modest wedding dress, or they must alter their chosen dress until it is modest. You would think that of all the dresses in the world, wedding dresses should communicate purity, chastity, and modesty. They don't. How sad that young brides are forced to cut off the hem of their dresses in order to make suitable tops that keep them from appearing immodest in the sight of God and in the presence of the company gathered to celebrate their marriage.

This problem is not relegated only to wedding dresses. Even I, the father of three sons, have often heard women complain that their daughters are unable to find suitable clothing in the stores. Christian parents do not want their daughters to be sensual, nor do they want them to be frumpy and "back-woodsish." What is a mother to do? Furthermore, Christian wives do not desire to tempt other men by what they wear. Nor do their Christian husbands want them to tempt other men!

But these same Christian men and women live in a culture that is so saturated with lust that it is fully expected that women will dress in order to catch men's attention. One woman in a recent interview confessed, "I love to dress up, and 90 percent of the time, I do it for men. I'm single, and it's a no-brainer that sexy clothing attracts them." At least she was honest. How is a Christian woman supposed to respond in a society that honestly expects her to look and act sexy?

The best response is for her to think and act according to the principles of God's Word. God is never taken by surprise with such downturns in cultures. In fact, the unrighteous philosophy that Christians are facing in the American system of thought right now was quite popular in the Roman system of thought almost two thousand years ago. It is rather amusing, and almost astonishing, to read ancient literature and discover that the women of Rome in Paul's day were under the same burden of licentious living that women must endure today.

Therefore, the instruction that God gave to pastor Timothy through Paul the apostle is as fresh as yesterday's news. No doubt women who were saved out of the pagan Roman culture wondered if they should continue to dress and act the way they did before they were born again. Obviously, the Holy Spirit convicted them of the sinfulness of some of their past practices. Obviously, the born-again husband was not comfortable with his wife living according to Rome's standard. What should she do? How should she dress? What should her character be like now that she belonged to Christ?

God answered questions like that by laying down a few simple principles to help channel a woman's thinking about how she should dress and act. While the instruction of this text deals specifically with conduct in the church, the principles apply in every single circumstance of life. Christian women can know how God expects them to dress.

PUT INTO PRACTICE FOUR SIMPLE PRINCIPLES

God established some simple guidelines for women who desire to please Him in the way they dress and act. In 1 Timothy 2:9–10 the sincere Christian woman finds four simple principles to help her know and achieve God's will in this matter.

First, God inspired Paul to write that the Christian woman must adorn herself with adornment (v. 9). That sounds like a strange requirement. The reason for this odd translation is that essentially the same word is used twice in quick succession in this statement. The Greek word translated "adorn" describes the action of putting things in order, arranging something, or getting ready for action. It is no surprise that the word was used to describe military preparations for battle. However, the word is also found to describe common everyday practices like what the virgins did when they trimmed their lamps (Matthew 25:7). Jesus told a parable about the demon that left a man. The man was never born again, and when the demon came back with seven more demons, they discovered the "house" put in order (Matthew 12:44).

God expects "a putting in order" when women who claim to love Him get dressed. The same Greek word (kosmein) is the basis for the English word "cosmetics." Therefore, the plain idea is that God's standard for women is to get dressed with a plan and purpose. In other words, the Christian woman must think about what she is doing. She must make choices about clothing and appearance with a purpose. As the English Standard Version translates the verb, the Christian woman must make choices to put on respectable apparel. She must realize that there is supposed to be an orderliness to her choices in clothing and appearance. She is getting ready for "something!" What is it?

Second, God desires for women who claim to love Him to adorn themselves with modesty (v. 9). Originally this Greek word referred to shame or disgrace. Does God want women to be ashamed when they get dressed? No. We might wonder if the "shame" concept was the reason that this particular word lost favor with Hellenists who preferred to fit into their world system. That is not necessarily the case. The idea of "shame" was brought back by Stoics who taught the need for men and women alike to be bashful or fearful of breaking divine authority.

Therefore, the word in Paul's day talked about reverence before God or the priest, as well as respect and reverence for other people. The standard for a Christian woman should be a fear of doing that which blemishes her godly testimony before others. While this principle has broad application, it certainly applies to how the Christian woman dresses. The only other time the word appears in the New Testament is in Hebrews 12:28, where the writer told Christians, "Therefore let us be grateful for receiving a kingdom that cannot be shaken, and thus let us offer to God acceptable worship, with reverence and awe" (Hebrews 12:28 ESV). Isn't it interesting that the same attitude that undergirds a woman's worship of God should motivate her choice of clothing?

> A woman's appearance and deportment always say something about her.

The connection between a woman's attitude toward God and her attitude toward dress is important because a woman's appearance and deportment always say something about her. Do your appearance and the way you carry yourself say that you think life is about you and that you could not care any less about what others think? Or do your appearance and deportment say that you have respect for other Christians, for authorities, and for God Himself in Whose presence you live moment by moment?

The third principle requires that the Christian woman adorn herself with self-control (v. 9). This word speaks of reasonableness, rationality, and mental soundness. The root of the word used in this text means to be prudent, thoughtful, and self-controlled. In other words, it requires the woman who belongs to God to know what is the right and acceptable action in any given situation. But more than knowing, she also must practice the proper measure. This expectation is broader than some of the others because God requires thoughtful self-control in every aspect of life for His people. It is a God-ordained characteristic of Christian women in that they are "to be discreet [self-controlled], chaste, keepers at home, good, obedient to their own husbands, that the word of God be not blasphemed" (Titus 2:5). It is supposed to be the characteristic of all people whom Christ has changed. God's people are to be like the one-time demoniac who, when the people came "to Jesus, and saw him that was possessed with the devil, and had the legion, sitting, and clothed, and in his right mind . . . they were afraid" (Mark 5:15). It should especially be an obvious trait of God's people in sinful days. Peter reminded Christians, "But the end of all things is at hand: be ye therefore sober, and watch unto prayer" (1 Peter 4:7).

Therefore, Christian women should dress in a way that indicates that they have carefully considered what their choice of clothing says about their relationship with God and their relationship to other men. A woman might stand before the mirror and think, "I wear this particular outfit because it makes me feel so _____." If her feeling is carnal, she has yielded her reasoning and is out of control. She has just yielded her reasoning process to the desires of her flesh. Feeling good about herself is not the highest standard God has for His women. Rather she should reason like this: "I do not wear that, even though it makes feel good about myself, because it also sends the wrong message." That is the thinking of a woman who is self-controlled.

Finally, God requires that Christian women adorn themselves in a way that is proper for women who profess godliness (v. 10). The assumption here is that a Christian woman professes godliness. To profess is to promise or offer something to someone. Often the word is used in connection with preaching or declaring a message loudly and publicly. God illustrates the principle well when He makes a promise and then always fulfills what He promises. Paul reminds his readers that Abraham was a hero of faith because he was "fully persuaded that, what he had promised, he was able also to perform" (Romans 4:21).

According to this principle, God expects Christian woman to actually display what they claim to have. Their claim is godliness, which is a reverence for God, piety, or, in a general sense, religion. There is a propriety, a properness of dress, that affirms such claims. There is a "fitting" way to dress for the woman who claims to be godly. She wears what is proper or fitting for the occasion so that she always declares by her clothing, "I want the world to see God in me." Her clothing should be an outward substantiation of an inward relationship with God. Modesty begins with an attitude. A woman's relationship with God will overshadow her choice of clothing.

These guidelines cut across the grain of normal cultural guidelines (v. 9b). Having established four positive principles governing how Christian women ought to dress, Paul briefly mentioned the negative example from his culture. The norm, or at least a common sighting, in Rome was "braided hair, gold, pearls, and costly attire." Paul was not opposed to a woman looking proper, orderly, or neat. That is obvious from the requirement for women to adorn themselves with adornment. Nor did Paul condemn properly arranged hair. His argument is against ostentation. Roman women would braid jewels and gold into their hair in order to call attention to themselves. They would wear costly clothing to declare to others that they were on the cutting edge. Obviously, high-priced clothes were a status symbol in Rome just as they are in twenty-first-century America. An article entitled "The Ancient World—Dress—Rome" states,

> Roman women are frequently pictured with elaborate hairstyles. Hair was braided and dyed blonde. Wigs made from the fair hair of slaves were worn. The Tutulus hairstyle had many variations and was built up into a cone-shape with pads of false hair, and decorated with wrought metal diadems and interlaced lengths of braided hair. Gold jewelry reached a high level of craftsmanship, and quantities of gold earrings, armlets, rings, and filets have been found. Men and women alike used makeup to reduce the effects of age.[1]

Some things never change. The norm for women in America is also to call attention to self. For example, one young woman who was interviewed about her clothing decisions said, "My fun, hip sense of style emerged in college, when I realized that clothes are just another way of communicating. When I dress, I aim to get a reaction from women—whether it's appreciation or envy." How common is that scary, selfish attitude among American women? It is probably very common because it is also obvious that women's fashion publications almost exclusively encourage appearance that draws attention to self. Christian women are under constant pressure to abandon God's principles and embrace the world's standard. What should they do? They should apply God's four principles for honorable appearance.

WHY IS IT IMPORTANT TO SUBMIT TO GOD'S STANDARD?

One important reason for the Christian woman to dress God's way is that someone is watching her. I hope it will not be shocking for the God-professing woman to realize that men naturally appreciate good-looking women. Men naturally respond to physical beauty. No one has to teach a natural man to do that. It is not something they have to learn at the feet of teachers. The male's enjoyment of the beauty of a good-looking woman is a God-given desire in order to fulfill God's command to the first humans to be "fruitful and multiply" (Genesis 1:28).

This common, natural response is acknowledged many times in the Bible. Way back in the really ancient times "the sons of God saw that the daughters of man were attractive" (Genesis 6:2 ESV). Abraham took a trip south one day, and "when he was about to enter Egypt, he said to Sarai his wife, 'I know that you are a woman beautiful in appearance'" (Genesis 12:11 ESV). His son Isaac learned well from dear old Dad and told Rebekah to lie about being his wife "lest the men of the place should kill [him] . . . because she was attractive in appearance" (Genesis 26:7 ESV). God even told the men of Israel when they were about to enter the Promised Land that if "you see among the captives a beautiful woman, and you desire to take her to be your wife" (Deuteronomy 21:11 ESV), they could take her. Then there was "Absalom, David's son, [who] had a beautiful sister, whose name was Tamar" (2 Samuel 13:1 ESV). And King Ahasuerus ordered his servants "to bring Queen Vashti before the king with her royal crown, in order to show the peoples and the princes her beauty, for she was lovely to look at" (Esther 1:11 ESV). Because men naturally respond to a woman's physical appearance, Solomon warned about the sensual woman, teaching his son, "Do not desire her beauty in your heart" (Proverbs 6:25 ESV).

Even the godliest men struggle with this natural desire. Job, whom God acknowledged was the most righteous man on earth, was determined not to sin by gazing at the physical beauty of a young woman. He confessed, "I made a covenant with mine eyes; why then should I think upon a maid?" (Job 31:1). David, the man after God's heart, succumbed to this pressure. "And it came to pass in an eveningtide, that David arose from off his bed, and walked upon the roof of the king's house: and from the roof he saw a woman washing herself; and the woman was very beautiful to look upon" (2 Samuel 11:2). Because the attraction is so natural, God warns men not to respond improperly to a beautiful woman. Jesus taught "that whosoever looketh on a woman to lust after her hath committed adultery with her already in his heart" (Matthew 5:28).

Therefore, Christian women must be very careful to take this natural desire of men into consideration and determine not to contribute to the problem. The sinful woman's thinking is characterized by the woman who responded to an interview question by saying, "Clothes have a big impact on my self-esteem. When I'm well put-together, I feel powerful and strong. That confidence gives me a desirable, sexy glow that men really respond to." Yikes! If a woman knows that her appearance is sensual and will cause men to respond, she should change her appearance! A woman who loves God abhors that kind of reasoning.

Furthermore, there are other Christian women, often younger women (teens and pre-teens), who are watching older women (twenty-somethings) to learn how to make the difficult decisions about clothing in a mixed-up, sinful world. God's woman must guard her decisions carefully.

Instead of being a stumbling block for men, the Christian woman is supposed to glorify God in her appearance and deportment (v. 9*b*). Paul concluded that the Christian woman professes godliness—"with good works." Good works are not just done in church. All the saint's practices, including getting dressed, ought to declare that she belongs to God and desires to demonstrate Him to the world.

It is fitting for a woman to determine whether her appearance helps sinners see Christ or causes them to be satisfied to look at her. Modesty begins with an attitude. A woman's relationship with God will overshadow her choice of clothing.

Syndicated columnist Sally Fields drew a few comparisons between ancient Rome and modern America in her editorial in the *Greenville News* on July 4, 2007. She barely scratched the surface in pointing out how America today stands at the same brink where Rome stood before her meteoric decline. The similarities are too obvious to ignore—even in women's habits of appearance and deportment.

Philo, a Jewish philosopher who died twenty-three years before Paul wrote to pastor Timothy, wrote a satire entitled *The Sacrifice of Abel and Cain* in which he criticized the sensual, gaudy practices of Roman women, comparing them to common prostitutes. He wrote:

> Accordingly, the one comes to us luxuriously dressed in the guise of a harlot and prostitute, with mincing steps, rolling her eyes about with excessive licentiousness and desire, by which baits she entraps the souls of the young, looking about with a mixture of boldness and impudence, holding up her head, and raising herself above her natural height,

fawning and giggling, having the hair of her head dressed with most superfluous elaborateness, having her eyes penciled, her eyebrows covered over, using incessant warm baths, painted with a fictitious color, exquisitely dressed with costly garments, richly embroidered, adorned with armlets, and bracelets, and necklaces, and all other ornaments which can be made of gold, and precious stones, and all kinds of female decorations; loosely girdled, breathing of most fragrant perfumes, thinking the whole market her home; a marvel to be seen in the public roads, out of the scarcity of any genuine beauty, pursuing a [perverted] elegance.[2]

First century Philo sounds almost like a reporter who is commenting on yesterday's Oscars or some other gathering of trendsetters in America. God has a better standard for Christian women. His principles are simple: Dress yourself in orderly fashion, showing respect, self-control, and godly desires. Do this because men are watching you, and other women who need Christ want to see how Christ changes the life of a sinner.

PUT IT TO WORK

1. What are the four principles for modest dressing according to 1 Timothy 2:9-10?

2. What questions do you answer when you get dressed?

3. What motivates your choice in appearance, "how you will please others" or "how you will demonstrate God"?

4. Do you appreciate attention from men? Is that acceptable to God?

5. Who is watching you?

PRINCIPLE 19
The head of the home must provide for the home.

But if anyone does not provide for his relatives, and especially for members of his household, he has denied the faith and is worse than an unbeliever. (1 Timothy 5:8 ESV)

Harland David Sanders was born in Henryville, Indiana. His father died when he was five years old, forcing his mother to work outside the home. Sanders dropped out of school in the seventh grade and began the first of many jobs, including firefighter, steamboat pilot, insurance salesman, and farmer. At the age of forty, Sanders acquired a service station in Corbin, Kentucky. Having been forced to learn to cook in his mother's absence, Harland began cooking chicken dishes for people who stopped by his station. Business grew and before long he had to move to an old motel that seated 142 people. The rest is history. Colonel Sanders could have used the excuse that he was virtually an orphan and had abandoned education, but he chose to apply himself in honorable labor.

Sanders had a profound influence on a young man from a similar background. Dave Thomas was born in Atlantic City, New Jersey, and was adopted by Rex and Auleva Thomas at the age of six months. His mother died when he was five, and he spent the next several years hopping from state to state with his adoptive father, who seemed to have difficulty holding down a job. When he was fifteen, Dave dropped out of high school to pursue his dream of owning his own restaurant. In 1962 Dave took over four failing KFC restaurants, turned them into profitable ventures in four years, sold them back to KFC, and became a millionaire at age thirty-five.

He could have used the excuse that he came from a troubled childhood and gone on welfare. But Thomas was motivated by higher principles.

Christian men need to be motivated by higher principles. Of course, many Christian men hear stories like those of Sanders and Thomas and think that they too can start out with meager beginnings and become millionaires. Yes, that is possible in America. However, Christian men should have a higher motivation to go to work and provide for their families than the prospect of becoming millionaires. Christian men have the command of God. We don't need a greater reason for getting a job.

However, some Christians apparently never got the memo that God has clearly expressed His will for them in this matter. They claim that they would take care of their families financially if they could only find a job. There is seldom a valid excuse for an able-bodied Christian man not having a job. While some might say, "I can't find a job," what they really mean is "I can't find the kind of job I want," or "I can't find the kind of work I like at the kind of pay I want to make." Sometimes a fellow has to begin working in something he does not prefer to do in order to get the opportunity to work in his dream job.

That kind of scenario might be particularly true for the Christian husband/father. God commanded that all heads of the home must be careful to provide for those under them. Who does that include? Those are the people for whom the heads of the household are responsible. In Paul's day, that circle was quite large and we might seriously question if the circle of responsibility should be smaller in our day. The context of this command revolves around the issue of widows. Who was responsible for taking care of those who could not care for themselves? Paul gave sage advice to pastor Timothy about this matter. In the process, he established God's principle that a man's neglecting to provide care for his family is tantamount to denying the faith. How can that be? We discover in this text that God is very serious about fathers and husbands taking care of people who look to them for provision. Christian heads of the household honor God when they provide for their families. They dishonor God when they fail to take care of those who depend on them.

PROVIDE FOR YOUR RELATIVES

It does not require extended theological training to realize that this simple text requires Christians to be responsible for the care of their relatives. The command falls within the context of instructions from Paul to Timothy about church matters. One of the pressing issues of that day was how much responsibility the local church should take in caring for needy widows. If a family did not step up to provide for their widowed relatives, it could create a hardship on the church.

The context of the command indicates that there were needy widows in the church. Some of these women were made widows in the most natural way when their husbands died. However, according to some Bible students, it was also possible (and unique compared to our experiences) that a woman might have been widowed because her husband, who had multiple wives before he was born again, divorced all but one after he was saved. No doubt that situation arose on occasion.

Women who were in such circumstances would often be needy. Paul called them "widows who are truly widows" (v. 3). Typically a widow like this would be older and not have the strength necessary to hold down a regular job. At that time it was difficult for any woman to find regular work to support herself. In ancient cultures women were especially subject to abuse or unfair practices. That is why God always encouraged His people to care for the helpless and protect the unprotected. When He formed the nation of Israel, God required in the law, "Ye shall not afflict any widow, or fatherless child" (Exodus 22:22). In fact, God promised that He Himself goes to bat for needy people. "He doth execute the judgment of the fatherless and widow, and loveth the stranger, in giving him food and raiment" (Deuteronomy 10:18).

Because God's heart is toward the needy, the early church desired to help widows meet their needs. One of the first conflicts in the church arose over the fact that Greek widows were not receiving the same kind of care Hebrew widows received from the church (Acts 6:1). As a result of this problem, some of the first office holders in the church, the deacons, were made responsible to assure that this provision was distributed fairly (Acts 6:2–6). Obviously, the church was concerned to take care of the needy widows.

However, there were widows in the church who were not needy. Some of the women had lost their husbands, but they were still young enough to work (v. 9). According to God's plan, the church should not provide for the needs of such women. Other women had indeed become widows when their husbands died, but they were more interested in pleasure than in trusting God (vv. 5, 13). The church was not responsible to take care of them. Some women had lost their husbands—which certainly made them widows—but they were not "truly widows" because they were still young enough to remarry (v. 11). The church should not provide for widows like that. They were not truly needy. Finally, there were women who had lost their husbands and were, therefore, widows. However, these women had children and grandchildren who should care for them (v. 4). The church should not be responsible to care for such widows.

That brings us to the heart of the issue. God expects Christians to do what they can to meet the needs of their relatives. While the flesh might recoil at the idea because it disdains sacrificing for others, God considers care for a widow to be a show of godliness (v. 4). God said that when children or grandchildren take care of widows it gives them the opportunity to show godliness to the entire household. Furthermore, God commends this sacrificial kindness because He does not wish for people to push their needy relatives off on the church (v. 16).

> **God expects Christians to do what they can to meet the needs of their relatives.**

That is not to say that a child or grandchild must have a widow or needy person move in with them. That is indeed the case sometimes. However, the principle requires that Christians must make sure that their relative, the widow, is cared for. That is not a difficult thing to assure in modern America. In Timothy's day, it was a different story. In first-century Roman culture there was no insurance or Social Security. A widow who was truly needy required the intercession of family members. Maybe some of the best care someone can give in this age of insurance, retirement funds, and Social Security is to give sound instruction regarding preparation for the inevitable. The time will almost certainly come when a loved one cannot care for himself or herself. Maybe an ounce of prevention is still worth a pound of cure.

Since God requires His people to take care of relatives once removed (i.e., grandchildren caring for grandparent), it stands to reason that Christians are even more responsible to care for their immediate households. This means that a Christian leader must take the responsibility to provide for his own family. Since that is true, it must also be true that it is wrong for the head of the home to expect a government program to provide for his family if he is not willing to do what God requires. Paul warned the believers in Thessalonica that people who won't work should not eat (2 Thessalonians 3:10). A sincere Christian should have no problem applying that rule to the lazy husband. But it is rather difficult to apply the rule to the lazy husband's needy family.

Nevertheless, God does not require the church to subsidize sloth. It is wrong for a husband and father to expect the church to provide for his family if he refuses to work. It is a different story when a head of the household is incapacitated. Then he or she has no choice but to lean on programs and the help of others. But sloth or even depression is not a valid excuse for failing to provide for the family. In fact, God condemns laziness. Also, God provides means in His Word for overcoming depression.

Typically, the means for providing is work, which sounds like too much work to some lazy fellows. Work is the kind of thing some guys avoid at all costs. But God commends work. The wise man understands the need for work. Solomon said, "Go to the ant, thou sluggard; consider her ways, and be wise" (Proverbs 6:6). From the ant we learn how to be diligent and to plan ahead. That is what the Greek word translated "provide" in the text (1 Timothy 5:8) actually means. God is all for planning ahead and doing the work that is necessary to meet needs. It is important to realize that God commended work even before the curse of sin fell upon the creation. Sometimes it is tempting to think that work is part of the curse. But that is not the case. Futility in work is the curse, not work itself. "And the Lord God took the man, and put him into the garden of Eden to dress it and to keep it" (Genesis 2:15).

At the same time, God also requires employers to be fair with employees. If a man works long hours but makes subminimum wage, he may still not be able to meet the needs of his family. If an employer is fair with the employee, the man ought to be able to make ends meet. That assumes, of course, that the wage earner manages his wages wisely. Often the reason a head of the house cannot provide for the needs in the home is due to poor spending habits. Why does good financial practice escape some people? Sound money management is generally as simple as self-discipline. It boils down to a matter of knowing how much money a person makes, knowing where the money must go, and, finally, making sure it goes there—and only there!

FAILURE TO PROVIDE IS TANTAMOUNT TO HERESY

God said in this text that the person who does not take care of his family has denied the faith and is worse than an unbeliever. Those are pretty strong words. Why would God say that? The faith is built on the love of God. We must realize that the New Testament uses the idea of faith in two different ways. One meaning of faith refers to the believer's salvation. It is impossible for a true Christian to reject the faith of salvation. Through grace, God has given faith to the believer so that he can trust God's finished work in Christ. That is what Paul meant when he wrote, "For by grace are ye saved through faith; and that not of yourselves: it is the gift of God" (Ephesians 2:8). Salvation is God's work, not the individual's work. Can a mere human undo God's work? No.

Salvation is the result of God's work that allows the believer to have faith. It is because of God's righteousness, not because of the sinner's own abilities. Peter taught that marvelous truth in his simple introduction to his second epistle. He began the letter by introducing himself as "Simon Peter, a servant and an apostle of Jesus Christ." But he wrote "to them that have obtained like precious faith with us through the righteousness of God and our Saviour Jesus Christ" (2 Peter 1:1). Since the Christian did not create that faith, he cannot abandon it. Therefore, Paul did not tell Timothy that the person who fails to take care of his own family has lost his salvation. A Christian cannot reject the faith of salvation, but he can reject faith in another sense.

A second way the New Testament uses the term *faith* is to speak of the Bible. A Christian can live contrary to the principles of God's Word. In this sense, "the faith" is the body of God's teaching. Jude used the word in this way when he warned, "Beloved, when I gave all diligence to write unto you of the common salvation, it was needful for me to write unto you, and exhort you that ye should earnestly contend for the faith which was once delivered unto the saints" (Jude 3). Even a Christian can reject this faith. However, real disciples who remember Christ's work in their behalf embrace the "faith." This was evident in the church at the beginning as "the word of God increased; and the number of the disciples multiplied in Jerusalem greatly; and a great company of the priests were obedient to the faith" (Acts 6:7).

The problem that Paul mentioned to Timothy (heads of the home rejecting the faith because they would not provide) is obvious when sin and sinners interfere with this faith. When sin influences a Christian's thinking, he may very well deny God's principle of taking care of his family. That is the same kind of thing Paul had to deal with in the case of Elymas. "Elymas the magician (for that is the meaning of his name) opposed them, seeking to turn the proconsul away from the faith" (Acts 13:8 ESV).

Since the essence of "the faith" is God's love, we can readily see how the head of the home who refuses to take care of his family rejects that love. The faith, the Word of God, describes God's love. In fact, the faith is known because of God's love. John argued, "And we have known and believed the love that God hath to us. God is love; and he that dwelleth in love dwelleth in God, and God in him" (1 John 4:16). The faith also expects believers to demonstrate God's love. Jesus taught, "By this shall all men know that ye are my disciples, if ye have love one to another" (John 13:35). As believers demonstrate the truth of God's Word, the faith is revealed to the world through love. Jesus taught,

> For if ye love them which love you, what thank have ye? for sinners also love those that love them. And if ye do good to them which do good to you, what thank have ye? for sinners also do even the same. And if ye lend to them of whom ye hope to receive, what thank have ye? for sinners also lend to sinners, to receive as much again. But love ye your enemies, and do good, and lend, hoping for nothing again; and your reward shall be great, and ye shall be the children of the Highest: for he is kind unto the unthankful and to the evil.
> (Luke 6:32–35)

Surely, love for family will motivate a person to work, earn a wage, and carefully provide for their needs. Love compels God's leaders to work. Love compels Christians to manage God's money wisely. Love allows the head of the house to sacrifice personal desires for the good of the family. To decide not to work or not to provide for the family is tantamount to turning against the true principles of God's Word. Even most unbelievers have a better standard than that.

That is what Paul meant when he warned that a Christian's failure to support his family renders him worse than unbelievers. Unbelievers typically show concern for their own. Taking care of one's household was expected in ancient times. Plato, the great Greek philosopher (427–347 BC), wrote,

"Next comes the honor of loving parents, to whom, as is meet, we have to pay the first and greatest and oldest of debts, considering that all which a man has belongs to those who gave him birth and brought him up."[1]

> Only in the most selfish modern cultures do people abandon their responsibilities to care for family.

Aeschines was an Athenian orator who lived a few years after Plato (389–318 BC). He wrote, "And whom does our lawmaker (Solon) condemn to silence in the Assembly of the people? . . . 'Let there be,' he says, 'a scrutiny of public speakers, in case there be any speaker in the Assembly of the people who is a striker of his father or mother, or who neglects to maintain them or to give them a home.'"[2] Demosthenes was a Greek statesman and orator, a contemporary of Aeschines (384–322 BC), who said, "I regard the man who neglects his parents as unbelieving in and hateful to the gods, as well as to men."[3] Aristotle, the famous Greek philosopher (384–322 BC), wrote, "It would be thought in the matter of food we should help our parents before all others, since we owe our nourishment to them, and it is more honorable to help in this respect the authors of our being, even before our selves." Philo, a first century AD Jewish philosopher, concluded, "When old storks become unable to fly, they remain in their nests and are fed by their children, who go to endless exertions to provide their food because of their piety."[4] Obviously, the ancient cultures believed for many centuries that it was noble for people to take care of their families—and even their extended families.

Only in the most selfish modern cultures do people abandon their responsibilities to care for family. We are part of one of the most selfish cultures to have populated the earth. Proof of such selfishness is manifested in the fact that mothers kill their babies because they pose an inconvenience to their desired lifestyle. The average abortion rate has been 1.5 million per year since 1973. Ninety-eight percent of the abortions are for reasons other than rape, incest, or the mother's life being endangered. One third of the abortions are performed on teens without their parents' knowledge.

That is a most horrendous expression of selfishness, especially in light of the fact that two million American couples are waiting for the opportunity to adopt. Due to selfishness, Americans have killed a total of 44,469,819 babies since 1973. That was as of Wednesday, July 11, 2007 at 8:30 a.m. This slaughter is equivalent to the total current population of Argentina, Chile, Bolivia, and Venezuela combined. What would the world do to a crazed dictator who obliterated the entire population of four significant nations?

In another display of selfishness we discover, according to the 2005 census, that there are 4.85 million couples living together out of wedlock. That is 10 million people. The rate is up 1,000 percent from 1960. Why? Selfish young people are unwilling to make a commitment for life.

In 2005, before Congress changed the bankruptcy laws, 1 out of every 60 families in the U.S. voluntarily filed for bankruptcy. They refused to pay their bills because it was inconvenient.

That is the modern American culture. God's heads of the households must stand out as unique. Many people in the culture are overly concerned for self. Christians, on the other hand, must be driven by God's love to take care of those who look to them for provision. Get a job, keep a job, pay your bills, and meet the needs of your family.

A true Christian has received the love of God. His love has removed the penalty and power of sin. That love should motivate the believer to love others like Christ loves him. Because of Christ's love the Christian father and husband is able to sacrifice for the benefit of others. The best place to begin showing the fruit of such loving sacrifice is in one's own family. Then the love will extend to the care of outlying family members and even strangers like concentric ripples in the pond. The world is watching and needs to see someone who sacrifices in order to provide for those who depend on him.

PUT IT TO WORK

1. Do you provide for your family or do you just give them money?

2. Have you expressed faith unto salvation?

3. How important is the Bible to you?

4. What kind of sacrifices have you made for your family in the past six months?

5. Does your family know that you love them? Have you told them? Have you showed them?

PRINCIPLE 20
Train the young women to love their husbands, to love their families.

Older women likewise are to be reverent in behavior, not slanderers or slaves to much wine. They are to teach what is good, and so train the young women to love their husbands and children, to be self-controlled, pure, working at home, kind, and submissive to their own husbands, that the word of God may not be reviled. (Titus 2:3–5 ESV)

Women's rights is such a foundational part of the American society that most people never stop to think that it is a somewhat modern movement in America. That women have the right to compete with men in the workplace, on the political field, in the clergy, and almost any other place we can imagine is taken for granted. However, it was not always that way.

The Women's Rights Movement marks July 13, 1848, as its beginning. On that summer day in upstate New York, a young housewife and mother, Elizabeth Stanton, was commiserating the lot of women in society with some friends over tea. Stanton poured out her discontent with the restrictions she felt were imposed on her because she was a woman. She wondered why she did not have the same freedoms to work, to succeed, to compete, that men enjoyed. Stanton's friends agreed with her, passionately. These women decided to do something about it and within two days the modern Women's Rights Movement was up and running.

The women announced that the movement would meet at the Wesleyan Chapel in Seneca Falls on July 19–20, 1848. They planned to hold "a convention to discuss the social, civil, and religious condition and rights of woman." Stanton declared, "The history of mankind is a history of repeated injuries and usurpations on the part of man toward woman, having in direct object the establishment of an absolute tyranny over her. To prove this, let facts be submitted to a candid world." Specifically, she was concerned about things such as the fact that women had to submit to laws when they had no voice in their formation. Or the fact that women had to pay property taxes although they had no representation in the levying of these taxes. Stanton was upset that most occupations were closed to women, and when women did work, they were paid only a fraction of what men earned. Furthermore, women were not allowed to enter professions such as medicine or law. Ultimately, she felt that women were robbed of their self-confidence and self-respect and were made totally dependent on men.

The women met, and the rest is history. By the time World War II engulfed the American society, it became obvious that the tools of war had to be manufactured, and the defense factories were in desperate need of laborers. Women now had the opportunity to become part of the workforce. Before the war, it was uncommon for women to work outside the home. During the war, about half of all American women worked outside their homes. The work of women during World War II proved that they could learn to do the same industrial work as men. The number of working women rose from 14.6 million in 1941 to 19.4 million in 1944.

Today it is rare to find a woman who does not compete in the work world with men. It appears that the women of Mary Stanton's philosophy got what they wanted, and now everyone is happy. Well, maybe not everyone. Whenever people turn God's plan on its head, they are not happy for very long. There is no lasting satisfaction in snubbing God's plan. God created the woman to fit perfectly into His ordained hierarchy. In Paradise, Eve was a helper that was suitable for Adam. Adam was her head, and she worked in perfect harmony with him. Then one day, the suitable helper sinned because she heeded Satan's convincing argument.

Because Eve sinned and Adam joined her in sinning, God leveled curses against His creation that exist to this day. God warned the woman (Genesis 3:16) that she would desire to have her husband's position as the head of the home. Nevertheless, God's plan is for the husband to rule over the wife. That is still God's plan in this age of human enlightenment. Because sin drives the flesh to be number one, God had to ordain a structure for orderliness. God's structure is that the husband will be the head of the wife, and the wife will complement his work.

That kind of thinking is definitely politically incorrect, and the modern world laughs it to scorn. But God's plan for the family has not changed. It is interesting that the Woman's Rights Movement came into being in this nation at the same time that Higher Criticism from Europe found a place in American seminaries. Higher Criticism attempts to debunk the authority of the Bible and leaves it as a collection of the writings of mere men with no more power than the writings of Shakespeare. Indeed, when people reject the authority of God's Word and God's plan, they will stand the family on its head. The results are predictable. We live with them every day in a culture that is rapidly declining toward anarchy and chaos.

What America is experiencing today is nothing new. The Roman culture declined while holding to many of the same debilitating kinds of philosophies the people of this nation hold dear. That is why God told Timothy to make sure that the older women teach the younger women about God's plan. If young Christian wives refuse to order their lives according to God's ideas, they will tarnish the reputation of the Bible and give sinners good reason to reject it. In short, God challenges young Christian wives to affirm the truth of the Bible by living according to His plan.

GOD'S PLAN IS PRACTICAL (Titus 2:3b-5a)

Paul instructed pastor Titus that the older women should instruct the younger wives in the church how to follow God's plan (vv. 3b–4a). Like most plans, God's plan will not be effective until someone teaches it to the people who need to do it (v. 4a). So, in a short and to-the-point word, Paul told Titus that the older women need to bring the young wives to their senses. The verb translated "train" means to advise or encourage. But since the word is virtually the same as the Greek word that means to think soberly, the word means more exactly to bring someone to his or her senses. The goal of this activity is reasonableness, rationality, and mental soundness. The verb is in the present tense, which means that this must be an ongoing process.

The instruction certainly does not imply that all young wives are mentally unbalanced and in need of therapy. Rather, the admonition is to instruct young wives to work against their natural tendencies and fleshly desires. By nature their flesh teaches young wives to step out of God's path, to live contrary to God's standard of sound thinking. Therefore, Paul's suggested teaching is corrective. It is like Wisdom crying out in the streets, encouraging the naive to come to her, as it is portrayed in the Proverbs. The continual fleshly influence of the ungodly world, coupled with the natural inclinations of the flesh, put young women out of balance regarding God's plan. God's desire is for them to be helped back into the right path.

God's plan is for experienced teachers to teach His principles to the young wives (v. 3*b*). Older women are those who have been down the road and have learned much through hands-on experience. Along the way, they have learned the lessons that make up God's plan. These teachers have learned how to behave in reverence. Their very lives demonstrate godliness. These saintly women know from years of maturing and growing spiritually how to conform to God's plan. They may not know how to operate an iPhone®, or they might be unaware of who is the latest American idol, and they certainly don't wear low-rise Diesel® jeans. But they have learned by God's grace how to demonstrate reverence for God, His Word, and His work. They can and must teach what they have learned to younger wives.

The older women need to teach God's plan. But it is the responsibility of younger wives to learn the seven principles (vv. 4–5*a*). First, the experienced teachers must teach the young wives how to be husband lovers (v. 4). The teachers need to train young wives to be brought to the right senses in the matter of loving their husbands. Why is this so important? The part of the word that is translated "love" means to love or show deep affection for someone or something. It means to have a desire for something or someone. It is the kind of love someone might have for a parent. It is also the kind of love the Pharisees had for things they should not have wanted. Jesus confronted those religious hypocrites because they loved the best rooms and seats at feasts and because they loved greetings in the market (Matthew 23:6; Luke 20:46). A good illustration of this kind of love is the feeling Christ Himself had for His friend Lazarus (John 11:36). Jesus also explained that God the Father loves the disciples like this (John 16:27).

One might rightly conclude that it is easy to have this kind of love for a friend you don't live with. It is easy to love when you can walk away from idiosyncrasies that wear on your nerves. It's easy to love when you don't have to dwell on the glaring differences between you and the one you have to live with. It is difficult to really love a person you live with. This is partly due to the fact that living together makes it impossible to avoid the other person's bad habits. No two people who live together ever agree on all things at all times. But the wife cannot just walk away from the husband

and forget about the matter. Furthermore, the young wife's husband will always seem to get in the way of progress. Her progress, that is. Why? She might conclude that he is a bad guy because he won't let her have her way.

> God's plan is for experienced teachers to teach His principles to the young wives.

So it is really true that love means sacrifice! Love requires that the lover says no to herself and yes to her husband. That is contrary to human nature. Infatuation comes quite naturally. Lust is as natural and predictable as the rising sun. But real love—now that is a different story. It takes work. That is why teachers must train young wives to love their husbands.

Second, teachers must train young wives to love children (v. 4). This word is like the previous word. It is one Greek word that requires young wives to sacrifice for their children. That is the rub. Children require incredible amounts of time and energy. From the moment the child is conceived in the womb until he or she leaves home, the mother/wife must sacrifice. The instant the child is born, he or she demands countless hours of attention that rob the mother of sleep. And as the children grow, Mom discovers that she must be in all places at all times to keep them from hurting themselves.

On top of the required daily maintenance, mothers must also train their children. Children come into the world as needy creatures. Who will teach them not to be selfish, not to lie, and not to throw temper tantrums? Who teaches them to share, to be respectful of others, and not to pick their noses in public? Does the childcare really care, or do they simply offer services for money?

Wives (mothers) must learn how to love their children so they can teach the children how to live out God's will for them. There is grave danger that, apart from personal sacrifice, a mom will shape the children to do her will. Human nature wants to be god and create little images of itself. Therefore, it takes incredible sacrifice to shape a child for twenty years to love God and serve Him only—and then to let the child go and do that! Only genuine love can meet these needs. Only love is willing to make the sacrifices necessary to love children. Someone must train the young wives to do this.

Third, teachers must train young wives how to be sober minded (v. 5). To be sober minded is to be temperate, controlled, or thinking correctly. This is essentially the same word that is translated "train" in verse 4. In this case, it is a compound word made up of *sozo*, meaning to save or keep safe, and the word *phren*, an old Greek word that refers to the mind. So the word simply means to keep the mind safe. Teachers need to teach young wives how to make decisions through a controlled thinking process as opposed to making decisions based on how they feel.

Fourth, teachers must train young wives to be pure (v. 5). This word comes from the same Greek word that gives us the English *holy*. In this particular context, it refers to sexual purity, fidelity. The flesh says, "Don't worry about being faithful; rather fulfill your desires." The world says, "It's okay because everyone else finds joy, satisfaction, and fun outside the marriage relationship." Those influences exert tremendous pressure on women. That is why the experienced teachers need to train young wives how to set up the fences. The world needs to see holy, young women and recognize their desire to be faithful.

Fifth, teachers must train young wives to be house-workers (v. 5). The focus of the young wife's labors should be the home. This is especially important while she has a young family depending on her. In those formative years, the wife needs to see the home as her castle. Her world tells her that she is a failure for staying at home to train her children to love God. But God's plan states otherwise. Experienced teachers need to train young wives how to make their home their chief ministry.

Sixth, teachers must train young wives to be good (v. 5). The word is simple. The requirement is not simple. In a general sense, this word refers to something or someone who is pleasing. In the context, the requirement is for a young wife to be good, pleasing to God. Also, if she is good, she will be pleasing to those who love God. Godly, older women need to train young wives how to render service that is pleasing to God first, to a godly family second, and to godly people third.

Finally, teachers must train young wives to be subject to their own husbands (v. 5). A young wife moves from being subject to her father to being subject to her husband at marriage. Does she never have freedom? The whole idea of being subject to any man cuts across the grain of the Women's Rights Movement. Being subject to her husband is not restrictive as the world describes it. Rather, this submission sets the Christian wife free to carry out God's plan for God's glory. Sinners cannot do that. Notice the emphasis on submitting to her own husband. When a woman works for another man, there is sometimes conflict with the order of submission. Godly employers are sensitive to God's plan. Older women must train young wives to be subject to their husbands in practical ways on a daily basis.

That is not to conclude that older women must teach young wives that they are inferior to their husband. Indeed, God declares that husband and wife are equal on the spiritual plane. "In declaring the spiritual equality of the woman before God (Galatians 3:28), Christianity immeasurably elevated her status but did not thereby abolish her functional position as the complement and support of her husband as the head of the house."[1]

RESPONSE TO GOD'S PLAN REFLECTS ON GOD'S WORD (v. 5b)

To ignore God's plan is to insult His Word. God does not approve of the life lived in conflict with His Word. Jesus applied that principle to the Jewish hypocrites who claimed to live according to God's law but who were sinful. Paul told Christians that because of such people "the name of God is blasphemed among the Gentiles through you" (Romans 2:24). Likewise, God issued a warning to young widows who might be tempted to become gossips and busybodies. He said through Paul, "I will therefore that the younger women marry, bear children, guide the house, give none occasion to the adversary to speak reproachfully" (1 Timothy 5:14). Even servants, who faced a more intense situation than modern employees face, must order their lives in a way that affirms God's Word. Paul told Pastor Tim to "let as many servants as are under the yoke count their own masters worthy of all honour, that the name of God and his doctrine be not blasphemed" (1 Timothy 6:1).

In all these cases, a slipshod lifestyle brought dishonor to God's Word.

Likewise, Christians who fail to live what they claim to believe gives sinners reason to reject God's Word. Why should they embrace a body of teaching that does not make God's people different from the world's people? The people of the world are wise enough to know that Christians ought to be distinct because of what the Bible teaches.

To live out God's plan is to affirm the truth of His Word. When a Christian (young wives included) attempts to live by God's plan, he or she declares that he or she really trusts God's Word. Some young wives have tried to live according to the foregoing principles and have stumbled. Did they give up? Few people ever live in perfect conformity to the Bible standard. God does not ask for perfection. He knows that such is not going to happen in this life. Christians know from experience that God is right on this issue. Mature Christians do not attempt perfection; rather, they live with the sincere desire to order their lives as closely as possible to God's standard so that others will know that they believe the Bible. Slavish insistence on rules similar to God's standard leads to pride. It is human nature to take principles to a level of nonnegotiable law. For example, if a young woman decides that "loving her children" is demonstrated by having twenty children, she will be proud of her large family and will despise anyone who does not agree with her. God's standard does not require human enhancement. Simply living out the principles as they appear in the Bible is sufficient to affirm God's truth.

Conformity to God's plan can be the best testimony of the gospel that many people will experience. Some people never go to church and have always turned away from tracts or sermons on the radio. But a life lived in conformity to God's principles speaks too loudly to be ignored.

God's plan is clear and simple. His plan contradicts the plan of the modern Women's Rights Movement. Or is it that the plan of the modern Women's Rights Movement contradicts God's plan? While God's instruction sounds archaic to the modern ear, it is the only plan that results in peace and satisfaction both in the individual and the home. When husbands love their wives as God instructed, and wives love their husbands as God instructed, the whole world sees a demonstration of godliness. The world needs to see the gospel in action. Young wives have an opportunity to show the world what God is like. God can draw sinners to Himself through their testimony. But they must conform to God's plan for it to happen.

PUT IT TO WORK

1. Who taught (or is teaching) you how to live out these principles from the Bible?

2. Which of these seven principles characterize your life best?

3. How do you demonstrate love to your family?

4. What, if anything, is more important to you than your home?

5. What practical evidence in your daily life reveals that you believe the Bible?

Likewise, wives, be submissive to your own husbands, so that even if some do not obey the word, they may be won without a word by the conduct of their wives—when they see your respectful and pure conduct. Do not let your adorning be external—the braiding of hair, the wearing of gold, or the putting on of clothing—but let your adorning be the hidden person of the heart with the imperishable beauty of a gentle and quiet spirit, which in God's sight is very precious. For this is how the holy women who hoped in God used to adorn themselves, by submitting to their husbands, as Sarah obeyed Abraham, calling him lord. And you are her children, if you do good and do not fear anything that is frightening. (1 Peter 3:1–6 ESV)

Peter wrote this letter, while being borne along by the Holy Spirit, in order to encourage and instruct Christians who had been scattered by persecution throughout the region we know today as modern Turkey. Often the persecution forced them to forsake family and home. They loved God and refused to renounce their faith in Christ. Sometimes their love for Him cost them everything. No doubt some of the Christians perceived themselves to be, as Paul called us, "the scum of the world, the refuse of all things" (1 Corinthians 4:13). Generally, it appeared that their world would not have them. They were not the authorities of the world but were the weak things that God had chosen for His own glory (1 Corinthians 1:27).

How should Christians respond when it becomes obvious that they are not in charge and that others have the right, by position or rank, to tell them what to do? Human nature tends to rebel against such authority. It is natural to strive to be the best, to be number one, to be the one who is in control. It takes special grace from God to be able to respond humbly to a tyrant.

Much of Peter's letter addresses circumstances like that. This part of the letter begins with the words "In the same way." The phrase calls to mind that Peter is giving much practical advice that focuses on those who have little or no authority in their circumstances. For example, Christians who have lost their homes, jobs, and families must submit to governors (2:13–17). God's plan is for His people to be the best citizens in order "to silence the ignorance of foolish people" (2:15). Christian slaves must submit to the authority of their masters even if they are unjust (2:18–22). In fact, all Christians have been called to suffer and endure as did Christ (2:21).

In light of the focus of this letter on the need for downtrodden people to submit to their authorities, it is not surprising that God would have Peter address the wife's submission to her husband. It is significant that Peter dedicated six verses to the issue of the wife's submission (3:1–6) but only one verse to the husband's proper relationship with his wife (3:7). Like the persecuted church, like citizens living under a dictator, like slaves working for an unfair master, many wives lived—and many still live—in difficult circumstances.

The place of wives in the first-century Roman Empire was not always a pleasant pasture. In Greek culture, the wife was expected to remain indoors and be obedient to her husband. Later, in Roman culture, the wife had virtually no rights at all. While she was a child, she was under the absolute authority of her father. When she married, she was under the absolute authority of her husband, who was allowed to divorce her according to his caprice. The Jewish wives were not much better off. On the one hand, the Jewish wife was a piece of property owned much like a goat or herd of sheep. On the other hand, some rabbis attempted to exalt her position. For example, one teacher concluded, "It is as if Adam had exchanged a pot of earth for a precious jewel" (Shab. 23). This idea was thrust into a culture that was, at best, ambivalent about the station in life called "wife." The same Jewish mind that concluded that the wife was a precious jewel also said, "God has cursed woman, yet all the world runs after her; He has cursed the ground, yet all the world lives of it."[1] In other words, men can't live with them and they can't live without them.

Peter wrote these words of instruction to wives who lived in that unpleasant cultural setting. It was not an enviable situation. Most wives lived in difficult circumstances. Some wives today live in difficult circumstances. They live with men who are unconcerned at best or implacable tyrants at worst. How should the Christian wife respond to a difficult husband? God instructed such a wife, through Peter, to respond quietly, submissively, and respectfully. Does that sound impossible? It is impossible in human strength alone, but the woman who hopes in God is able to do right with the goal of winning her husband.

WIVES WHO LIVE WITH DIFFICULT HUSBANDS SHOULD SEEK TO WIN THEM THROUGH QUIET RESPECT (1 Peter 3:1-4)

The sage advice of the first two verses is "Be more concerned with what you are than what you say." More precisely the text requires the Christian wife to submit to her husband even if he does not believe (v. 1*a*). Most modern believers are familiar with this kind of scenario. A believing wife living with an unbelieving husband is so common that we don't even react when we hear about such a relationship. Maybe a mixed couple, in this sense, is more common in modern America because in this culture many men have relegated religion to the women and children. It is obvious in many churches that women are more likely to respond to or be involved in the functions and services.

However, in the first-century Roman culture it was more of an unusual thing to find a believing wife living with an unbelieving husband. The rarity might be explained by the fact that most people in the culture lived as Plutarch described when he wrote:

> A wife should not acquire her own friends, but should make her husband's friends her own. The gods are the first and most significant friends. For this reason, it is proper for a wife to recognize only those gods whom her husband worships and to shut the door to superstitious cults and strange relationships. (Greek historian, AD 46–112)

Typically, a wife would simply adopt the gods or religion of her husband.

But what if a wife was truly born again? She could not worship a false god. Therefore, a conflict could erupt immediately upon the wife's conversion. That would create a fearful situation because Christianity was an outlawed religion by the time Peter wrote this letter. Of course it seems likely that the phrase "even if" indicates that most husbands who were married to Christian women were also Christians themselves.

> The Christian wife submits to her unbelieving husband because she seeks to win him without a word.

At any rate, the issue here is a born-again wife living with a husband who is characterized by "not obeying the Word." This is more than a simple statement that the guy didn't go to church. Rather, the phrase boldly points out that the husband avoided salvation. The Word always has been and always will be the source of salvation. Earlier in this letter, Peter reminded Christians that they were supposed to purify their souls, "Being born again, not of corruptible seed, but of incorruptible, by the word of God, which liveth and abideth for ever" (1 Peter 1:23). Did not Paul establish the nonnegotiable standard when he wrote, "So then faith cometh by hearing, and hearing by the word of God" (Romans 10:17)? Without hearing the Word, no one is a believer. Obviously then the husband who is not born again has never obeyed the first and most important matter of the Word.

Obedience to the Word is expected because of salvation. A very important principle that is often repeated throughout the Scripture is that where there is no obedience to the Word, there is obviously no salvation. In Peter's day, a husband who was not obedient to the Word would almost certainly harass his wife if she was born again. In this day, unsaved husbands are often glad to have a Christian wife because they think she will at least be faithful and dependable.

In a secondary sense, the phrase "some do not obey the word" can apply to husbands who claim to be Christians. Sometimes even husbands who profess to be Christians do not obey the Word. They might truly be born again but have not grown in Christ or have let sin into their lives. Men like that do not obey the Word. Such a husband will often be hard to please or might resent his wife's dedication to Christ.

It is also true that many so-called Christian American husbands are not even born again. They rest the hope of their salvation on a family tradition or on an emotional decision or experience. But the Holy Spirit has never changed their hearts. Because that is true, they do not live out God's principles. Because they do not live out God's principles, there will be conflict when the wife does. The question addressed by the text is "How does the Christian wife handle this conflict?"

The Christian wife must seek to win her unbelieving husband by her example (vv. 1*b*–2). This begins by the wife being submissive to her own husband. This submission is a voluntary selflessness. As William Barclay said, "It is a submission that is based on the death of pride and the desire to serve. It is the submission, not of fear but of perfect love."[2]

Peter never intended to establish a principle here that all women must be submissive to all men. That idea contradicts the clear instruction of Ephesians 5:22 and Titus 2:5, which require wives to submit to their "own husband." Furthermore, the principle does not require a Christian wife to submit to her husband if he requires her to sin. She must submit only as it is fitting with God (Colossians 3:18). Unsaved husbands might desire for their wives to share in their sin. No Christian wife should do that.

The Christian wife submits to her unbelieving husband because she seeks to win him without a word. The goal is to win the husband to Christ, or to obedience to His Word. The method she adopts to achieve this goal is by quiet, respectful, pure conduct. Her life is characterized by respect. She respects God first, her husband second. Thus, she primarily does what she does out of love and respect for God. She does not quietly submit in order to stroke her husband's ego or to manipulate him into doing her desires. She believes God's Word and out of respect for Him obeys it.

This woman's quiet respect is obvious. Yea, the husband cannot deny it. Therefore, the godly wife's testimony is invaluable for leading the unbelieving husband to the gospel. That kind of man needs to hear the Word of God, but it may well be the observation of His wife's behavior that leads him to hear the Bible. The old saying applies here: "What you do speaks so loudly that I can't hear what you say." A submissive spirit can be the most effective means for a wife to lead her husband to Christ.

Actually, living with a respectful and pure conduct is God's plan for all Christians in all relationships. Jesus taught His followers to "let your light so shine before men, that they may see your good works, and glorify your Father which is in heaven" (Matthew 5:16). A few verses earlier in this letter, Peter told Christians to "[have] your conversation honest among the Gentiles: that, whereas they speak against you as evildoers, they may by your good works, which they shall behold, glorify God in the day of visitation" (1 Peter 2:12). This kind of life is necessary because "every man that hath this hope in him purifieth himself, even as he is pure" (1 John 3:3).

In order to win her unbelieving husband to the Word, the Christian wife must also be more concerned with internal adornment than outward adornment (vv. 3–4). Verse 3 requires her to avoid an overemphasis of external appearance. In the Roman culture, which set the stage for this letter, gaudy ostentation was not unusual—especially among the wealthy class. One writer illustrated this fact when he wrote, "Why should men grudge women their ornaments and their dress? Women cannot hold public offices, or priesthoods, or gain triumphs; they hold no public occupations. What, then, can they do but devote their time to adornment and to dress?" (Lucius Valerius). It is documented that Julius Caesar, who lived a generation before Christ, bought a pearl for Servilia that cost the equivalent of about $120,000. Seneca, a contemporary of Nero, spoke of women whose pearl earrings amounted to two or three fortunes in their ears. Lollina Paulina, wife of Caligula (reigned from 12–41), owned a dress that was so covered with emeralds and pearls that it would have cost about $900,000 in today's money. Hollywood has nothing on first-century Rome. Christian women were not ignorant of this finery.

God warns that overemphasis on the external is an indication of a wrong attitude within. The problem actually preceded Peter's day by six centuries. God warned rebellious Israelites,

> In that day the LORD will take away the finery of the anklets, the headbands, and the crescents; the pendants, the bracelets, and the scarves; the headdresses, the armlets, the sashes, the perfume boxes, and the amulets; the signet rings and nose rings; the festal robes, the mantles, the cloaks, and the handbags; the mirrors, the linen garments, the turbans, and the veils. Instead of perfume there will be rottenness; and instead of a belt, a rope; and instead of well-set hair, baldness; and instead of a rich robe, a skirt of sackcloth; and branding instead of beauty. (Isaiah 3:18–24 ESV)

To proscribe avoiding ostentation in appearance in no way means to imply that there is virtue in being ugly, unkempt, frumpy, or just plain sloppy. A good wife must take care of the externals so that she does not give her husband an excuse to be unfaithful or so that she does not give the world reason to criticize her God. But she must not get out of balance to the point of focusing on external appearance.

Instead of focusing on externals, the Christian wife must focus on adorning the hidden person (v. 4). She might impress other people with the externals for a while, but God knows the truth. When God sent Samuel to pick a new king, He warned him, "Look not on his countenance, or on the height of his stature; because I have refused him: for the Lord seeth not as man seeth; for man looketh on the outward appearance, but the Lord looketh on the heart" (1 Samuel 16:7).

Eventually even unbelievers recognize this genuine inner beauty, even if they cannot explain its source. Thus, Peter explained that when the wife prepares her heart, she is genuine as opposed to superficial. He said that when she prepares her heart, it is permanent as opposed to transient. The word translated "incorruptible" is the same Greek word Peter used when he explained that Christians are born again "to an inheritance incorruptible, and undefiled, and that fadeth not away, reserved in heaven for you" (1 Peter 1:4). God concluded that the result of a heart so adorned is precious because it demonstrates the value of the regenerated heart.

THERE ARE EXAMPLES OF WIVES WHO HAVE DONE THIS (vv. 5-6)

Holy wives hope in God. Holy wives who hope in God adorn themselves according to His principles (v. 5). That is why an unbelieving husband ought to be able to observe a gentle and quiet spirit in His holy wife. God sets aside these people for His own purposes. A holy wife is a saved wife. A holy wife understands her relationship with God and desires to glorify Him in everything. An unholy wife, who exhibits the traits of an unsaved wife, takes her cues from society and, patterning her life accordingly, lives contrary to the gentle and quiet spirit.

Conversely, the unbelieving husband should observe a gentle and quiet spirit in a wife who hopes in God. Wives like that are also like Sarah, Rebecca, Rachel, and Leah, who trusted God. They were not always perfect, but their hope was in the Lord. They did not submit to their husbands because they thought their husbands were superior. They submitted because they knew that it was God's plan for them to do so. Ultimately, they saw God as their authority. They practiced Isaiah's principle: "For thy Maker is thine husband; the Lord of hosts is his name; and thy Redeemer the Holy One of Israel; the God of the whole earth shall he be called" (Isaiah 54:5).

Holy wives purposely adorn themselves a particular way. They prepare their hearts to a particular end. They adorn themselves by submitting to their husbands, which is to accept God-ordained authority. By trusting in God so completely, they eliminate much cause for fear and struggle from their lives. Verse 6 teaches that wives like Sarah illustrate how to do good without fear (v. 6). Sarah obeyed Abraham. The story of her life includes times when she doubted and argued, but God used her to illustrate what a respectful woman is. She referred to her husband as "lord" (Genesis 18:12) and apparently lived with that attitude. She obeyed him, which is the evidence of a submissive spirit.

As a result, wives like Sarah have no cause to fear. They have no fear because their hope is firmly fixed in God. A wife like Sarah understands her relationship with God. She knows that He is her Father and she is His child. That eliminates the kind of fear that can come from being married to an unsaved husband. Ultimately, all fear is removed when a wife is able to see her relationship to God as a real relationship with the perfect husband.

The wife who lives with a contrary husband might often think that he will never change. Often he doesn't. But God gives the grace necessary for that wife to be an example to the sinner. She can trust God for that grace as Augustine's mother did. Augustine, the ancient bishop of Hippo, wrote about his mother's example to his unsaved father in *The Confessions of Augustine*:

> When she had arrived at a marriageable age, she was given to a husband whom she served as lord. And she busied herself to gain him to Thee, preaching Thee unto him by her behavior; by which Thou madest her fair, and reverently amiable, and admirable to her husband. . . . As he was as earnest in friendship, so was he violent in anger; but she had learned that an angry husband should not be resisted neither in deed nor even in word. But so soon as he was grown calm and tranquil, and she saw a fitting moment, she would give him a reason for her conduct, should he have been excited without cause. . . . Whenever she could she showed herself such a peacemaker between any differing and discordant

spirits. . . . Finally, her own husband, now towards the end of his earthly existence, did she gain over unto Thee; and she had not to complain of that to him, as one of the faithful, which, before he became so, she had endured.[3]

When it seems as though you have to endure—endure by trusting God. Endure while living out Christ and winning the contrary soul without a word. Christian wives through the ages have learned that God's plan works, that His Word is true, and that He is true to His Word. Therefore, attempting to win the stubborn or wayward husband to a right relationship with God is more likely through gracious and respectful behavior than by trying to fight fire with fire.

PUT IT TO WORK

1. In what ways does your husband fail to obey God's Word?

2. How have you attempted to bring your husband into conformity to God's Word?

3. If your husband emulated your life precisely, would he be in fellowship with God?

4. What changes could you make in your spirit and conduct that would cause you to be more submissive to your husband?

5. Do you love your husband enough to help him or do you tolerate him?

PRINCIPLE 22
Husbands must live with their wives in an understanding way.

Likewise, husbands, live with your wives in an understanding way, showing honor to the woman as the weaker vessel, since they are heirs with you of the grace of life, so that your prayers may not be hindered. (1 Peter 3:7 ESV)

I read somewhere that there are only two times when a man does not understand a woman: before he marries her and after he marries her. Maybe you husbands have felt that way on occasion. Whose fault is it? The problem is not anyone's fault, except maybe Adam's, whose sin affects everyone. Before sin entered the world, all relationships were perfect. God understood the humans He had created, and they understood Him. The man fully understood the woman, and the woman fully understood the man. It is hard to imagine what life was like in presin Eden.

However, everything changed when sin infected the world. God still understands His creatures perfectly, but His creatures struggle to know Him and to know about each other. There are times when it seems as though everyone in the world has skewed thinking—everyone except me of course! That is why husbands and wives must work at their relationships. They should not expect to fall in love, say "I do," and live happily ever after. That is Mother Goose and Fairyland Forest stuff. Those things happen only on television and in the so-called Christian romance novels that seem to have found and exploited a needy spot among Christian womendom.

God's instruction for husbands to think rightly about their wives falls within the context of tribulations and humiliation. Peter addressed the letter to Christians who were scattered across the Roman Empire because of persecution. He reminded them that they faced tribulations because they were holy people living in an unholy world (1:3–2:12). He reminded them that, in spite of the fact that authorities would cause trouble for them, they needed to respond with proper respect (2:12). He wrote that Christians must show respect for governing authorities (2:13); Christian servants must show respect for their masters, even when they are unjust (2:18); and Christian wives must show respect for their husbands, even when their husbands are unsaved (3:1–6).

In the same vein of thinking, a Christian husband must show deep respect for his wife—even if he happens to be married to a woman who is not perfect. Probably the central theme of this entire letter is contained in one verse. Peter wrote to Christians, "Finally, all of you, have unity of mind, sympathy, brotherly love, a tender heart, and a humble mind" (1 Peter 3:8 ESV). That statement is the key for making relationships work in a world that stumbles under the influence of sin. No one is perfect. Each person has a sin nature, and each person yields to that nature at various times. Yielding to the sin nature is what causes conflicts between husbands and wives. Yielding to the sin nature is the opposite of working toward a "unity of mind, sympathy, brotherly love, a tender heart, and a humble mind."

The husband who declares that he is the head of the wife and that she must do whatever he demands is a man who is yielding to his sin nature and shows little concern for God's standard of unity, love, sympathy, and a humble mind. Conversely, the husband who seeks to live with his wife in an understanding way will assign value to her and will enjoy God's reward. That way of living is contrary to natural tendencies and is, not surprisingly, contrary to the world's advice. However, God's standard is always right regardless of the world's opinion. God's standard for husbands is for them to be understanding and respectful toward their wives. God promised the reward of hearing that husband's prayers.

BE UNDERSTANDING

When Peter encouraged Christian husbands to live with their wives in an understanding way, he used the very common Greek word that is almost always translated "to know." What must a husband know if he would live with his wife according to God's will?

First, the husband must know God. This almost goes without saying. However, life proves that there are many husbands who claim to be Christians who, at the same time, live as though they hardly know God. To know God, the husband must learn what God says about His relationship with humanity in general and with the husband in particular. How can a husband get to know God?

The Bible reveals the person of God. By God's design, His Word tells the reader that He alone is the creator of all things and all people. Therefore, God is the supreme authority to whom everyone must give an account. In the Bible, God reveals that every person inherits Adam's sin nature, and, therefore, everyone is an offense to God. It tells quite clearly that the penalty for the sinner's offense against God is His judgment in this life and eternal judgment in hell forever. The Bible reveals the painful truth that God is undebatably justified to condemn all sinners. The husband needs to know this God, Who reveals Himself in this book. But the good news is that the Bible reveals so clearly that God is also love and that out of His love, mercy, and grace He has provided the price to pay the penalty for the husband's sins.

God has chosen to describe His loving, but just character in the Bible. He has also chosen to reveal the parameters of fellowship with Him. No husband has the prerogative to walk up to God and slap Him on the back as if He were a good buddy. The first step in establishing any fellowship at all with God is to receive God's provision of salvation through Christ's sacrifice by faith. Then, because the resulting salvation demonstrates God's amazing love, the redeemed husband loves Him in return. He loves God above everyone else and everything else. Because the husband loves God, he will seek to know more about Him by reading His Word. Also, because he loves God, the born-again husband desires to talk to Him through prayer. Because He loves God, the redeemed husband will become more and more like Him as he lives in fellowship with Him.

The husband who does not know God in this way fails this requirement from the outset and, at best, can only stumble along in his relationship with his wife, copying this requirement as much as his human ability alone will allow him to copy it. No husband can live with his wife according to understanding until he first knows God.

Knowledge about God is not the only knowledge a person gains from reading the Bible. The Christian husband needs to learn God's plan regarding women from the pages of the eternal book. Authors by the hundreds continue to write books about the secret, subtle intricacies of women. But no one can reveal the truth about woman's nature like her Creator does in His Bible. There the reader discovers that the wife is spiritually equal to her husband. That is what Paul meant when he wrote, "There is neither Jew nor Greek, there is neither bond nor free, there is neither male nor female: for ye are all one in Christ Jesus" (Galatians 3:28). Because

> The husband who lives in an understanding way with his wife must learn about her from God.

she is on a level playing field with her husband, the wife is also capable of committing sin just like he is. The husband who lives in an understanding way with his wife must learn about her from God.

He also must search God's Word in order to discover God's plan for the wife. There he discovers that God created the first wife to be a helper. Moses recorded the opening days of man's history by saying, "Then the Lord God said, It is not good that the man should be alone; I will make him a helper fit for him" (Genesis 2:18 ESV). That has been God's plan for wives ever since. But she is not only to be a helper according to God's plan. He also intends for the wife to show respect for, to submit to, and to love her husband. Ultimately, of course, God created the wife for His glory. Therefore, He gave spiritual gifts to redeemed wives so they can serve Him first by serving others of His people. A husband must read his Bible if he would ever hope to dwell with his wife in understanding. That is the first step.

Living with a wife in an understanding way also demands that the husband know his wife. He is to know his wife in a general way, realizing that she is the weaker vessel, according to this text. The word translated "vessel" in many English versions is the Greek word that speaks of a useful utensil like a jar or a dish. Usefulness is God's plan for each person of His creation. However, as it works out in this world infected by sin, some jars are used for sin while others are submitted to God for His use. In fact, God creates different kinds of vessels for different purposes. Paul explained this idea while writing about God's prerogatives as the Creator. Paul argued, "Hath not the potter power over the clay, of the same lump to make one vessel unto honour, and another unto dishonour" (Romans 9:21)? That is also God's right.

Notice that the word *vessel* is used in a comparative sense at this point. God did not say that the wife is the "weak" vessel, but the "weaker" one. It is like comparing pots and pans in the wife's kitchen. Some are bigger and some are smaller. That is all part of God's plan. Paul reminded Timothy that "in a great house there are not only vessels of gold and of silver, but also of wood and of earth; and some to honour, and some to dishonour" (2 Timothy 2:20). In the godly family, there is the husband pot and the wife pot. The wife is the weaker pot.

That is not to say that the husband is not weak. Everyone is weak in the flesh and unable to live sinless lives. However, that God called the wife "weaker" than the husband does not imply that she is more sinful than he is. Much of the time the opposite is true. Nor does it indicate that the wife is less intelligent, less spiritual, or less moral than her husband. What does it mean? This statement refers to the fact that the wife is typically weaker than her husband in the physical arena. Sometimes she is also weaker than her husband emotionally. As such she is unable to withstand the amount of pressure her husband can endure. Some wives think that their husbands don't respond like they do because they are just obtuse, or dense, or without feelings. Occasionally that might be the case. Nevertheless, the Christian husband must know that his wife is weaker than he is and respond to her accordingly.

Specifically, this requirement can mean that the husband must know his wife's idiosyncrasies. This idea is quite forceful in light of the fact that the understanding husband is "housing together with her." Housing together is actually a very good way for a husband to learn that his wife is different than he is. Youngsters in love and about to be married really do not know what their future spouse is like. But a few months of housing together begins to uncover the deep mysteries. Does it make them want to bail out and start over? Apparently, that is quite a common response. However, the understanding husband dwells in harmony with his wife in spite of the fact that she is different. Actually it is a good thing that the husband and wife are different because if they were exactly alike, one of them is not necessary. To live in understanding is to accept, yea, to embrace differences that are insignificant.

BE RESPECTFUL

The Christian husband must not only live in an understanding way with his wife, but he must also assign value to his wife. Respect should be a chief characteristic of the husband's attitude toward his wife. Granted, love is more chief than respect, but respect is important. In fact, mutual respect is supposed to be a characteristic of all Christians. "Be kindly affectioned one to another with brotherly love; in honour preferring one another" (Romans 12:10), Paul told the Roman Christians. In the next breath after this chapter's text, Peter told Christians, "Finally, be ye all of one mind, having compassion one of another, love as brethren, be pitiful, be courteous" (1 Peter 3:8).

God's plan for the family is unity, but unity does not require that we all be exactly alike. That is uniformity. Unity requires that the husband and wife respect differences and assign value to others as we would like to have them assign value to us. Love is a good thing to have in a marriage, but it is not critical. Mutual respect is critical for a successful marriage. A marriage can survive without love. Many marriages have survived without love. Even more obvious is the fact that a marriage does not have to have romance in order to continue. But in order for a marriage to survive, the husband and wife must respect each other.

The husband who shows honor to his wife, who shows respect to her, will honestly assess her value. How many husbands have ever sat down with pen in hand and written down the value of their wives? One fellow in a letter to *The Economist* website wondered about this. He wrote:

Dear Economist,

I live in a strange European Union country where one of our members of parliament declared his wife, who is a housewife, an economic asset in the wealth statement required by parliament. Was he right to do so? Was he fair towards his wife, who is also a human being?

Miroslaw Wasilewski
Warsaw, Poland

Dear Mr. Wasilewski,

You raise two questions: the first is whether a housewife can be an economic asset. The answer, surely, is yes. An economic asset is defined by its ability to produce a valuable flow of services. These could be financial (a portfolio of shares) or physical (a car) or both (a house). Presumably your man in Warsaw derives both financial and non-financial benefits from his wife. Even if she does not earn monetary income, her unpaid labour reduces his financial outgoings—a financial benefit. If she is nice to have around the house then that is a non-financial benefit too.

But is this definition fair to the wife? There is no contradiction between being valuable and being human. So the question is whether this valuable human being should be regarded as property. I don't see a problem in that. Property is something to be cherished.[1]

That is an example of literally attaching value to a wife. But more important than financial value is the fact that a man's wife is God's gift of grace to serve alongside him as his helper. A husband's wife is the recipient of his greatest sacrifices if he is following all God's plan for the husband and wife relationship. God requires, "Husbands, love your wives, even as Christ also loved the church, and gave himself for it" (Ephesians 5:25). Why would a man make real sacrifices for someone who is not valuable to him?

One of the best ways for a husband to honor his wife is to acknowledge that she is a co-inheritor of God's grace. She too receives God's favor in this life, just as the husband does. God grants her common grace (air, rain, light, etc.) the same way He gives it to everyone else on earth. However, God also gives a Christian wife special sanctifying grace as she matures to be like Him. God even gives some wives extra grace to live with their ornery husbands. How valuable is God's grace? The Christian wife is a recipient of the invaluable grace throughout life. How valuable does that make her? How much should a husband respect such a woman?

Even more important is that the Christian wife also receives God's favor regarding eternal life. Nothing is more valuable than eternal life. Therefore, the Christian husband who has a Christian wife does well to respect the woman who shares the very thing he counts most valuable in all the earth and in eternity.

BE HEARD

Peter ended this challenge by offering a great reason for the Christian husband to do what God's plan expects. If a husband decides that it is not important for him to follow God's plan and live with his wife in an understanding way, he is cutting himself off from God. That's right! Wrong attitudes hinder effective prayer. God listens to His creature's prayers because He is gracious. He is not obligated to hear our prayers. Rather, out of His mercy and kindness, God invites His children to bring their petitions to Him. Jesus taught the disciples this wonderful truth when He asked them, "If ye then, being evil, know how to give good gifts unto your children, how much more shall your Father which is in heaven give good things to them that ask him" (Matthew 7:11)? He invites His children who sometimes must live in a troubling world to cast their burdens on Him in prayer. But prayer is a privilege, not a right.

God warns through Peter's letter that sin interrupts prayer. Sin separates the child of God from God so that He is not obligated to listen. Solomon learned from his own sinful experience, "The Lord is far from the wicked: but he heareth the prayer of the righteous" (Proverbs 15:29). He also learned that lesson from his father, David, who acknowledged, "If I had cherished iniquity in my heart, the Lord would not have listened" (Psalm 66:18 ESV). Disrespect for a wife and refusal to live with her according to understanding is sin and causes ineffective prayer.

The great danger then is that a husband who is powerless in prayer is a detriment to his family. He cannot lead successfully if he is out of fellowship with God. His duty is to direct the family to a right relationship with God. He is responsible to show the family God's will. If he cannot even pray to God, how will he show God's will? That kind of husband cannot intercede for the people for whom he is supposed to provide. Intercession is critical for the physical and spiritual well-being of wife and children. If the father does not pray for them, who will? If the husband will not live in an understanding way with his wife, he cannot pray effectively.

God's plan for the successful family requires husbands to understand their wives, show respect for them, and experience an effective prayer life. Human nature mitigates against all those things. A wise husband will seek fellowship with God first so that he can direct his wife and family in that same walk with God.

PUT IT TO WORK

1. What evidence is there in your life to prove fellowship with God?

2. How do you know that God hears your prayers?

3. Name three truths you have learned about your wife since you were married that help you understand her better.

4. How much time have you spent in the last six months talking to your wife in order to learn more about her?

5. Does your wife think that you try to understand her? If not, why?

After these things God tested Abraham and said to him, "Abraham!" And he said, "Here am I." He said, "Take your son, your only son Isaac, whom you love, and go to the land of Moriah, and offer him there as a burnt offering on one of the mountains of which I shall tell you." So Abraham rose early in the morning. (Genesis 22:3 ESV)

I t is good to have Bible heroes. Most people choose a Bible hero while they are children in Sunday school. Probably everyone who is a Christian has heard a Bible story and thought, "I would like to be like that person." No doubt little girls learn about Esther or Ruth or Deborah and think that such characters make good models to emulate. Boys read about the exploits of Joshua or David and hope to be such brave warriors. Some might even think that it would be nice to be wise like Solomon (or, unfortunately, rich like Solomon) or to be determined like Nehemiah. Probably only a few think that it would be honorable for them to be meek like Moses.

But who ever picked Abraham for a hero? Abraham does not strike us as a hero kind of guy. Rather the typical view of Abraham is that of an old, slumped-over man in a long robe with long white hair, and a long white beard, who is wandering all over ancient Canaan looking for a city not made with hands. The old patriarch doesn't make for a popular object of hero worship. After all, Abraham was not a brave warrior, was he? Actually, he was. According to Genesis 14:1–16, Abraham put together an army of three hundred warriors from among his own servants and defeated an alliance of four kings and their armies. That seems like a pretty brave and heroic deed.

Fathers in the church today do well to desire to be fathers like Abraham.

Okay, Abraham wasn't always an old patriarch. It is true that he was adventurous. He left his home and extended family in Ur of the Chaldeans when he accompanied his father to Haran. Then he left Haran and went wherever God led him. That seems like hero kind of stuff. In fact, Abraham's original step of faith, to follow the instruction of the one true God, Whom Abraham had not known heretofore, and to step outside his comfort zone by faith in God's Word are the very reason Abraham makes a good hero.

Abraham is one of the all-time great examples of a man of faith. His faith was so settled that it drove him to obey God. And yet, at the same time, the person who has studied the Bible knows that Abraham was not always perfectly obedient to God. There was that time in Gerar that Abraham lied to Abimelech and told him that Sarah was his sister instead of admitting that she was his wife. He had done the same thing in Egypt earlier. Should a liar be a hero? And didn't he go along with his wife's bad idea of having a child through her handmaid Hagar? Things like this often cause men to choose Daniel, who appears to have been virtually faultless, or Joseph, who at worse was arrogant, to be their heroes.

However, most Christians must truly identify with Abraham's atypical slips. He was not characterized as a liar and certainly not as an adulterer. He simply fell into sin because he was afraid, or because his limited human wisdom could not comprehend how God could possibly keep His promise. Who among us has not done the same kinds of things? Yes, Abraham was very much like modern believers. But how much are modern believers like him?

Maybe being a great father was the one area in which Abraham sets the best example to follow. He was a man who did not become a father until the twilight of life. And then, once his son was grown into adulthood, he attempted to kill him and burn his body as a sacrifice to God. Is that a good example of fatherhood? Common sense demands that this act was a terrible example of what fathers should be. Or was it a good example? Did Abraham actually intend to kill Isaac? In this amazing display of faith, Abraham simply trusted God, obeyed God's instruction to the letter of the law, and fully expected God to do what human wisdom could neither do nor comprehend. That is astonishing faith. Abraham demonstrated extreme faith to his son in a way that Isaac would never forget. It is no wonder that Isaac was also a man of faith in God. His father was a good example to follow. Fathers in the church today do well to desire to be fathers like Abraham—fathers with great faith.

GOD GAVE ABRAHAM CLEAR INSTRUCTION (Genesis 22:1-2)

This is the unusual story of how God chose to test Abraham (v. 1). This is the same God and the same Abraham whose story began at the outset of chapter 12 in Genesis. This is the same Abraham whom God had chosen previously to receive His blessing. In the beginning of their relationship, God called this man out of Ur. That blessing is so unusual in light of the fact that God could have chosen to speak to any one of the thousands of people who lived in the land of the Chaldeans. But God chose to bless this particular man. In a greater sense, God could have chosen any one of the millions of people who lived in the world. But God chose Abraham.

God revealed part of His blessing when He led Abraham out of his family's homeland into the land He would give to His posterity. The fact that God promised to give the land to Abraham's posterity presupposes the fact that God would also grant the man the blessing of a large posterity. Furthermore, the story tells how God prospered Abraham greatly. Genesis 13:2 says matter-of-factly that "Abram was very rich in cattle, in silver, and in gold" (Genesis 13:2). That was because God had blessed the man as He had promised to do. Abraham was living proof that God is faithful to His Word. Abraham proved that fathers can trust God.

But now, at this time in his life, God chose Abraham for a special test. There is plenty of evidence in the broader story that God had allowed Abraham to be tested previously. Surely it was a test of faith for Abraham to leave home and family. It was a test for Abraham to trust God to give him and Sarah a son. In fact, the patriarch failed that test the first time around when he succumbed to having relations with Hagar. It was a test for Abe to tell the truth to Pharaoh and Abimelech about his wife. Could he trust God to protect Sarah and him in order to fulfill His promise regarding a son and posterity? It was a test for Uncle Abraham to allow Lot to choose the well-watered plains. In that test, once again, Abraham discovered that God is faithful as He protected His chosen servant from the sin of Sodom. It was a test for Abraham and his band of weekend warriors to attack the allied kings. But again, he discovered that God gave the victory.

Finally, when it seemed impossible, God had provided the promised son, Isaac. Little by little along the way God kept growing Abraham's faith through tests and faithful provision. But now God allowed a test that eclipsed anything Abraham had experienced. This part of the Abraham and God story begins with the words "After these things," referring to all the previous trials and tests and after the blessings and lessons of life that God had given. How many years had God been silent before He allowed this test to come into Abraham's life? It had probably been many years since God had spoken to Abraham. Now God spoke and the message was not the kind of thing Abe wanted to hear.

When God finally spoke, He came with a test for Abraham. This is not the same thing as God presenting a temptation to sin. It is Satan's practice to tempt people to commit sin. He knows that sin brings retribution, and his malicious nature loves to see people suffering under that retribution. Satan tempted Job to sin. God tested Job's faith but God never tempts anyone to sin. James warned in his letter, "Let no man say when he is tempted, I am tempted of God: for God cannot be tempted with evil, neither tempteth he any man" (James 1:13). Rather than tempting His creation, God, Who designed us, proves us through testing, which allows His children to be strengthened in faith.

This was God's test for Abraham to prove who or what was the object of his greatest love. It is easy for folks to slip into loving the gift more than the giver. As a result, it is possible for a father to love his children more than he loves God, Who gave the children to him. A child continually begs his father to buy him a new video game system. Finally, the father concedes because he loves his child so much and he wants the child to be happy. When the child receives the gift, he is very thankful and tells dear old dad over and over that he loves him. The son enjoys the game and is happy. The father is happy. But the son enjoys the game so much that he virtually becomes addicted to it. He loves the father's gift so much that he spends hours with it every day. His father says, "Son, let's go outside and shoot some hoops." But the son replies, "I would rather stay here and play this game you provided." Before long it is obvious from the amount of attention the boy gives to the gift that he has little affection for the father, the giver of the gift. It is easy for people to do that to God. Did Abraham do that regarding Isaac?

In this specially designed test, God required Abraham to sacrifice that which was dearest to him (v. 2). God knew what was nearest and dearest to Abraham, just as He knows the object of His children's deepest love and affection. Therefore, God acknowledged that Abraham loved Isaac. Genesis 23:1 reveals that Isaac was about thirty-seven years old when his mother died a few years after this event. Therefore, he had probably lived with Abraham for about thirty-five years when the test came. As far as the Bible record shows, he was a model son. There is no indication of rebellion or trouble. It appears that Isaac was a wonderful, obedient, submissive child. It is really easy for a dad to love such a child.

God reminded Abraham how much he loved his son. Notice that God called Isaac "your son." In fact, He said that Isaac was "your only son," the one who makes you laugh. It is no wonder that God reminded Abraham that Isaac was "the one you love." This is the first mention of love in the Bible. It is interesting that one should read this far in the Bible before discovering a statement about love. Love is the chief trait of God the Creator, the trait that God Himself defines. Chronologically, it is possible that between two and four thousand years had passed since God created the world. Yet this is the first mention of love. However, we must also bear in mind that the events in Job took place during that two-to-four-thousand-year period before Abraham, and love is mentioned three times in that writing.

It is also significant that this mention of love is in a story that demonstrates God's love. The greatest expression of love is when God the Father showed His love for the world through His unique Son, God the Son. Indeed, God's greatest demonstration of love is when He killed the Son for sinners. That is the whole story of John 3:16: "For God so loved the world, that he gave his only begotten Son, that whosoever believeth in him should not perish, but have everlasting life." That story is complete in that God illustrated His love for the Son and us by raising Him from the dead. Those same principles all come to bear in this test of Abraham's faith. The symbolism is too obvious to ignore.

Nevertheless, God proposed a test that was senseless to Abraham. In the Patriarch's thinking, it was senseless to kill the promised son. How would God be able to fulfill His promise of a nation of people from Abraham's seed if the promised son were dead? It was also senseless, as far as Abraham was concerned, for God to kill the source of worldwide blessing. When God had called Abraham out of Ur, He promised, "And I will make of thee a great nation, and I will bless thee, and make thy name great; and thou shalt be a blessing: and I will bless them that bless thee, and curse him that curseth thee: and in thee shall all families of the earth be blessed" (Genesis 12:2–3). How could God bless the earth through Abraham's seed if the seed were killed?

Furthermore, it must have seemed senseless to Abraham for God to expect him to act like the pagans who worshiped their gods through child sacrifice. Surely it was senseless to do what God condemned (Leviticus 18:21; 20:2; Deuteronomy 12:31; 18:10). It was senseless to offer his son as an offering, the smoke of which ascends to God and pleases Him. In the most practical terms, it was senseless to travel three days (that is forty-five miles) from Beersheba to Mount Moriah, the spot where the future city of Jerusalem would be.

What does the child of God do when it appears that God requires something that is senseless? Some Christian fathers think that it is senseless for them to take their children to meet with God's people on Sunday morning, Sunday evening, and Wednesday evening when they are so tired and busy? Why would God expect such a thing? Some fathers think it is senseless for them to teach their children, by example, to give an offering when the family doesn't seem to have enough money to make ends meet. Others think it is senseless for them to demonstrate devotion to God by reading their Bible and praying when it seems such a sissy thing to do. Or is it senseless for a father to show his children how to love their mother when she actually irritates him? Is it senseless for Dad to sacrifice his time in order to spend it with his children when he would rather please himself with his hobbies? Do fathers find it impossible to trust God's teaching on such matters? Fathers must learn to respond as Abraham did even if it is on a much smaller scale.

ABRAHAM OBEYED GOD'S CLEAR INSTRUCTION (vv. 3-10)

Comprehensible or not, senseless or not, Abraham went to the place God had identified (vv. 3–6). According to verse 3, he did all the work necessary to prepare for an actual offering (or at least he had his servants do it). That would have been quite foolish if Abraham never intended to offer a sacrifice. Having gathered everything necessary for the sacrifice, Abraham then went to the appointed place with purpose (vv. 4–6). He told his servants that he planned to go with Isaac to worship (v. 5). The Hebrew word translated "worship" speaks of bowing before the Superior. It speaks of humility. In his heart, Abraham was already humbled before God. He would manifest that humility in obedience and reverence. He took all the items necessary for the sacrifice (v. 6).

> A father's faith in God causes him to pray, read his Bible, and train his children for God's glory.

It is obvious that, as much as he possibly could, Abraham attempted to do what God had required (vv. 7–10). Imagine that loving father trudging up the hillside of Mount Moriah, not knowing for sure what to expect. In his heart he trusted God to provide (vv. 7–8). On the one hand, he knew what God had instructed and he acted accordingly.

On the other hand, he knew that in some unusual way God would have to do a miracle of provision. That is what Abraham told Isaac when Isaac queried about the sacrificial lamb. No doubt the term *lamb* is full of symbolism, in light of the rest of the revelation in God's Word. But Abraham must have thought of it literally.

With complete confidence in God, but almost certainly with some anxiety in his heart, Abraham carried out God's plan precisely (vv. 9–10). He went up the mountain and built the altar. He was experienced in building altars as a place where he would worship God for God's glory (v. 9). Then Abraham did an amazing thing. Having laid the wood in order on the altar, he put his thirty-five-year-old son on top of the wood (v. 9). Even more amazing, the man who trusted God implicitly raised his knife in order to thrust it into his son (v. 10). This would have made a great movie! At what point was he going to stop? How much faith in God did Abraham have? How illustrative Abraham's faith is.

A father's faith in God causes him to pray, read his Bible, and train his children for God's glory. His faith in God allows the father to do what might seem senseless to human wisdom. In the end, it is the father's faith in God that allows him to send the children he has trained to go to serve God. The father who is compelled to micromanage his sons and daughters proves that he lacks faith in his training process. Did the father train them to serve God? Then let them do it! Micromanagement proves lack of faith in God's Word. Did Dad teach the Bible to the children? Let them learn to obey it on their own. Fathers with faith in God must train the children

God has given and then gradually let go more and more until they are on their own with God. They must learn to trust God, not Dad. They must develop a personal fellowship with God, not rely on Dad's fellowship. Too many fathers do not trust God enough to lay their children on the altar. Apparently, they think that they know better than God does.

GOD HONORED ABRAHAM'S FAITH (vv. 11-14)

God commended Abraham's faith (vv. 11–12). The good news is that God stopped Abraham's progress of sacrificing Isaac (v. 11).

The Angel of the Lord called out and stopped him in midswing. The Angel of the Lord is God the Son. How thankful was Abraham to hear from the Savior of sinful humanity?

God the Son told Abraham that He knew the level of Abraham's faith (v. 12). That is not to say that this test was a revelation to God. God is omniscient and eternal. He knows all things for all eternity. He always knew Abraham's faith. But now Abraham also understood what God had known. Abraham had just proved that he loved and trusted the Giver more than he loved the gift.

Then God did an amazing thing. He provided a substitute sacrifice (vv. 13–14). God revealed the ram in the thicket and Abraham sacrificed it in the place of Isaac (v. 13). Isn't that just what Abraham had told Isaac God would do? Abraham concluded what he had confidently asserted earlier (v. 14). When Isaac had asked about the sacrifice, father Abraham had assured him that God would provide (v. 7). So he named that place "Jehovah Jireh," which means "the Lord will provide." God had provided indeed. It was a beautiful illustration of God's provision of His own unique Son, Jesus Christ, as the sacrifice to cover sins. If Abraham is our example, we must trust God's provision, especially in the matter of salvation. If Abraham is our example, we must live as though we trust God by placing everything at His disposal. If Abraham is our hero, our children ought to be assured that our faith in God trumps everything else in life.

PUT IT TO WORK

1. According to your children's observations, how much do you trust God?

2. Do you trust God enough to do the hard things like meeting with His people, supporting His work, finding Him daily in quiet time?

3. What do you withhold from God because you don't trust Him?

4. How would you respond if your daughter told you God wants her to be a missionary?

5. Has God ever allowed you to endure testing so that you would trust Him more?

PRINCIPLE 24
Teach God's principles to your children.

"**Now this is** the commandment, the statutes and the rules that the LORD your God commanded me to teach you, that you may do them in the land to which you are going over, to possess it, that you may fear the LORD your God, you and your son and your son's son, by keeping all his statutes and his commandments, which I command you, all the days of your life, and that your days may be long. Hear therefore, O Israel, and be careful to do them, that it may go well with you, and that you may multiply greatly, as the LORD, the God of your fathers, has promised you, in a land flowing with milk and honey. Hear, O Israel: The LORD our God, the LORD is one. You shall love the LORD your God with all your heart and with all your soul and with all your might. And these words that I command you today shall be on your heart. You shall teach them diligently to your children, and shall talk of them when you sit in your house, and when you walk by the way, and when you lie down, and when you rise. You shall bind them as a sign on your hand, and they shall be as frontlets between your eyes. You shall write them on the doorposts of your house and on your gates." (Deuteronomy 6:1–9 ESV)

O n a recent flight into Detroit, I sat beside a young girl and her little three-year-old brother. Their mother sat a few rows ahead of us. I noticed the family shortly after they entered the plane but did not notice anything particularly unique about them. They were just another family of the world traveling from point "A" to point "B." Eventually I struck up a conversation with this girl and discovered that she lived in Florida and they were going to visit her father in a large northern city. He was a very successful businessman and throughout the summer the mom and children often flew to where he was in order to spend some quality time together.

The main reason I struck up a conversation with this girl was the book she was reading. It was entitled *In Jesus' Footsteps*. I asked the girl why she was reading that particular book, and she told me that it was required reading for her school. As you can imagine, that made me more curious. I continued to ask questions and the girl explained that she was about to enter the seventh grade in a Christian school. This was going to be her first year in the school, but she was glad to go there because this was the school many of her friends attended. Why did her parents decide to send her to a Christian school? They were concerned about the gangs and crime in the public school. Was the girl a Christian herself? No, but apparently that didn't matter. Where did she attend church? She and her family did not attend church regularly.

This short conversation reminded me of a trend I have observed for several years now. Parents who have little or no concern for the things of God are willing to spend good money hoping that an underpaid, and often unappreciated, teacher in a Christian school will teach their children how to succeed in life. It has become an American thing to push the children off on sincere teachers who really are not able to, nor should they try to, fix all the children's problems.

Even sadder is when parents, who insist that they really are born-again followers of Christ, are not concerned enough to teach their children to fear God. They conclude that teaching the children to respect God is the job of the Sunday school teacher, the pastor, or the Christian schoolteacher. Apparently, parents like this are content to work hard and make enough money to provide the finer things for their children so that they will fit in with their culture. Heaven knows we don't want young people who are not accepted by their world! Parents like this do not realize the conflict they create with their errant philosophy. They work hard to make sure their children fit into the world system and then send these same children to the church or Christian school so that the servants of God can teach the children how not to fit into their world. No wonder the culture has reared a generation of confused youth.

Folks are folks in any generation. Therefore, it is not surprising that God dealt with the same kind of issues with the ancient Israelites as He prepared them to enter the Promised Land. True, they did not have a lot of

Christian schools or Sunday schools in that day, but the principles were the same. God knows that each succeeding generation must learn the principles of respect for God. Without those principles firmly in hand, the whole nation would drift from God. Who was responsible to teach these principles to the succeeding generations? The parents were. God expected them to establish a right relationship with Him first and then to teach the children how to establish and maintain that same kind of relationship with God on their own.

Nothing has changed. The need is the same today. Who is teaching the children how to have a right relationship with God?

DEMONSTRATE LOVE FOR GOD (Deuteronomy 6:1-5)

God's plan for His people, according to Moses, was that they should learn to respect Him by doing His commands (vv. 1–3). Moses understood that this was God's plan when he told the people, "God commanded me to teach you." Moses knew that when a person is diligent to know and do God's commands those commands will teach the person respect for Him (vv. 1–2). This is also a reminder that God taught Moses, face to face, the things He wanted the people to know. Moses, the man who first resisted God by appealing to the fact that he was not an orator, faithfully taught all God's law to the people for forty years.

What exactly did Moses teach? What lends itself to a growing respect for God? The terms *statutes* and *the rules* must include all God's law. How can all the different laws recorded in Exodus through Deuteronomy contribute to a greater respect for God? Many of those laws revealed God's character and teach God's people how to view and respond to Him. In a nutshell the first half of the Ten Commands tells the reader what God is like and how he should relate to Him. Many of those laws also taught the Israelites (and continue to teach believers) how to get along with their neighbors. In a nutshell this was the second half of the Ten Commands.

These words from Moses contend that familiarity with and practice of God's laws should lead a person to a mature respect of God. How would that happen? The laws reveal God's holy character. The laws reveal God's high expectations. The laws reveal promised punishment for disobedience. Therefore, the laws, or commands, help God's people understand that He desires for them to live differently from the rest of the world and that He will punish those who don't. Initially, therefore, one ought to have a healthy fear of God, knowing that He will punish those who ignore His law. In a mature sense, respect for God causes the child of God to seek to live in a way that pleases Him.

Doing God's commands not only leads to greater respect for Him but results in tangible blessings (v. 3). This was especially true for the Israelites, who were about to cross the Jordan to possess the land that flowed with milk and honey. God commanded Moses to teach these things so that the people, their sons, and their grandsons might have long days in a wonderful land (v. 2*b*). God wanted life to go well for His people in the new land (v. 3). God wanted them to enjoy, to the fullest, the land that gushed out milk and honey.

The phrase "flowing with milk and honey" was a well-known phrase in that day. It certainly sounds metaphorical to the twenty-first-century ear, but the ancients used the phrase to describe a unique and rich land. Like other well-known phrases in ancient cultures it lost its meaning in later cultures. To modern people it is like the phrase "putting on the dog." What does a person who is just learning English think when they hear that someone is putting on the dog?

The phrase "a land flowing with milk and honey" was found in an ancient Egyptian text to describe the land of northern Palestine, just as God described it. A similar phrase appears in an ancient Canaanite text.

> The skies will rain down milk
> And the valleys will flow with honey.[1]

In fact, the description of the Promised Land as that kind of country is found many times in the Pentateuch. God used it four times in Exodus (3:8, 17; 13:5; 33:3), once in Leviticus (20:24), four times in Numbers (13:27; 14:8; 16:13, 14), and five times in Deuteronomy (11:9; 26:9, 15; 27:3; 31:20). It was a wonderful promise about a wonderful place.

However, only a strong society could enjoy such blessing. Even while Moses declared this great promise to the people, God was poised to drive out of the Promised Land nations who had become terribly vile. God was ready to replace them with the strong nation of Israel. A strong society is built on knowing and doing what God commands. Israel was like that for a while. However, her history reveals that Israel quickly adopted the ways of their pagan neighbors and forfeited the pleasant land. In a similar fashion, America once was a culture that respected God. The forefathers of this great nation loved and trusted God so much that they abandoned homes, jobs, and families in Europe to come to this land. They built a society on respect for God and reaped astonishing blessings. But their posterity has forsaken God and disrespected Him. As a result, the society is reaping the fruit of judgment, and it is hard to imagine that the once-great America is rapidly becoming a third-world nation because of her disrespect for God.

> Good parents learn that the knowledge and practice of God's commands lead to great respect of God.

Good parents learn that the knowledge and practice of God's commands lead to great respect of God. They also learn to do God's commands from a heart of love (vv. 4–5). This is a critical practice because the true God is one (v. 4). The phrase means that the God of Israel is incomparable. Pagan neighbors held to other gods, but Israel learned that those gods do not compare to the true God. After the people had observed God's drowning of the Egyptian army, they sang, "Who is like unto thee, O Lord, among the gods? Who is like thee, glorious in holiness, fearful in praises, doing wonders" (Exodus 15:11)? In fact other gods are only the creations of man's hands or imaginations. That was Hannah's conclusion when she prayed, "There is none holy as the Lord: for there is none beside thee: neither is there any rock like our God" (1 Samuel 2:2).

The principle still applies. It is part of human nature to create things to replace God. Modern thinkers are not illiterate and backward like the ancients were. Or were the ancients actually illiterate and backward? Some of their artifacts testify of great abilities. Nevertheless, citizens of modern society put pleasure, possessions, or people in the place of God just like the ancients replaced Him with their idols. Modern pagans give time, energy, love, and loyalty to the gods of pleasure and possessions. Parents are wise to wonder if the object of their love and respect can truly deliver them from trouble. Can false gods comfort them in time of loss? Can their preferred god offer grace in time of need? Can their god give eternal life? Maybe this is why Americans quickly forget about love and loyalty to their chosen gods and pray to the true God when tragedy strikes. When the next 9/11 hits, as it probably will in a matter of time, will the true God listen as suffering people cry out to Him? God is one and will share His glory with no other lesser gods.

The God of Israel is singular. That is also the idea contained in the words "The Lord our God, the Lord is one." There is a oneness with God—a oneness in the Godhead. Though He exists and ministers in three persons (Father, Son, Holy Spirit), He is one God.

He is one God in a way that supersedes human comprehension. Human pride seeks to remove God's unique nature by explaining Him in terms human wisdom can grasp. Thus, Islam insists that Jesus of Nazareth cannot be God the Son. There is only one God they claim. Christians claim the same truth.

Because there is unity, or oneness, with God, there must also be a unity of purpose and will with God. God has one will for His glory.

God has one purpose for His glory. Therefore, God's people must love God singularly (v. 5). Moses put it like this: "You shall love the Lord your God with all your heart, and with all your soul and with all your might." *Heart*, *soul*, and *might* are essentially synonyms speaking of the total being. The heart of a person is the seat of the intellect, the will, and the emotions. In other words, God challenges people to think about why they must love God and then love God supremely! The soul is the true person. The might is the whole person. Therefore, love God with the entire, the whole person—no part withheld. Only the individual can make this decision.

Because God is Who and what He is, His people have every possible compelling reason to love Him fully. If this love is missing, God's commands become an undoable burden. Love for God makes His command a natural desire and response for Christians. Jesus told the lawyer who asked about the most important command, "Thou shalt love the Lord thy God with all thy heart, and with all thy soul, and with all thy mind. This is the first and great commandment" (Matthew 22:37–38). That seems clear enough. Nothing changed between God's plan regarding His peoples' love in the Old Testament and God's plan for them in the New Testament. That is why Jesus told the disciples, "If ye love me, keep my commandments" (John 14:15). The same truth drove John to conclude, "By this we know that we love the children of God, when we love God and obey his commandments. For this is the love of God, that we keep his commandments. And his commandments are not burdensome" (1 John 5:2–3 ESV).

God requires the people who are related to Him to establish this awesome respect and love for Him because, as parents, they must teach their children how to do it. A leader cannot lead where he has never been. Parents must not send their children to church, Sunday school, or the Christian school so they can learn how to love God. Parents must show the children how they love God.

PASS IT ON (vv. 6-9)

God commands parents to teach their children what is on their heart (v. 6). Obviously, it is critical at this point that God's commands would be on the parent's heart. But that is not always the case. Worse is that it is not often the case. What is naturally on a person's heart? Self! Ways to enjoy pleasure are often the important thing on the hearts of many people. They continually think about the things they think will bring them pleasure from any number of resources. Essentially, people by nature want the focus of life to be on the individual. This unbridled selfishness is why many parents, even Christian parents, try to live their children's lives for them. They sense that their own life is, or was, unfulfilled and seek to make decisions for their grown children. It causes me to wonder how many lives a person will disrupt before he or she realizes that he or she doesn't know best.

It is far better for parents to have a heart full of God's commands. When God proclaimed through Moses that the parents must have the words He commands them on their hearts, it is not an admonition for the parents to be legalists. Rather, this is a challenge to know God intimately. If a parent knows God's laws in his brain only, he can be pretty sure that he will be a legalist. Conversely, to have God's commands residing in the heart makes a parent godly. His commands influence the way the parent thinks, the way he or she responds, and that parent's love for Him.

But, it is not enough for the parent to have a right view of God and a right relationship with Him. The parent must also teach God's commands diligently. The word *teach* means to make them plain. The root word means to make sharp. The parent must teach God's commands so that the words will penetrate the child's natural selfish resistance. This is a daunting task. It is difficult because God's commands are unpopular. Making matters worse is the fact that sin, as it is continually demonstrated in the world, is wildly popular. It would be very easy to teach children how to sin, if indeed they needed someone to teach such a natural response. Also, it is a daunting task to teach God's commands to them because God's commands cut across human sensibility. How shall the parents ever get their children to understand? It will not happen in a moment or even in a matter of days. Godly parents must be willing to dig in for the long haul.

But the methodology for teaching God's commands is not complicated. Parents should teach the children naturally (vv. 7–9). That was God's instruction for His people. He told them to teach His commands by living them (v. 7). More specifically God told parents to talk about His ways when they sat in their houses. In order to carry out this task, the parent must first take time to sit in his house. When he or she does, each one should talk naturally to the children about God's principles. The children should not be surprised to sit and hear Mom and Dad talk about God.

Second, the parent must teach God's principles when he walks by the way. This idea involves traveling from one place to another. So talk about God while traveling over the river and through the woods to grandmother's house. Talk about God while driving around town.

Third, talk about God while lying down and while rising up. This command means that parents should start the day and end the day talking about God. This is a good argument for family devotions.

Since God commanded it, parents should be able to do it. But a parent might recoil and say, "No, it is not natural." It should be. Verse 6 reminds that people talk about whatever is on their hearts. Maybe that is the problem. Maybe the topic of discussion between the parent and the children really is whatever is on the heart at the time. In that case the general topic of conversation indicates that something needs to change. Mom or Dad needs to think of something more godly.

Finally, God revealed that parents who honor Him must teach the spirit of His commands, not the letter (vv. 8–9). God used a metaphor to explain how His truths are supposed to be an integral part of His people. He told the people to bind His principles on their hands so that whatever they did was influenced by His truth. They were also supposed to bind His principles between their eyes so that they would see all things through His principles. Third, they were to write them on the doorposts of their houses so that God's principles would rule their home.

> God revealed that parents who honor Him must teach the spirit of His commands, not the letter.

The metaphor was easy enough to understand. But, as they often did, God's people went to extremes so that they could be proud of keeping His laws. They made phylacteries, little boxes in which they placed written words of the Torah. They literally placed written words in mezuzahs they attached to doorways. And yet these same people broke God's commands constantly.

God doesn't want parents to teach their child a lot of rules that will not apply ten years from now. Rather, parents must learn about God from His commands. This knowledge must drive them to a deep and abiding respect. That respect brings about deep and genuine love for God. When parents love God, they want to live in a way that is pleasing to Him. Godly parents learn how to live in a pleasing way from His truth. Then, having learned the right way, parents must live accordingly every day. Living rightly shows the children how to do it. Good parents talk about God naturally to their children. They must not preach, must not demand, and must not check off the rules as they keep them. People who wear phylacteries live like that. God wants His people to show their children what the true, loving, forgiving, and merciful God is like by the way they live.

PUT IT TO WORK

1. List three ways that you demonstrate your love for God to your children.

2. What is the most recent lesson about loving God that you have learned from the Bible?

3. How much time did you spend with your children last week?

4. What principles about fellowship with God did you teach them during that time?

5. What did your family talk about while driving on the most recent trip?

PRINCIPLE 25
Be careful what you teach the children by your life.

"**You shall not** make for yourself a carved image, or any likeness of anything that is in heaven above, or that is in the earth beneath, or that is in the water under the earth. You shall not bow down to them or serve them, for I the LORD your God am a jealous God, visiting the iniquity of the fathers on the children to the third and the fourth generation of those who hate me, but showing steadfast love to thousands of those who love me and keep my commandments." (Exodus 20:4–6 ESV)

When our colt, Malachi, was born a few years ago, within a few minutes of his birth, he was nursing from his mother. As I watched this phenomenon of nature unfold, I could not help but wonder how he knew that mom was a good source of food. Who taught him to do that in such a short time? Of course, the answer to that question is instinct. Animals are born with innate instincts, inherent dispositions toward a particular behavior. Instincts are natural responses that an animal will predictably do, unless overridden by intelligence or knowledge. Thus, while it is a colt's instinct to find food from his mother, it is also his instinct as he gets older to eat whatever looks edible. To a horse, that can be just about anything. Simple observation of a mare's relationship with her foal reveals her careful methodology for teaching the youngster that some plants are good for food and other plants are not good for food or can be poisonous. It is a beautiful lesson of the parent horse teaching the child horse important lessons of life.

People are a lot like horses. They too have instincts, natural responses to particular stimuli. People will respond according to those instincts unless they have learned to override them through intelligence and knowledge. One of the strongest, most obvious instincts found in humans is selfishness. It is the manifestation of pride that lurks deep within the soul of every human. It is the root of sin. All people are born with pride, and they will naturally express it. Because of this instinct, folks want to do what they want to do. Most parents have learned that the antidote to natural selfishness is intelligence and knowledge. Some might conclude at this point that current culture desperately lacks such intelligence and knowledge.

God explained throughout Proverbs that He is the source of intelligence and knowledge—that is wisdom. He graciously offers wisdom to His created beings, who by nature are simpletons. His created beings are tainted by sin and now are people impressed with themselves, and, therefore, determined to satisfy themselves at all costs. Some people recognize such intrinsic selfishness and conclude that it is wrong. Others acknowledge the same kind of selfishness and conclude that, because it is so natural, it must be right.

The expressions of selfishness opposed to God's wisdom are as multiplied as the number of sins and vices that can be imagined. Murder, theft, lying, fornication, infidelity, sensuality, and the list goes on and on, are all demonstrations of an unhealthy emphasis on selfish desires. Do the progressive thinkers of the day approve of all such behavior simply because it is natural?

God warned His people Israel on the day He made them a nation that they must guard against the natural propensity toward idolatry. The second command warns that none of God's people should ever be guilty of worshiping a symbol or a substitute for God. It is easy to make this command apply so specifically that one can miss the real point. While it is true that God forbids His people in every age from bowing down to and worshiping idols that belong to false gods and false religions, it is also true that God forbids His people to praise and exalt any of their natural desires in place of Him.

The reader cannot help but notice that this is the first command that is accompanied by a warning. After God warned people not to exalt anything in His place, He added the warning that He visits the iniquities of the fathers on the third and fourth generation of those who hate Him. The teaching is simply this: People who claim to be God's people, but who respect or exalt other things in place of Him, actually prove by their actions that they do not honor Him. The children of these people learn to live just like their parents. The result is a natural outflow. People teach their children to not honor God, and God responds by allowing them to reap the natural consequences that always accompany sin.

The challenge of the text is clear. Parents must be very careful about what they honor and exalt in life because their children will adopt their standards. A wise parent is careful to discern if his or her standards will put the children in the path of God's blessing or in the path of sin's painful consequences. It does not take a very perceptive person to realize that the culture, as a whole, is standing in the middle of a six-lane highway of sins' consequences. Indeed, the future is going to be very exciting because the culture has exalted everything but God. Worse, the culture has outlawed God. Guess what lies in store for God's people who live in this kind of environment? Christian parents must be wise and disciplined to offer a solution to the problem and not contribute to the problem.

THE EXPLANATION OF THE PRINCIPLE

This principle, as it appears in verses 4–5, is the second of the Ten Commands. In it, God forbids His people to worship any image of any sort. An image might be the representation of a false deity. That was no doubt a very common understanding of the application of the law in ancient Israel because idols were so prolific among their neighbors. That might help explain why there are fourteen synonyms in the Old Testament translated "idols" or "images."

Here the word *likeness* refers to a real or imagined pictorial representation, a form, an image, or semblance. Most of Israel's contemporaries worshiped false gods that were represented by these forms, images, or idols. The people of Israel surely must have understood what God told them through Moses. They didn't have any difficulty making the application. God's people knew from their experience in life that these false gods and images were always the product of man's imagination. Were they able to deduce like you and I are that because the false god was the product of their imagination, it made the creator of the god the actual authority? This is why God commanded His people to destroy all such expressions of man's sinful instincts when they entered the Promised Land. Joshua reminded the invading Israelites, "You may not mix with these nations remaining among you or make mention of the names of their gods or swear by them or serve them or bow down to them" (Joshua 23:7 ESV). God prohibited His people from worshiping an idol.

However, this prohibition also includes symbols of the true God. It is not a prohibition against art. After all, God required the construction of ornate furniture and objects for the tabernacle and temple. Was that not art? He intended that these symbols would facilitate worship and point to His holiness. God's plan was that the temple furnishings would help to emphasize the nature of worship. But the presence of the invisible God was to remain unsymbolized. When the objects intended to facilitate worship became a substitute for worship, it was sin which brought God's judgments. This is obvious in the later history of Israel when the ark itself became an image of God. The people went to battle against the Philistines and decided that they needed to have the symbol of God in their camp. The unwise people brought the ark to the battle front, and God judged them by letting the Philistines take the symbol (1 Samuel 4).

That was also Aaron's sin when he made the golden calf to "represent" God (Exodus 32:4). He did not mean that the golden calf was a god that brought the people out of Egypt. He meant that the calf represented the God of the Israelites. That was the kind of thing his pagan neighbors did regularly. God judged Aaron and the people. In a similar fashion, the objects that ought to facilitate modern worship of God can replace God. For example, church buildings, rituals, or traditions must never become the purpose or the focus of worship.

God imbedded some very good reasons for the prohibition in these verses. First, to make an image would be tantamount to "having other gods before the true God" (20:3). God expressly forbade that in the first command. Second, no image can adequately represent God. It is true that God created man in His image (Genesis 1:26), but that does not mean that God is like man. In fact, God cleared up that possible misunderstanding when He declared through Isaiah, "For as the heavens are higher than the earth, so are my ways higher than your ways, and my thoughts than your thoughts" (Isaiah 55:9). Because this is true, any attempt to illustrate God in images is to impute the image or philosophy with human weaknesses on God. That is to attempt to make God in the likeness of man. That would be a gross sin.

Before these people entered the Promised Land in order to possess it, Moses warned them again that God had good reasons for prohibiting them from trying to make an image of Him.

> And the Lord spake unto you out of the midst of the fire:
> ye heard the voice of the words, but saw no similitude; only
> ye heard a voice. And he declared unto you his covenant,
> which he commanded you to perform, even ten command-
> ments; and he wrote them upon two tables of stone. And
> the Lord commanded me at that time to teach you statutes
> and judgments, that ye might do them in the land whither
> ye go over to possess it. Take ye therefore good heed unto
> yourselves; for ye saw no manner of similitude on the day
> that the Lord spake unto you in Horeb out of the midst of
> the fire: lest ye corrupt yourselves, and make you a graven
> image, the similitude of any figure, the likeness of male or
> female, the likeness of any beast that is on the earth, the
> likeness of any winged fowl that flieth in the air, the likeness
> of any thing that creepeth on the ground, the likeness of
> any fish that is in the waters beneath the earth: and lest thou
> lift up thine eyes unto heaven, and when thou seest the sun,
> and the moon, and the stars, even all the host of heaven,
> shouldest be driven to worship them, and serve them, which
> the Lord thy God hath divided unto all nations under the
> whole heaven. (Deuteronomy 4:12–19)

No one saw God as He gave these commands, therefore, no one can make an accurate image.

But the greatest reason for not making images of God is expressed when God said, "For I the Lord your God am a jealous God" (v. 5*b*). One might prefer the word *zealous* instead of *jealous* in this verse because the state-ment does not refer to an emotion but a mindset resulting in action. In English, the idea of *jealous* includes suspicious, distrustful, envious—none of which characterize God. However, zeal does characterize God well. In the Old Testament, it is clear that there are at least three applications of the concept with God.

First is the idea of exclusive devotion (Exodus 34:14; Deuteronomy 4:24). That God requires faithful, sincere devotion to Him alone is clear when He warned the people, "For thou shalt worship no other god: for the Lord, whose name is Jealous, is a jealous God" (Exodus 34:14).

Second, zeal is obvious in God when He directs His anger against His enemies who oppose Him (Numbers 25:11; Deuteronomy 29:20; Psalm 79:5). This anger was explained when God told the people through Moses,

> Beware lest there be among you a root bearing poisonous and bitter fruit, one who, when he hears the words of this sworn covenant, blesses himself in his heart, saying, "I shall be safe, though I walk in the stubbornness of my heart." This will lead to the sweeping away of moist and dry alike. The LORD will not be willing to forgive him, but rather the anger of the LORD and his jealousy will smoke against that man, and the curses written in this book will settle upon him, and the LORD will blot out his name from under heaven. (Deuteronomy 29:18–20 ESV)

Third, God displays zeal when He expends energy to vindicate His people (2 Kings 19:31; Isaiah 9:7). That is precisely what God promised in Jesus Christ, the eternal King of Kings. "Of the increase of his government and peace there shall be no end, upon the throne of David, and upon his kingdom, to order it, and to establish it with judgment and with justice from henceforth even for ever. The zeal of the Lord of hosts will perform this" (Isaiah 9:7).

God is jealous because He ordains that His people should have an exclusive relationship with Him.

God is zealous. Or one could conclude that God is jealous if the word is used in a way similar to the way *love* and *hate* are often used in the Old Testament. Love and hate are typically not presented as emotions but as attitudes that result in particular actions. Love is an action. Hate is an action. Therefore, God is jealous because He ordains that His people should have an exclusive relationship with Him. His standard for a relationship with His people is much like the relationship of a husband and wife. He thinks and acts in order to protect that relationship. That is jealousy without the emotion. It is what God expressed when He asked His people, "How shall I pardon thee for this? thy children have forsaken me, and sworn by them that are no gods: when I had fed them to the full, they then committed adultery, and assembled themselves by troops in the harlots' houses" (Jeremiah 5:7). God wants to protect the relationship with His people.

Imagine a handsome young man who woos a young woman and then married her. One day she hires a famous artist to paint a portrait of her husband. As soon as she sees the finished product, she falls in love with it. The color is deep and rich. The hues are breathtaking. The man in the portrait looks as real as life. Because the wife loves the portrait so much, she spends an inordinate amount of time with it to the neglect of her husband. In fact, she is so enamored with the painting that she falls in love with the artist who created it. Finally, the silly woman runs off with the artist and the painting. Should her husband be zealous for her? God is zealous for His people.

Therefore, if God's people exalt an object or even a philosophy above Him, they do so with the knowledge that their sin brings serious results (vv. 5*b*–6). The negative results are stated in the end of verse 5. God promises to visit iniquity to the third and fourth generations. That does not mean that a mathematician can figure out how long God's judgment will last. It is simply a promise of continuity. Since that is true, what can we conclude about God's promise that "the fathers shall not be put to death for the children, neither shall the children be put to death for the fathers: every man shall be put to death for his own sin" (Deuteronomy 24:16)? That God will visit iniquity is not a promise of justified punishment that God Himself enacts. Rather this is a promise of the outworking of natural consequences when one generation teaches the next generation to breach their relationship with God. That happens with regularity.

The good news is that there are also positive results with God (v. 6). God's mercy is highlighted against the backdrop of sin's consequences. He shows mercy (*chesed*) for myriads of people. He freely displays kindness and faithfulness for innumerable people. What kind of person would prefer to receive God's judgment instead of His loving loyalty?

THE APPLICATION OF THE PRINCIPLE

A wise person is able to see this principle coming to play in real life. Some people offend God by replacing Him with tangible objects. For example, a person might see all his possessions as things he owns rather than as resources that God has loaned to him in order to do His work for His glory. Some parents think about, dream about, pursue, and spend all their time and energy gaining that which is passing away while at the same time ignoring God. These are typically the traits of unsaved people and are passed down from one generation to the next.

Other parents are apt to teach their children to replace worship of God with worship of lesser things. One writer concluded, "The nature of the sin . . . [is] the attempt to make the worship of the Lord something that relates to the senses rather than to the spirit."[1] That idea is demonstrated when parents teach children by their practice that observing traditions is the same thing as worshiping God. The Catholic church is a chief proponent of this error. But even genuine Christians can pass on such error. Even Christians can errantly teach their children that reciting the Lord's Prayer and the Apostles' Creed, observing communion, singing hymns, taking an offering, or going on visitation is worshiping God. If the spirit of the participant is enthralled with other things, no worship of God has occurred.

It is also possible for Christian parents to teach their children that if their human senses are heightened, they are worshiping God. This error is observable in many church services. It is not unusual to find instrumentalists playing with thumping loud noise, worship leaders literally jumping up and down, the choir dancing, and the lights flashing. Such attempts at worship replace God with a focus on the senses. God is a spirit, and those who worship Him must avoid exalting human senses and make sure the hidden spirit is in fellowship with Him. This is a fine line and difficult to maintain. If the parents err, they pass their error to their children, who will reap the consequences of the parents' sin.

The command is still valid, and, therefore, the consequences of the principle will also come to pass. A parent passes disloyalty to God to his child as the child observes it. Does the parent "hate" God? Such a parent would deny the accusation. Nonetheless, his actions prove he does not love God. It is so easy for a parent to teach a child to love this passing world. Parents teach this when they conclude that making money is more important than loving God. They conclude that being an "influence" for kindness and morality in the world is more important than obeying God. God disdains such action. He said, "Ye adulterers and adulteresses, know ye not that the friendship of the world is enmity with God? whosoever therefore will be a friend of the world is the enemy of God" (James 4:4).

As a result of such practices, the children stand for nothing, fearing they will offend sinners, and call their fear an open door to influence others. And then their children, the next generation, will often go the next step and be gross sinners because God visits the iniquity of the parents. They reap the consequences of sin, which is to be more deeply sunk in sin. They also reap untold heartache.

On the bright side, the children can learn to love God by watching their parents' love for God. Love is an action, not just an emotion. People can spend the whole day talking about an emotion, but an action requires sacrifice. Do the children know from observing their parents' lives that the parents truly worship God alone?

If this culture's forefathers from the mid-nineteenth century could come back and observe what has developed from their lives, what would they think? Would they be happy to see marriages ripped apart by divorce? Would they be satisfied to see young couples living together out of wedlock, aborting their accidental babies? Would they rejoice to see the proliferation of Hollywood's sins being lived out in nearly every home in America? Would they agree with the American philosophy that he who has the most toys when he dies wins? It is not likely that the founding fathers would be satisfied. This culture's unbridled hedonism is the result of parents being careless about their relationship with the one true God. He is indeed appointing the iniquity of the fathers on the generations that follow. Christian parents desperately need to stand in the face of the onrushing sin and show their children how to honor God and how to exalt Him with their lives. They should look forward to rejoicing as their children experience the loving kindness of the true God.

PUT IT TO WORK

1. Can your children point to anything in your life that looks like an image that replaces the true God?

2. If your children love God as much as you do, will you be satisfied?

3. If you knew for sure that your sin would affect your children, what would you change?

4. Do you see any weak traits in your children that they have picked up from you?

5. What steps can you take to be sure your children will enjoy God's blessing?

PRINCIPLE 26
Do not hide God's wonderful works from the children.

Give ear, O my people, to my teaching; incline your ears to the words of my mouth! I will open my mouth in a parable; I will utter dark sayings from of old, things that we have heard and known, that our fathers have told us. We will not hide them from their children, but tell to the coming generation the glorious deeds of the LORD, and his might, and the wonders that he has done. He established a testimony in Jacob and appointed a law in Israel, which he commanded our fathers to teach to their children, that the next generation might know them, the children yet unborn, and arise and tell them to their children, so that they should set their hope in God and not forget the works of God, but keep his commandments; and that they should not be like their fathers, a stubborn and rebellious generation, a generation whose heart was not steadfast, whose spirit was not faithful to God. (Psalm 78:1–8 ESV)

An article appeared in the *Greenville News* recently that posed the possibility that the United States is going down the same path Rome followed to her destruction about fifteen hundred years ago. That is not a novel idea to many people. Philosophers and historians have been wondering and warning about that connection for at least a generation. This brings to mind the old saying, "Those who will not learn from history are destined to repeat it." Apparently Americans don't learn and so they repeat. For some reason the human race either cannot or will not learn the lessons of history. As a result, nations, societies, families, churches, schools, businesses, and individuals often walk the same path to demise that their predecessors walked just a few generations earlier.

Several years ago I was talking with a man about family reunions. He told me that his family celebrated a huge family reunion each year in a state in the north. Each year the extended family, amounting to over one hundred people, gathered at a relative's house, ate, fellowshiped, and caught up on the latest family gossip. One of the highlights for the older folks was when the matriarch of the family rehearsed the family's roots. He said that the family had been in America for several generations and that the forefather had been a deacon in a Puritan community.

The issue that caught my attention was that this man was clueless about what a deacon was and more clueless about who the Puritans were. He was admittedly not a Christian—or even religious for that matter. As far as he knew, he had a couple of aunts and uncles who attended church somewhat regularly, but for the most part his family had little knowledge of God and little concern to gain any knowledge of God.

How does a family that began with a deacon in a Puritan church end up in rank paganism within a few generations? Someone, somewhere along the line, neglected to tell the children the testimony of God. Someone failed to stress the importance of knowing and doing God's commands. Someone forgot God's works just like the people of Israel tended to do.

It seems likely that the psalmist Asaph wrote the song recorded as Psalm 78 to be an instructive song. It was to be sung publicly and was intended to convey the importance of parents teaching God's truths to each new generation. It is proof that each generation of God's people must be challenged to pass on the knowledge and experience they have of God. It is proof that we tend to neglect the important teaching of God's Word to our children. Spurgeon said of this psalm:

> It is a singular proof of the obtuseness of mind of many professors that they will object to sermons and expositions upon the historical parts of Scripture, as if they contained no instruction in spiritual matters; were such persons truly enlightened by the Spirit of God, they would perceive that all Scripture is profitable, and would blush at their own folly in undervaluing any portion of the inspired volume.[1]

Parents, are you teaching God's Word to the next generation? Grandparents, are you teaching what God has taught you to your grandchildren? How will they know unless someone teaches them? Forgetfulness and neglect are inexcusable for God's people. If God's people have seen, if we have heard, if we have come to know the God of the Bible, we must not, by any means, hide these things from the children.

PARENTS MUST DETERMINE TO TEACH THEIR CHILDREN (Psalm 78:1-4)

This psalm challenges God's people, particularly the parents, to determine that they will teach things they have heard and known (vv. 1–3). Parents do well to develop a desire for others to hear important things (v. 1). Some folks are naturally reserved and not interested in telling other people what they know. Other folks are the opposite. They think that everyone in the world wants to hear their words of wisdom. When the psalmist announced to the people, "Give ear to my teaching," he taught that the one speaking, especially the parent, realizes that he or she has something important to say. Parents need to tell this important information to this new generation.

It is very important for parents to learn not to blabber on just because they are impressed with the sound of their own voice. That seems to be the case sometimes. The danger with mindless jabber is that children know when Mom or Dad is rambling and has nothing of any real value to say. Children also know when the folks are arrogant and wrongly presume that they can correct the sinful child. Most important is the fact that children know when a parent is demanding something from them that the parent is not willing to do himself. Children see that as hypocrisy.

Parents must not speak just to hear themselves speak, but they must speak things heard and known (vv. 2–3). The psalmist was determined to teach in parables and dark sayings (v. 2). What parent knows how to do that? The words sound deep and mysterious, but actually these are concepts any parent should be familiar with, concepts all Christian parents should implement in life. Parables are simply comparisons. To teach by parable is to teach that which is generally unknown by comparing it to that which is known. Anyone who studies the Bible realizes that this was one of the chief methods Jesus used for teaching. Matthew observed, "That it might be fulfilled which was spoken by the prophet, saying, I will open my mouth in parables; I will utter things which have been kept secret from the foundation of the world" (Matthew 13:35). Sometimes children's songs and Sunday school stories do this well.

Parents are also able to teach by using dark sayings. This term really sounds foreboding. The word is a little sinister in that dark sayings are the confusing things of antiquity. However, these things do not remain confusing or secret. These are truths that current knowledge has helped to uncover so that the past actions become useful teachers in the present. To teach with dark sayings is to use the mirror of the past to reflect the condition of the present. Parents can use this method to unfold their child's needs by pulling up the lessons of the past.

Ultimately, this must be a matter of teaching the things we have heard and known. These are the things "our fathers have told us." But such teaching must be more than the traditions of the past. Long-held traditions might not even be accurate or true. Rather, these are the things God has taught in His Word.

The parent who has determined to teach what he or she has learned from God will not hide those things from the coming generations (v. 4). Parents must tell the glorious deeds of the Lord. Of course, before a parent can tell the children about the glorious deeds of the Lord, he or she must know them first. It is difficult to teach others something you do not know personally. Parents ought to be intimately familiar with the glorious deeds of the Lord, such as the miracles of creation, the flood, the exodus, and all the other amazing works of God. Christian parents should know well the stories about the miracles God performed as He worked with people to direct them to do His will. Most important, the parent who teaches God's wonders should be very familiar with the most glorious miracle of God's salvation. Have you ever told your children the circumstances of your new birth? These wonderful truths are learned from the Bible and understood more when Bible truth is applied to everyday circumstances.

The psalmist's challenge is for godly parents to learn about these glorious deeds and then tell them to the generations. Do not hide the wonderful stories. What Christian parent would hide the truths of the Bible? A parent may not purposely hide truth from her children, but failing to tell the children the wonderful news is to hide it from them. In a similar fashion, to be sidetracked by telling only stories of human exploits also results in hiding the wonders of God. Even Christian parents can be easily impressed with the passing fancies of humanity. Those things quickly grab human attention. So it is with the children.

Parents must tell the glorious deeds of the Lord.

How can an old Bible story compete with an exciting video game? It is difficult to capture the modern child's attention. But the parent who knows the God of the Bible stories well will be so impressed with Him that they will give life to His stories. To those parents, the wonders of God eclipse everything else in importance.

PARENTS MUST DETERMINE TO TEACH THEIR CHILDREN GOD'S TESTIMONY (vv. 5–8)

Sincere parents may wonder what should be the best lesson to teach their children. The answer to that question is clearly answered in verses 5–6. God appointed the matters that parents should teach the children. He established a testimony and appointed a law. God established a testimony in Jacob. Does God really expect Christian parents to teach God's testimony to the children? What is the content of His testimony? How does the parent know what to say to the children? When the psalmist wrote that God established a testimony with Jacob, He meant that God made His truth known through the sons of Jacob. The whole history of Israel is God's unfolding of the truth about Himself. Much of what modern Christians know about God comes through the context of His working with the nation of Israel. Therefore, in simple terms, God's story about Himself is what parents must teach their children. His testimony is the truth about Him.

Sometimes it is good to simply sit down and recall the great stories of how God worked with the ancient people. God did not record these in the eternal Scripture to serve as entertainment. He reveals what kind of God He is in the testimony.

Another portion of that body of knowledge that parents must consistently give to their children is the law. God appointed a law in Israel for a reason. We might understand the need for Jewish parents to rehearse the Mosaic law to their children over and over. But surely God does not expect twenty-first-century American parents to teach that kind of boring stuff to their children, does He? This is not a reference per se to the Mosaic law. Rather, this idea of law refers to the revelation of God's will. In other words, twenty-first-century American parents know what God desires, what He expects, because of His law. That is the kind of stuff children need to hear from their parents. In fact, according to verse 5, God commands His people to teach His will to the children. How much more should Christian parents be concerned about doing that?

The modern approach is to tell the children that there is a God Who loves them, which is true. Then Mom and Dad tell them that this God of love wants them to go to heaven to live with Him. So what is to keep the children out of heaven? Sin. How do the children know what sin is? Good parents teach their children that sin is everything contrary to God's will. Unfortunately, this is where the breakdown occurs in modern families. Parents hesitate to define sin for fear of being labeled legalists. Nevertheless, God's law is still defined by God's law. Paul explained this connection when he told the Christians in Rome, "What then shall we say? That the law is sin? By no means! Yet if it had not been for the law, I would not have known sin. I would not have known what it is to covet if the law had not said, 'You shall not covet'" (Romans 7:7 ESV). The law explains God's will. Teach it to the children.

God intends for each successive generation to know His testimony and law (v. 6). It is not right that one generation should know the will of God, live according to it, enjoy the rewards of obeying God, and then let the succeeding generation fend for themselves. Each generation must tell the testimony and law of God to the children of that generation. When the chain breaks, a generation goes without knowledge. The results are tragic. What causes the chain to break?

Parents fail to continue the process when the things of a passing world distract them. When this happens, the children grow up hoping they will be rich and famous, or hoping they will make money, or hoping they will live in a nice house in a nice neighborhood, or hoping they will be popular. Those hopes consume their thinking and energy.

However, according to God's plan, knowledge of God's testimony should stimulate steadfast hope in God (vv. 7–8). Those who learn this great truth must take care not to forget it. Remembering God's testimony and law is critical if the children would set their hope in God—and they must. Having learned the truth about God from the parents, how can the children do anything but set their hope in God? The sad truth is that many children from Christian homes have no greater hope in God than pagan children do. Maybe the parents have been faithful to communicate the truth about God to the children, but the children have forgotten the works of God.

The psalmist warned in verse 7 that the children must not forget what their parents teach them about the works of God. These are the works He has done at all times for all people as recorded in the Bible. Most

The children, having learned from the parents, must keep God's commands.

important the children must not forget the works God has done in their hearts.

Furthermore, the children, having learned from the parents, must keep God's commands. Human nature almost cringes to hear such a challenge. Christians hate the thought of trying to keep a list of human commands in order to please God. But this is not a challenge to keep the law in an effort to win God's favor. The children already have God's favor if they are born again. Rather, this is an admonition to show the evidence that God's law is written on the heart. When a sinner repents of sin and receives Christ as Savior, he or she establishes a mature, intimate relationship with God. To keep His commands is to learn the importance of a right and mature relationship with God. It begins with the confession of sin, is rooted in trusting Christ alone for salvation, and establishes a love relationship. Because of that relationship, the Christian child keeps God's commands out of love for Him.

The other side of the coin is what parents hope to prevent by teaching their children about God's testimony and law. Stubbornness flows from a heart that is not steadfast (v. 8). The people in Asaph's day understood this well. Asaph's song reminded them and reminds the modern reader that the fathers illustrated this attitude of stubbornness all too well. What was their problem? According to verse 22 in this psalm, they did not believe God. No doubt those fathers would have argued that they, more than any of their neighbors, believed God. It is true that they knew a lot about God. It is also true that they had witnessed more amazing works of God than any previous generation. But they really did not trust God. They trusted their own judgment. That is why they made a golden calf and concluded that it represented the gods who brought them out of Egypt. That is the conclusion of human wisdom. They did not believe God, and that is why they tried to enter the Promised Land after disobeying God and were defeated (Numbers 14).

Many second and third generation Christian homes know much about God. They have heard the gospel and the testimony about God all their lives. They have memorized Scripture. They know God well—but they do not trust Him. They do not "trust his saving power" (v. 22).

Another evidence of the fathers' stubborn hearts was found in the fact that they remembered God, but not genuinely (vv. 35–39). They remembered that they had been told that God is their rock, their safe haven (v. 35). They remembered that God was the redeemer of the nation (v. 35). But their hearts were not right toward Him. They flattered God and said nice things about Him that they didn't really believe (v. 36). In short, they lied to Him (v. 36). If those ancient Israelites were like modern religious people, they might have sung praises and hymns to God even though they did not believe what they articulated. Did they sing

> I am Thine, O Lord,
> I have heard Thy voice,
> And it told Thy love to me;
> But I long to rise in the arms of faith,
> And be closer drawn to Thee
>
> ("Draw Me Nearer," Fanny Crosby)

when they really were not the Lord's and did not long to have closer fellowship with Him? Christians express such untruths regularly.

How do these things happen? Their heart was not steadfast toward God (v. 37). They were not faithful to the covenant (v. 37). This same kind of attitude and sin are reaffirmed by James as a New Testament–age problem. He said:

> If any of you lack wisdom, let him ask of God, that giveth to all men liberally, and upbraideth not; and it shall be given him. But let him ask in faith, nothing wavering. For he that wavereth is like a wave of the sea driven with the wind and tossed. For let not that man think that he shall receive any thing of the Lord. A double minded man is unstable in all his ways. (James 1:5–8)

An unfaithful spirit is not a stable spirit. This person knows about God. Maybe he or she knows a lot about God and the Bible. But he or she is not devoted to Christ. Folks like this might be very religious but are subject to all kinds of beliefs, whims, and fads. Probably this person is not born again.

Therefore, the parent must teach this kind of double-minded child that he or she needs to come to God through Christ. Later in his letter, James admonished sinners to "draw nigh to God, and he will draw nigh to you. Cleanse your hands, ye sinners; and purify your hearts, ye double minded"

(James 4:8). Parents do well to teach the lesson of James to their children so that they will not be stubborn and rebellious. They need to teach the children to confess sin and abandon it. They need to teach the children to yield to God for the purifying of their hearts.

Children who do not learn from history are destined to repeat it. History is God's story. Tell it to this new generation so that the children will know God. They will never love God if they do not know Him. Tell them the wonderful story that culminates in the salvation of the soul.

PUT IT TO WORK

1. Name five unfamiliar stories (i.e., not Noah's ark, Jonah in the whale, etc.) from the Bible that demonstrate God's power and might.

2. What principle or principles did God reveal about Himself in those stories?

3. What truth about God's testimony did you teach your children last week?

4. Do you enjoy an ongoing, intimate relationship with Christ?

5. Have you shared the story of your salvation with your children?

PRINCIPLE 27
Unless God builds the home, the effort is futile.

Unless the LORD builds the house, those who build it labor in vain. Unless the LORD watches over the city, the watchman stays awake in vain. It is in vain that you rise up early and go late to rest, eating the bread of anxious toil; for he gives to his beloved sleep. Behold, children are a heritage from the LORD, the fruit of the womb a reward. Like arrows in the hand of a warrior are the children of one's youth. Blessed is the man who fills his quiver with them! He shall not be put to shame when he speaks with his enemies in the gate. (Psalm 127:1–5 ESV)

Dilapidated houses tell interesting stories. An old, run-down house covered with weeds was probably someone's pride and joy in days past. Imagine the people who built that house. No doubt they were very proud of the finished product as it displayed their skill and hard work. Surely there were many joyous holidays and birthdays celebrated in that home. Maybe an entire generation of children grew up and left that home, or maybe even multiple generations.

But that was then and this is now. What happens to all the hard work, the craftsmanship that went into building a house after many years? Some houses, like those on the battery in Charleston, South Carolina, stand the test of time. But many houses are eventually abandoned, and, being left to the elements, soon deteriorate, leaving a testimony of temporalness regarding all humanity's efforts.

Families are like that too. A young husband and wife start out together with great dreams and aspirations. They plan to have a family, buy a house, rear the children and then . . . Well, we who are over fifty generally don't like to think about what happens when it is all over. It happens so quickly. But, in the process of time, this dreamy-eyed young couple has children. They are excited because their dreams are becoming a reality. Mom and Dad work their jobs, follow their careers, buy a house, buy a couple of cars and all the other necessary stuff. They even spend some time rearing the children. Sooner than they can imagine, the children are grown, and the parents are forced to assess the quality of the end product. How did they do in building their home?

There are many different standards of quality by which the world judges the home. For most of the people in American culture, financial success is the sole criterion of quality. If the children grow up to be wealthy, it is an indication that the parents built a successful home. Others appeal to the standard of education. If the children go on to earn advanced degrees in their field, the culture congratulates the parents on a job well done. Others gauge success on popularity. If the child can make it on television or in politics, friends might very well judge the parents to have been a smashing success.

However, the culture's standard of success is not always the same as God's standard. Solomon, the probable author of this psalm, concluded that if God doesn't build the home, the parents' labors will be futile. The home that is not built through God's guidance, by God's power, according to God's blueprint, is not a successful home. The world might praise such a home, but the world is passing away. In the end, a home that is not built by God will look like a typical ramshackle, rundown, useless home.

Wise parents will appeal to God for wisdom in growing and maturing the children God has placed in their home. Wise parents must recognize the need for God's influence and must train the children to embrace and rely on God's grace and guidance. One of the great paradoxes of the Bible is that the individual child is responsible to trust and obey God; but at the same time, God requires the parents to teach the children how to trust and obey God. Sometimes parents will faithfully build the home through God's wisdom only to have the children tear it down. At other times, the parents will rely on God's wisdom to build the home, and the children will follow their example and continue to build on the same foundation, according to the same blueprint. This psalm concludes that such parents are blessed. Christians should agree and rejoice to see such a home.

THE PRINCIPLE OF GOD'S SUPERINTENDING (Psalm 127:1-2)

Solomon's argument from the outset of this psalm is that it is useless to build without God (v. 1). Build what? Is it vain to build a house or a city or a family? Yes. All those ideas are covered by the challenge. More accurately, the idea of "build" in this psalm probably describes the process of living the typical life. In that sense, everyone is in a building process and needs to be aware of this principle. Life is a building process, and how one builds is vital. It is of critical importance for everyone to understand that God is the divine architect. As creator, it is His prerogative to determine the plan. That being true, a person is foolish to go about building his or her life without consulting the Designer and Architect.

As the designer, God has the right to give His created beings the plan. But as a loving Father, it is also His desire for everyone to build life according to His design. What is that design? God's design is revealed in the pages of the Bible. A short synopsis of that design is to say that God's plan requires everyone who builds to be in fellowship with Him. That requires faith in Christ and sins forgiven through Christ. Furthermore, God's design is for His people to build on the foundation of Christ. Paul pointed to this design when he told the Corinthian Christians, "For other foundation can no man lay than that is laid, which is Jesus Christ. Now if any man build upon this foundation gold, silver, precious stones, wood, hay, stubble; every man's work shall be made manifest: for the day shall declare it, because it shall be revealed by fire; and the fire shall try every man's work of what sort it is" (1 Corinthians 3:11–13). The primary application of this text is in the matter of service to God. But what is building a home if it is not service to God?

The principle, as Solomon stated it, includes human efforts in building structures, houses, institutions, businesses, cultures, and just about anything in life we can imagine. Nearly everyone does this—it is life! However, God warns people not to attempt this apart from Him. His warning is clear: To live life apart from God is vain. Therefore, the watchman's work in guarding the city is useless apart from God. That is because God exercises sovereign control over all things. As God exercises control over all things, He works all things for His glory.

That wonderful truth begs a question. If it is vain to guard a city unless God is also guarding it, then how can burglars break into the homes of God's people? If God was watching our church property, why did He allow burglars to break into it and steal equipment? Was He not watching? Should we have been here watching instead? The security of these buildings was not breached because God's people were careless. The alarms in the buildings were set, and, for a change, all of the doors were actually locked. In that sense, we were watching. We were guarding the building against attack. Nevertheless, God allowed thieves to break in and steal for His own purposes. Possibly God's purpose was to remind His people that the treasures of earth are always susceptible to destruction. Or maybe God wanted to remind His people how much they must depend on Him. Or God might have allowed the break-in to remind us that there is still much work for the gospel to save sinners who steal. Maybe God used this event to warn others to be more careful. Ultimately, God uses such sinful actions to allow stubborn sinners to heap up God's judgment against themselves. It is true for them as it will be for future Babylon: "For her sins have reached unto heaven, and God hath remembered her iniquities" (Revelation 18:5). God is in charge. His people are foolish to guard the city without God.

Therefore, it is also true that they labor in vain to build a house if they build without God. A perfect example of this truth is found in ancient Babylon. Those proud people thought they could succeed on their own. "And they said, Go to, let us build us a city and a tower, whose top may reach unto heaven; and let us make us a name, lest we be scattered abroad upon the face of the whole earth" (Genesis 11:4). They decided to build a monument to their own greatness, which naturally excluded God. In response, God showed the importance of this principle. They said, "Let us build. . . . And the Lord said, Behold, the people is one, and they have all one language; and this they begin to do: and now nothing will be restrained from them, which they have imagined to do. Go to, let us go down, and there confound their language, that they may not understand one another's speech" (Genesis 11:4, 6–7).

A contrast to the foolishness of the Babelites' building without God is Solomon's building the temple. Before he began the project, he prayed for God to guide him and to give him wisdom (2 Chronicles 1:10). God answered Solomon's prayer, gave him favor with the people, and provided him with the resources. When it was completed, God glorified Himself in the building. "Now when Solomon had made an end of praying, the fire came down from heaven, and consumed the burnt offering and the sacrifices; and the glory of the Lord filled the house" (2 Chronicles 7:1). What a difference it makes to include God in the process.

But in this psalm the principle applies specifically to the context of building the home. The term *house* is often used in the Old Testament to refer to family. For example, Abraham's house in Genesis 15:2 is his family. When God gave the midwives "houses," He gave them their own families (30:3). The households of Jacob's sons were their families (Exodus 1:21). When Ruth married Boaz, she came into his "family" (house) with the blessing that God would make their "family" like the "family" of Israel (Ruth 4:11). It is quite interesting that right after the Babel illustration (Genesis 11:1–9) God introduced the story of how He built the family of Abraham (Genesis 11:10–32). Therefore the principle is this: Whoever builds a family without God is wasting his time.

> Whoever builds a family without God is wasting his time.

Working harder does not solve the problem (v. 2). When human wisdom notices a problem in the family-building process, it tends to conclude that someone needs to work harder, work more hours, do more stuff, to make it work. But God warns that human effort does not make up for the lack of God's intervention. Therefore, parents read all the books men and women have written in order to know how to build their home. Parents go to seminars in order to get the right answers. Parents make the rules tougher and restrictions tighter to counter their teens' rebellion. The results of such conclusions shout, "Useless!" That is not to conclude that there is no value in books or seminars. Often God uses His servants to write books and hold seminars or lectures that are very helpful for parents who seek to build God's way. Rather, this is to say that books and seminars cannot replace God's part in the equation of home building. Extended human effort cannot replace God's absence in the process. Working more hours to solve the problem will not help if God is left out of the picture. A parent robbing himself of sleep because of worry will not help. Worry never makes up for the lack of God's intervention.

In fact, when parents yield to God's directing in the building process, they discover that along the way God gives them rest. When parents rest in God's wisdom, they sleep well. There will be times (many times) when parents will be, and should be, concerned for their children. But when they seek God's help and wisdom, He gives rest. A sign that parents are maturing in their walk with God is that they know how to turn difficult home-building issues over to God's control and then discover God's plan through the principles of His Word. The principle is clear: God must be involved in the home-building process. The question is "How?"

THE PRINCIPLE APPLIED (vv. 3-5)

The first step in making God's principle work is to acknowledge rightful ownership. Children are from the Lord (v. 3). God is kind to lend His property to parents so that they can manage His property for His glory. To a point, that is true. However, Solomon's word choice here might indicate more ownership rights than a mere steward would enjoy. The text says that sons (the most literal meaning of the Hebrew word), or children, are an inheritance from the Lord.

The word *inheritance* speaks of receiving a possession, generally from a parent or a relative. In this case, the parents receive a possession from God. That means that children are really not just the result of a natural biological process. Since that is true, the organism in the mother's womb is not just a fetus; it is a possession given by God. Children are His reward, just like the fruit in harvest time is His reward. God's reward is the pay that He gives to His people. God is kind to give children to parents with the agreement that they will build a home God's way.

Therefore, wise parents view children as an extremely valuable gift from God. In fact, a parent's view of his or her children will, in large measure, effect the way a child is reared. A parent who truly evaluates her child as a valuable gift from God will not think of her child as a nuisance. Granted, there will plenty of times when a child will agitate the parent's spirits. But even in those times, the parent's opinion is tempered by the fact that the child is God's reward. To value children as God's property motivates parents to invest extreme time and energy in the building process.

It is important to acknowledge at this point that God does not bless all families the same way. Some couples might wonder why, if children are God's reward, if they are His inheritance, God never gave them a reward or inheritance. It is obvious that God does not choose to give every couple children. That is God's choice, and He knows perfectly well why He makes it. It is wrong to conclude that childless couples are the objects of God's judgment, or that they are not blessed, or that they are not as fortunate as couples with children. Nothing could be further from the truth.

In the cases of childless couples, God chooses a special ministry for special people. Often couples without children are able to be a great help and assistance to parents. Sometimes childless couples become adoptive parents. Couples without children have greater liberty of time and possessions so that God can use them for His service. Someone might argue that the Old Testament model is clearly pro-big family. The Old Testament picture is not always the best picture to apply to every generation. In the Old Testament dispensation, God often blessed parents with children in order to grow the nation of Israel and thereby fulfill His promise to Abraham regarding a nation as numerous as the sand on the seashore. Modern Christians are God's people, but we are not Israel—and you are probably not a physical descendent of Abraham. Therefore, couples should not sense the same pressure to have children that the ancient Jews felt. Each couple must rejoice in the wisdom of God's blessing to them whether it is many children, few children, or no children.

Parents who have children must realize that children are a blessing, not a burden (vv. 4–5). Solomon likened children to arrows in the hands of a mighty warrior. This is a picture of a parent shaping the child for a particular end (v. 4). The ancient warrior did not buy his arrows at the local arrow supply. He shaped his own arrows. He shaped them for a particular task. He had a goal in mind while he worked with each arrow.

The parent's goal is to have the child fly straight for the glory of God when he lets him or her off the string of the bow. C. H. Spurgeon observed, "To this end we must have our children in hand while they are yet children, or they are never likely to be so when they are grown up; and we must try to point them and straighten them, so as to make arrows of them in their youth, lest they should prove crooked and unserviceable in after life."[1]

Solomon also said that the man is blessed who has a quiver full of these arrows. A quiver full can be a lot of work. We must remember that not all quivers are the same size. Some parents are not organized enough themselves to be able to build a large home for God's glory. What good is accomplished when parents who are slack in their relationship with God try to rear many children for God's glory? On the other hand, a large number of children means a large number of trials. But a large number of trials can mean deeper faith and greater maturity.

Maybe the most important result of building the family God's way is discovered after the task is completed. The parent is blessed in later years (v. 5). Good arrows are a defense against the enemy. But who is the enemy? Hannah saw her co-wife, her adversary Penninah, as her enemy. "And Hannah prayed, and said, My heart rejoiceth in the Lord, mine horn is exalted in the Lord: my mouth is enlarged over mine enemies; because I rejoice in thy salvation" (1 Samuel 2:1). The history states that "her adversary also provoked her sore, for to make her fret, because the Lord had shut up her womb" (1 Samuel 1:6).

Indeed, the enemy is often real people who, for whatever reason, become agitators, accusers, or talebearers. In this verse the enemy is in the gate. So the good children, who accompany their parents in the gate where court meets, prove to be a great defense. But the people did not always meet in the gate to hold court. Good children, who were in the gate where people gathered, silenced the criticism of the enemy. Enemies, often those who are jealous or envious, might attack the parent's character, his love for God, his sincerity of service, or even his ability to be a parent. There is no greater defense at such times than being able to say, "Here, let me introduce you to my children." When the children are flying straight, the enemy's attacks sound foolish. On the other hand, if the arrows are not flying straight, a parent under attack will tend to shrink at accusations, fearing that maybe the enemy is right. Likewise, good grown children will offer care in old age. That is a great defense.

God encourages parents to build their homes with Him so that we will not be put to shame by our children. When you have finished your building process, what will the house look like? Will it continue to be in good standing after you are gone? Arrows that fly straight shape arrows that also fly straight. And so the process continues generation after generation for God's glory.

PUT IT TO WORK

1. Which of your children did God give to you?

2. In what practical ways do you appeal to God for guidance in building your home?

3. If your "arrows" hit the target for which you have shaped them, what will the target be?

4. In your thinking, what standard will determine if your children are successful?

5. If you were attacked by the enemy as being ungodly or unrighteous, what kind of defense would your children's lives provide for you?

PRINCIPLE 28
Teach the children wisdom.

The proverbs of Solomon, son of David, king of Israel: To know wisdom and instruction, to understand words of insight, to receive instruction in wise dealing, in righteousness, justice, and equity; to give prudence to the simple, knowledge and discretion to the youth—Let the wise hear and increase in learning, and the one who understands obtain guidance, to understand a proverb and a saying, the words of the wise and their riddles. The fear of the LORD is the beginning of knowledge; fools despise wisdom and instruction. (Proverbs 1:1–7 ESV)

For many years I have said that you can't teach someone to have common sense. I came to this conclusion through a process of failure while trying to teach particular individuals to have common sense. Over the years I have preached, taught, and counseled men and women by giving out the Word of God. But over the years there were those people who never seemed to figure out how to make the truth of God's Word work in real life. Most people who have a heart to help others have had the same kind of experience. It is not uncommon for an encourager to have tried and tried to help a co-worker or a friend learn how to live by a budget, or practice self-discipline in eating, or just get his or her life organized. But in the end, it became obvious to the helper that he or she must have failed to teach common sense because the needy person still didn't seem to understand how to make wisdom work. We could assume that people are born either with common sense or without common sense. If that is the case, the person who was born without common sense has no choice but to flounder through life repeating the same mistakes over and over.

This text teaches the error of that kind of thinking. According to Solomon, who was the wisest of men, common sense is taught. Since common sense is taught, it must also be learned. Therefore, Solomon challenged his son to learn common sense. He challenged his son to learn how to discern problems and issues, to learn how to look at a situation and understand what caused it and what the end of it would be. That is common sense.

But the matter at hand is more than just common sense. Many people in the world have common sense even though they are not right with God. Many people have the ability to figure out common problems and come up with the solutions to problems. But at the same time these people cannot discern that they have a sin problem, nor can they figure out the solution to their sin problem. Common sense is that which the vast majority of people agree is sensible. It is a point that most people concur is prudent or wise. But most people do not agree that Jesus Christ is the Savior from sin.

Common sense explains how one thing is common with other things in life. It describes trends or connections. That is how John Locke defined it. Thomas Paine concluded that the overall connections in life and the opinion of the masses demanded that the colonies in America should be free from Britain's tyranny. But Thomas Paine was a deist, and both he and Locke denied the immortality of the soul.

According to Solomon common sense is taught.

Solomon taught that God is the author of all wisdom. He created the world by wisdom and in wisdom. His wisdom is evident in everything. However, that is not to say that every person who exercises any amount of wisdom in any kind of circumstance is right with God. God also created the human body, but that does not mean that all humans are right with God. Many people use God's creation in direct opposition to Him. In that sense, the sinful world also has wisdom but sinners do not use wisdom for God's glory. The wisdom of this world allows businessmen to make brilliant deals; it allows governing officials to make wise laws; it allows scientists to make helpful discoveries. But ultimately the world's wisdom falls short because that kind of wisdom denies God.

True wisdom, true common sense, is learned from God. It begins with a right relationship with God, and it grows through fellowship with God in His Word. Who will teach this principle to the children? God gives parents the responsibility to gain wisdom and exercise wisdom in their own lives so that they can show their children how to be wise.

THE PROVERBS (Proverbs 1:1)

The first verse in this ancient writing identifies it as Solomon's collection of proverbs. How fitting that the man who asked God for a special measure of wisdom would give the world a collection of that wisdom in words and example. When Solomon took over the throne of Israel from his famous father, David, God gave him the opportunity to ask for anything his heart desired. It was a very special opportunity. "In Gibeon the Lord appeared to Solomon in a dream by night: and God said, Ask what I shall give thee" (1 Kings 3:5). If God gave you the same kind of opportunity, for what would you ask?

Solomon asked for help.

> And Solomon said . . . "And now, O Lord my God, you have made your servant king in place of David my father, although I am but a little child. I do not know how to go out or come in. And your servant is in the midst of your people whom you have chosen, a great people, too many to be numbered or counted for multitude. Give your servant therefore an understanding mind to govern your people, that I may discern between good and evil, for who is able to govern this your great people?" (1 Kings 3:6–9 ESV)

His request revealed a right opinion about himself. His request revealed a right opinion about God.

God acknowledged that Solomon's request pleased Him (1 Kings 3:10). Therefore, "God gave Solomon wisdom and understanding beyond measure, and breadth of mind like the sand on the seashore, so that Solomon's wisdom surpassed the wisdom of all the people of the east and all the wisdom of Egypt" (1 Kings 4:29–30 ESV).

More than that, God inspired Solomon to write words that are included in the eternal Word of God, the Bible. The words in this book named Proverbs are those God-inspired wise sayings. Not all the sayings included in this book are Solomon's words, and not all the wise sayings Solomon spoke are in this book. Scholars speculate that some of the sayings come from Hezekiah, and there is obviously the section in chapter 31 that purports to come from King Lemuel, which is probably not a code name for Solomon.

These proverbs are object lessons. The word *proverb* means to represent or to be like. Therefore, a proverb is instruction that teaches by example, or a parable or an object lesson. Sometimes the proverbs can be short, pithy sayings of wisdom. Much of the instruction in this collection named Proverbs is like that. Sometimes the wise saying can be a full sentence. Sometimes it is a story, like the wise sayings of Jesus, which He gave in the form of parables. Proverbs are always a way of teaching wisdom.

THE PURPOSE OF THE PROVERBS (vv. 2-6)

The purpose for this collection of proverbs is stated in verses 2, 3, 4, and 6. This stated purpose also applies to the entire Bible in a general sense. In that sense, it is true that the Proverbs and the entire Word of God give wisdom (v. 2). By it (the Bible) the reader is able to know wisdom. The word translated "to know" means to perceive, discriminate, or distinguish. This is the way the word is used when the Bible says that Balaam knew that God blessed Israel. Balaam the prophet was able to distinguish rather quickly in the blessing/curse scenario that God was on Israel's side. The word also means to know by experience, or it can mean to be skillful. That was one of the traits of the elders who were chosen to lead Israel into the Promised Land (Deuteronomy 1:15).

What does the Bible (Proverbs) help the reader know? Solomon said that the Proverbs are written so that the one who reads and studies them will know wisdom. Wisdom is primarily an attribute of God. Applied to humanity, the word speaks of skill, shrewdness, prudence, or the ability to administrate. Therefore, this collection of wisdom reveals that by wisdom a man learns to work (6:6–11), by it he chooses good friends (13:20), by it he displays personal humility (11:2), and by using wisdom he gains more wisdom (19:20).

Furthermore, through the Word of God a person also comes to know instruction. The translation "to know instruction" is from an interesting Hebrew word, which basic meaning has to do with correction, chastisement, or discipline. How does the Bible teach the reader discipline or correction? Here the word is applied to learning. It is a reminder that learning must be accompanied by discipline. To some extent, discipline is necessary for the learning process to be effective. Those who teach in public schools comment on this truth regularly. Sometimes they experience a dilemma when there is no discipline in the classroom, which results in learning with difficulty at best—no learning at worst. God's Word teaches that those who would be wise must learn through discipline—especially mental discipline. Parents must teach children that learning requires discipline. This is the nature of homework. However the same principle is true in every aspect of life. Therefore, the fool in Proverbs is the guy who thinks that life should be easy and fun. He does not apply self-discipline to learn the important things and, as a result, he proves throughout life that he is indeed a fool. Parents need to teach children the principles of God's Word that reinforce the idea that self-discipline is necessary for learning. It is a theme repeated often in the Proverbs.

Also, by God's Word the reader learns to understand. Understanding is a very important concept in the wisdom literature of the Bible. To understand is to perceive or to discern. It is the ability to choose between right and wrong or between good and evil. A person with understanding is able to look at a situation and answer questions about the situation such as why it came about, where the idea came from, and what the probable results will be. That description of the word was illustrated when the angel Gabriel told Daniel to understand the vision he had received (Daniel 9:23). Gabriel expected Daniel to be able to discern God's plan regarding the seventy weeks.

The wise person must discern, perceive, or make a choice about words of insight. It might sound confusing, but the Hebrew word used here is actually the plural of the same word translated "understand" in this same verse. In other words, the person who would be wise must understand words of understanding. Does that sound confusing? The idea means that God's Word is full of words of discernment and perception, which only wisdom can grasp. How does it look in real life? Your child has friends in the neighborhood. One day they are bored and, looking for some fun, they decide to go to the store down the street to steal some cigarettes. Does your child participate? If not, is it because you have taught him how to discern good and evil? Have you taught him how to perceive a situation and realize that this action could lead to serious consequences? Or would your child have to say, "I can't do that because Mom won't let me"?

Parents must teach their children how to have mental discipline so that they can make wise choices.

God's Word also teaches the one who wishes to be wise how to receive instruction (v. 3). Of course the word translated "instruction" is again the word that talks about correction or discipline. It is a necessary part of gaining wisdom. The person who resists correction is destined to be a fool. The connection between discipline and the four following characteristics—wise dealings, righteousness, justice, equity—is undeniable.

God's Word is useful for receiving discipline in wise dealing. Wise dealings look like pondering or prudence. To practice wise dealings is to have insight into a situation or to comprehend it. While most of the people in Israel had no inkling that God planned to have a temple built in Jerusalem, David had wise dealings in the matter. He received instruction from God so that in later years he knew how to prepare for making furniture for the temple (1 Chronicles 28:19). Wise dealing describes the mental process that leads to wise activity. The young person who does not use the proper thinking process will probably not end up with the right actions.

God's Word is profitable to help God's people receive discipline in righteousness. This common Hebrew word speaks of ethical conduct toward others. It refers to being right with the law. Most important it speaks of having a right relationship with God. Practical righteousness is not an accident. It is learned. The child who is always at odds with others or who seems to have a lot of trouble with authorities or with the law is a child who is not right with God. He or she has not learned how to receive the wisdom of God's Word through self-imposed discipline.

Another characteristic that a person receives through disciplined learning is justice. The word describes that act of deciding a case. The person who has justice is able to govern or rule equitably. It is an important trait for leaders. Leaders have learned how to decide cases and make decisions fairly. Leaders must have wisdom. God's Word is the perfect source for wisdom.

Finally, the Proverbs are useful to make the reader receive discipline in equity. Equity refers to uprightness, straightness, and evenness. An unwise culture, like the American culture, fosters crookedness and perversion. Conversely, God's Word teaches children how to be straight and upright. Parents who teach their children how to receive discipline that makes them straight and upright will also teach them how to stand contrary to the flow of popularity.

According to verse 4, God's Word also teaches the seeker how to act in wisdom. Young people who have wisdom will act according to wisdom. Those who act contrary to wisdom do so because they are devoid of it. To act according to wisdom is to act with prudence. The Hebrew word speaks of shrewdness or craftiness. That sounds bad in the ear of one who is accustomed to the typical meaning of the word *shrewd*. But a shrewd person is not necessarily bad. Rather the person with this characteristic shrewdly evaluates advice (15:5), shrewdly regards circumstances (27:12), and is shrewd in experience (12:16). Prudence can be used positively to bring about good results, or it can be used negatively in a selfish or wicked way.

> The person who cannot figure out what he or she ought to do doesn't have this wisdom.

The Proverbs, and the entire Word of God, give this prudence to the simple. The reference to the simple person has nothing to do with mentally challenged people. The simple person is naive and must be taught or is immature to the point that he or she believes anything and everything. Worse, this child is stubborn, rejecting good advice. It is far better for parents to train their children to gain knowledge and discretion. Knowledge is perception or cunning. It is a theme in Proverbs. Discretion speaks of a purpose, plan, or scheme. The youth need to have someone teach them this ability. It is normal for youth to be lacking discretion. The person who cannot figure out what he or she ought to do in life doesn't have this wisdom.

God's Word also teaches how to understand (v. 6). It teaches the reader how to understand a proverb, which is expressed in examples, parables, or words of wisdom. The Word of God also teaches the reader to understand a saying. This word carries a negative connotation. It is like a scornful saying, a taunt, or satire. God's Word gives wisdom for understanding such negative statements and, at the same time, for understanding the words of the wise. The words of the wise are the words of people who have a reputation for having and exercising wisdom. The Bible also gives us understanding of the riddles of wise men. The riddles are the enigmatical sayings or difficult questions.

In a nutshell, the wisdom of God's Word teaches the reader how to look at a situation and understand its source and its consequences. This wisdom helps people get along with other people. It keeps people from sin and ruin. It is revealed in practical things such as using a budget, which prevents overspending. The simple wisdom of the Bible teaches practical truths such as the need to work forty hours to receive forty hours worth of pay. It even guides the reader in the decisions about what and how much to eat, where to live, what career to pursue, and who should be friends. A lot of folks don't have that kind of practical wisdom.

Having established the purpose of the Word of God, it is fitting for Solomon to offer a challenge to heed that wisdom (v. 5). The one who seeks wisdom will hear and gain more. This makes sense to the one who has understanding. But this does not make sense to the fool.

THE FOUNDATION OF THE PROVERBS (v. 7)

A right relationship with God is a prerequisite for wisdom. This is the ultimate goal of God's Word. Here Solomon wrote, "The fear of the Lord is the beginning of knowledge" (Proverbs 1:7). In chapter 9 he wrote, "The fear of the Lord is the beginning of wisdom: and the knowledge of the holy is understanding" (verse 10). In chapter 15, we discover that "the fear of the Lord is the instruction of wisdom; and before honour is humility" (verse 33). Job agreed when he said, "And unto man he said, Behold, the fear of the Lord, that is wisdom; and to depart from evil is understanding" (28:28). The psalmist agreed by writing, "The fear of the Lord is the beginning of wisdom: a good understanding have all they that do his commandments: his praise endureth for ever" (111:10). An awesome respect for God is the essence of salvation.

Solomon's request for wisdom was rooted in his awesome respect for the Lord. He trusted and obeyed His Word. Therefore, Solomon respected God. Conversely, fools see no reason to have God's wisdom and, therefore, have no desire to fear God. It is true that the foolish person often appears to be wise according to the world's standard. He or she appears to be happy and successful. Often these folks appear to be brighter than God's people. Sometimes they are. Jesus said, "The children of this world are in their generation wiser than the children of light" (Luke 16:8).

God's people are foolish to conclude that unredeemed people cannot have wisdom. Though God is the author of wisdom, sinful humanity can use it for ungodly purposes. Eve desired to be made "wise" but not for God's glory. The world has wisdom, but when it is pitted against God's wisdom, it fails (1 Corinthians 1). In the end, the fool reaps consequences for rejecting God's wisdom. Often in this life a foolish person will experience much pain and sorrow for his foolish decisions. Certainly in eternity that person will regret the rejection of God's wisdom.

Who is responsible to teach children how to make wise decisions? Obviously, parents are to take the initiative as did Solomon. He told his son, "My son, hear the instruction of thy father, and forsake not the law of thy mother" (Proverbs 1:8). It is not enough for parents to create and enforce rules without explaining the wisdom, the meaning, and the purpose behind those rules. If the parent cannot give a meaningful reason for standards, maybe the standards are not rooted in wisdom. Generally, parents teach wisdom or fail to teach wisdom by their own example. Children learn much about wisdom by watching their leaders. Are Mom and Dad discerning and perceptive? Can the parents tell where things came from and where they are going? Do the folks demonstrate the process of gaining wisdom through mental self-discipline? Do they illustrate wise dealing, righteousness, justice, and equity in their relations with others? Most of all, do the parents show their children that their relationship with God is the basis for wisdom?

God's plan is for parents to direct their children to the Word of God, where the children will find wisdom just like Mom and Dad did. If the father and the mother are not in fellowship with God and therefore lack God-given wisdom, the children will have difficulty discovering God's great repository of wisdom.

PUT IT TO WORK

1. Do you fear God?

2. What principles of wisdom have you demonstrated to your children in the past week?

3. Are you able to perceive the source of problems, the solution to problems, and the outcome of problems?

4. How many times have you read through the complete collection of proverbs?

5. Are you aware that there are thirty-one chapters in the Proverbs, which is generally the number of days in a month?

6. What would happen if you read one chapter each day?

PRINCIPLE 29
Wise child or foolish child? The difference is painfully obvious.

A wise son makes a glad father, but a foolish son is a sorrow to his mother. (Proverbs 10:1 ESV)

The good news is that, according to statistics compiled by the Federal Bureau of Investigation recently, the volume of violent crime in the nation from 2003 to 2004 declined 1.2 percent. The rate of violent crime also declined 1.1 percent. The numbers show that, in that year, only 465.5 violent offenses were committed per 100,000 in population. Now that is encouraging news—unless you were one of the 465.5 per 100,000 that was attacked. The bad news is that the crime rate among juveniles increased during the same time period—and it continues to rise.

Usually statistics like this do not cause much alarm to the typical citizen. They are just statistics, a lot of numbers without souls. People seldom get stirred about problems among young people until we, or someone we know, becomes their victim. Statistics about troubled young people are not too bothersome until the troubled person is our teen or the teen of someone we know. How did the parents of the 1,278,948 juveniles arrested in 2005 feel? Or more pointedly, how do the parents of Cho Seung-Hui, who murdered several students at Virginia Tech, feel today? Does crime matter to the mothers of criminals? Do thieves' mothers cringe to hear about their children's crime? Do the mothers of drug dealers ever cry?

It seems very unlikely that a young man would grow up in a good home, be taught morality and honesty by his mother, and then one day, out of the blue, decide to go out and break his mother's heart. Rather, young people who become great burdens to their mothers and fathers arrive at that destination through a slow process of foolish thinking and foolish acting. They refuse to think properly and then one day find that they cannot help but act according to their foolish thinking. Men and women like that shatter the hearts of a lot of people who had high hopes and aspirations for them.

The young man who decides that the petty theft of a few dollars here and a nice pen there is unimportant may one day be so enslaved to his habit of stealing that he cannot stop, even when it shatters his parents' heart. No doubt it makes him sad to hear his folks sob, but he cannot help but steal.

The young woman who enjoys the attention her flirting gains from men slides more deeply into that abyss as the years go by. One day her daddy learns that she is a dancer at the local club, where she thrives on the attention of men and their money. She knows that it is wrong, but she can't stop. She knows that her lifestyle embarrasses her dear father, but she is unable to break the chains of her folly.

The young man knows that he shouldn't look at pornography, but he enjoys the thrill and convinces himself that no one is hurt by his practice. But like all habits, this one takes the young man deeper and deeper into sin until one day he gets mixed up with an underage girl and the authorities come to take him away. He is sorry to hear his mother weeping with a broken heart, but how could he stop?

The beautiful young woman falls head over heels for the knight in shining armor. Her parents are more discerning than she is and warn their daughter of potential problems they see in the handsome man. But the daughter, being compelled by folly, is determined to snag this man to be her husband. She succeeds only to learn within five years that the man she thought loved her actually loves the attention of many women. His unfaithfulness destroys the marriage. The divorce breaks the heart of those discerning parents who warned their precious daughter. But what can be done about it after the marriage is destroyed?

In each of the above hypothetical cases the child should have learned how to choose to follow wisdom not foolishness. Life is full of choices, and the child who chooses folly will be a burden for his or her parents until she goes to the grave. Why would a child want to do that to the very ones who brought him or her into this world? Far better for children to learn early in life how to choose wisdom.

A WISE CHILD MAKES A FATHER AND MOTHER GLAD (Proverbs 10:1)

A wise son or daughter is one who chooses wisdom. This verse draws a simple picture of a parent/child relationship. The joy or the sorrow is experienced within the context of relationships. Obviously, the first noun speaks of the father, since the noun that refers to a parent is masculine gender. But the principle applies to the mother as well. It is also true that in several proverbs Solomon spoke of the mother and the father in parallel statements. What is true for one is true for the other. In this case we can certainly conclude that a child who chooses to think and act wisely makes both the father and the mother glad.

But is this a principle that applies only to a son or does it also apply to a daughter? The word translated "son" is also used to speak about children in a more general sense. Again, the noun in this case is in the masculine gender, which typically means it refers to a son. Indeed, it is clear that Solomon gave this collection to his son to help keep him out of trouble, especially regarding his relationship with women (Proverbs 5–7). However, there are cases in the Bible where even the masculine noun is translated "children" to include both sons and daughters. One example of that use is in Genesis 3:16, where God's curse promised Eve that "in pain you shall bring forth children." The word *children* in that verse is the same word and form of the word found in this text. Therefore, this proverb sets forth an important principle for a successful relationship between a mother (as well as father) and her children.

This proverb begins on a positive note by describing the child who chooses to be wise. But what exactly does such a child choose? Does it mean that she spends inordinate hours in the library seeking wisdom. No. The emphasis is on wise action, not necessarily on the pursuit of the concept of wisdom. Nor does it indicate intellectual stimulation as we might be prone to think of wisdom. Here the emphasis is on how the child acts.

To act wisely is to refrain from acting in an evil way. What is the evil way? In very simple terms, there are two ways in life: the good way and the evil way. Children will need to choose between the two paths. One is identified by that which is called evil. Says who? The question of evil is not a matter of opinion, nor is it up for debate. God's Word identifies evil. Godly parents apply God's Word to help identify evil. Spiritual leaders use God's Word to point out evil. The other path is identified by the traits of wisdom as they are spelled out in the collection of Proverbs.

The wise child chooses the wise path. While action is the key in this text, thinking almost always precedes acting. People live out the way they think. We can generally tell how a person thinks by the way he lives. So too, the essential idea behind the Hebrew word translated "wise" represents a manner of thinking and an attitude concerning life's experiences. The wise child thinks in line with God's wisdom before he or she acts wisely.

In a broader sense, to be wise relates to prudence in secular affairs, skills in the arts, moral sensitivity, and experience in the ways of the Lord. All of those ideas are found in the Old Testament's uses of "wisdom." In fact, some scholars argue that the Old Testament descriptions of wisdom are similar to the traits of wisdom from surrounding ancient cultures. However, the wisdom of the Old Testament is quite distinct from other ancient worldviews in that it reflects the teaching of a personal God,

> The wise child is a child who knows and understands Bible principles.

Who is holy and just. This holy and just God expects those who have a relationship with Him to exhibit His character in the way they live out life. It is a unique blend of the revealed will of a holy God with the practical human experiences of life. Unlike human wisdom, in which man is the measure of all things, Old Testament wisdom teaches that the human will, even in the realm of practical matters, must be subject to divine causes. Therefore, Hebrew wisdom was not theoretical and speculative. It was practical, based on revealed principles of right and wrong, to be lived out in daily life.

In other words, the wise child is a child who knows and understands Bible principles. He is able to identify actions or practices that are contrary to Bible principle and actions or practices that conform to the Bible principles. The wise child makes choices that reflect right thinking and acting in light of those Bible principles.

In practical terms it means that he or she has learned how to say no to the desires of the flesh, to peer pressure, and to the influence of the pagan worldview.

What does that kind of living do for the parents of such a child? The text concludes that the child who lives according to wisdom will make a glad father and mother. Glad parents are characterized by an ongoing joyful disposition. Their joy flows from a happy heart. Their life demonstrates the kind of feeling folks had when they attended the festivals in Jerusalem. The description of festival joy is one of the most common uses of this word in the Old Testament. It is not surprising to discover that this kind of joy is associated with kind words (Proverbs 12:25). It is the way someone feels when he meets a loved one he hasn't seen in a while (Exodus 4:14). It is the joy a godly person experiences when he or she observes the outliving of righteousness (Proverbs 27:9).

The parents of a wise child rejoice to see their child living out God's principles. These parents will feel a good kind of pride toward their child. While it is true that God condemns pride in human accomplishments, it might be possible for parents to be proud of the work God has done in the life of a child who is wise. That is to boast about God, which is not only allowed, but commanded: "That, according as it is written, He that glorieth, let him glory in the Lord" (1 Corinthians 1:31). The parents of a wise child know that the end of the road he or she has chosen is good for the child. Above all they know that God is getting the glory for righteous living. Parents whose children make choices based on the wisdom of God's Word ought to be a joyful. They ought to be glad.

A FOOLISH CHILD MAKES A MOTHER AND FATHER SAD

Some children choose to be foolish instead of choosing to be wise. Do they actually choose this path, or do they take it by default since they cannot do better? According to this proverb the child chooses to be foolish. The foolish child described throughout the Proverbs is not mentally deficient. A literal translation of the word found here (which is the most common Hebrew word translated in the Old Testament as fool or foolish) is "stupid fellow." The term refers to the dull or obstinate one. The word describes a propensity to make wrong choices.

Why does he or she make bad choices? There are several contributing factors to the fool's foolishness. This kind of person does not appreciate the knowledge that is gained from the Bible. Wisdom cries out, "How long, ye simple ones, will ye love simplicity? and the scorners delight in their scorning, and fools hate knowledge?" (Proverbs 1:22 ESV). Also, this person does not delight in pursuing understanding. "A fool takes no pleasure in understanding, but only in expressing his opinion" (Proverbs 18:2). Furthermore, this person enjoys doing the unacceptable. "Doing wrong is like a joke to a fool, but wisdom is pleasure to a man of understanding" (Proverbs 10:23 ESV). Finally, not only does this person do foolish things because he is convinced he is right but he enjoys talking about his foolish choices. "The tongue of the wise useth knowledge aright: but the mouth of fools poureth out foolishness" (Proverbs 15:2).

It is not that the foolish child just has a stretch of bad luck. Rather, the foolish child prefers to make bad choices. He has been acquainted with wisdom but has chosen not to live accordingly. The terrible end is that after he has practiced avoiding wisdom for a period of time, he becomes unable to see the right way. The right choice is not palatable to him. The bad choice really does seem to her like the best way to benefit herself. As a result of wrong practice that leads to bad habits, the child mistakenly thinks that he or she is wise. "Wherefore is there a price in the hand of a fool to get wisdom, seeing he hath no heart to it" (Proverbs 17:16), Solomon wondered. The fool becomes so absorbed in his foolish ways that wisdom eludes him in almost every way.

Ultimately, the foolish child chooses the bad paths in life because he has no fear of God. Solomon concluded that fools are fools, "for that they hated knowledge, and did not choose the fear of the Lord" (Proverbs 1:29). These children chose not to respect God. They assumed that they themselves are the measure of all things. Her failure to maintain a right relationship with God blinds her eyes to true wisdom. She really, truly, does not get it. Though you correct this child repeatedly, he continues to choose to do that which is harmful to himself. Worse is the fact that the foolish child continues to choose to do that which is harmful to his friends and family. When the picture is completed, it becomes clear that the foolish child continues to choose to do that which is harmful for society. That is why society must often put this kind of person out of circulation. How terribly tragic this is. How does the wrong path come to such a bitter end?

The fool is trapped in a downward cycle of destruction. All the while he is destroying himself, he is convinced that he is right. In fact, he comes to believe that he might be the only one who is right. Sadly, friends and family might, out of misguided love, support the fool in his folly. Only after the fool has damaged family and friend relationships will the family and friend admit that they were wrong to embrace his foolishness. Conversely, true love sees the problem, addresses the problem, and refuses to embrace the problem. True love for the foolish son is rooted in the fear of God, which is true love for God. Therefore, true love knows where the foolishness will lead and seeks to stop it short.

Bad fruit always leaves a bad taste in the eater's mouth. Foolish children are bad fruit. And the final fruit of their foolishness is a sad mother and father. The text uses a word that pictures this poor mother sunk in sorrow. The primary meaning of the word is a mental troubling that results from affliction. The affliction comes because of the foolish child. It is directed at the mother who experiences mental sorrow in affliction. The sorrow is so deep that this word accentuates the pain it brings. This kind of sorrow emphasizes humbling.

This is how Jeremiah felt as he observed the destruction of Jerusalem. He had warned the foolish people to stop being foolish or they would bring destruction on themselves. They rejected Jeremiah's warning. "Is it nothing to you, all ye that pass by? behold, and see if there be any sorrow like unto my sorrow, which is done unto me, wherewith the Lord hath afflicted me in the day of his fierce anger" (Lamentations 1:12). Many mothers can identify with Jeremiah's pain. They have warned, disciplined, chided, and prayed for a foolish son or daughter. It is heartbreak for a mother to watch the child she brought into this world walk a path of destruction. It is infinitely worse when the fruits of that walk come to bear, bringing agony and sorrow.

Mother, of all people, should not have to bear such sorrow. She is to be a source of comfort (Isaiah 66:13), a teacher (Proverbs 31:1), and a discipliner (Zechariah 13:3). Those duties should bring respect from her children. Indeed, according to God's standard the mother's children owe her obedience (Genesis 28:7), blessings (Proverbs 30:11), honor (Exodus 20:12), and respect (Leviticus 19:3). The Bible reveals a higher standard of respect for mother in the culture of God's people. Children should honor their parents, and especially their mother. Children should never be the source of agony and sorrow.

But it is too common an occurrence for fools to bring great sorrow and pain crashing down on their parents' heads. Where can the sorrowing mother and father of a fool turn for help? Only God's Word brings relief from this state of mind. David concluded, "My soul melteth for heaviness: strengthen thou me according unto thy word" (Psalm 119:28). Here is hope. The same Word of God that promises the tragic consequences of foolish decisions also promises to heal and strengthen those who are crushed by sin's results.

The two words—*glad* and *sorrow*—map out two extremes. A son who becomes a murderer or daughter who becomes a prostitute will certainly cause sorrow for the mother and father. They are contrasted to a son or daughter who becomes a wonderful servant of Christ and who exhibits few if any flaws. That child makes for glad parents. Reality generally flows somewhere between the extremes. Most children grow up to be in the general sphere of the moral/ethical failures or in the general sphere of the successful Christian. The parents' joy or sorrow is in response to where in those spheres their child chooses to live. Woe to the son or daughter who has little or no concern for Mom and Dad. Woe to that child who is so selfish that he or she makes choices that please him or her alone and end up breaking his or her folks' hearts. It is a blessing to have a child who chooses to fear God and keep His commands. That child will be wise and bring joy to his or her parents.

PUT IT TO WORK

1. Who is teaching your child which path to choose?

2. How are you teaching your child to discern between good and evil?

3. If your children continue on the path they are walking, will you be glad or sad in the end?

4. Can your children learn from your example how to choose the right path?

5. Did you make your parents glad?

Train up a child in the way he should go; even when he is old he will not depart from it. (Proverbs 22:6 ESV)

Some people train trees or shrubbery to grow in very interesting shapes. The person who does this does not normally go to a nursery and ask the salesperson for a tree that looks like a corkscrew. Normally, a person plants a tree in the ground, and if it gets sufficient water and sunlight, it grows straight up toward the sky. In order for a tree to end up with an interesting, artistic shape, someone had an idea or plan for the tree. That artist bought a particular kind of tree, planted it in dirt that she had prepared well, and then for many years, she shaped and trained the tree so that it would look like a corkscrew. The artist had a goal and dedicated the tree and herself to achieving that goal.

Other people train dogs to do amazing things. Left to itself a dog will be a scavenger and a nuisance. But dogs can be trained to be not only man's best friend but man's protector. Some dogs are trained to be bomb-sniffing or drug-sniffing dogs. The trainers of these dogs have a plan; they have a goal for an otherwise useless animal. Then for many months, maybe years, the trainer carefully, systematically teaches the dog how to identify a bomb with its olfactory senses, which are far superior to human sniffers.

Horses can also be trained to do amazing things. A wild horse is found running in the wilderness of the West. Horses of that kind are mixed breeds, scruffy looking, and not about to submit to a mere human. However, with a good plan and much careful labor, it is possible to train a horse to submit and use all its massive power according to the master's wishes. Royal Lipizzaner Stallions are trained meticulously to perform to the delight of audiences. These horses, originally bred and trained in the Spanish Riding School in Vienna, Austria, use their might and power to entertain audiences with beautiful prancing and acrobatics. The result of much training is impressive and a standard far from what these horses would be if they had been left to themselves.

If we can train trees, dogs, and horses to be beautiful, useful, and graceful, why can't we train children to reach a valuable end? In past generations, some worldly-wise thinkers concluded that children should be left to themselves so that they can grow without interference from jaded, biased adults. They concluded that misdirected, naive, bigoted parents caused children to fight, be selfish, be unkind, or just not like other people. The current chaotic atmosphere of America's inner cities proves how wrong those worldly-wise thinkers were.

God, our creator, has a better plan for His creation. He teaches in His Word that all children are born with a sin nature and, being subject to that nature, will act according to sin. He gives children to parents and then holds those parents responsible to train and direct the children away from the natural sinful propensities to a right relationship with God. When children are right with God, they will be right with others and that makes for a pleasant society.

In this proverb, Solomon gave an important challenge with an attached promise. The challenge is for parents to be dedicated to training their children according to God's way. The promise is that when the children are growing old, they will not waver from the plan the parent used for training them. Both the challenge and the promise are broader than they first appear.

TRAIN THE CHILDREN ACCORDING TO THEIR WAYS

Parents must be dedicated to child training. A dedicated parent has to make a conscious decision at some point to train the child (or children). It is not a haphazard response. Training doesn't just happen. It is the result of dedication. In fact, the word translated "train" is also used to refer to dedicating something such as a building. It means to inaugurate. The idea behind dedicating or inaugurating implies preparing something for use. When Community Baptist Church purchased a piece of property for a new building, the first thing we did in preparing it for a building site was to gather in the field and dedicate this property for God's use and to His glory.

Parents must have the same attitude regarding child rearing. They must determine to prepare each child to serve a useful purpose in society. It sounds easy enough. But in reality such dedication requires much work. Preparing a child to serve God faithfully requires superhuman work. That is why parents must be fully dedicated to the task. Yet, in reality, there is no choice in the matter. While it is important for parents to dedicate their children to the end that they will be used for God's glory, the decision to rear the children has already been made. The fact that a parent already has children predetermines what the parent needs to do.

Therefore, since the need to train the children is a foregone conclusion, parents must have a plan for training. Again, training doesn't just happen. Parenting should not be the big experiment. God's people do not need to shoot in the dark when it comes to training their children. The principles of the Bible should be the plan. The Bible is not only sufficient to establish the plan for training but the most reliable guide. Since it is God Who gives the command to train the children, since the command is found in God's Word, and since God's Word is the plan for everyone who would honor Him, the principles of His Word should be the map parents follow. That only stands to reason.

But what does it mean to train the children according to God's plan? What does God's plan require? Briefly, one can conclude from a study of the Bible that God's plan is for parents to teach the children the principles of God's Word. God's plan also requires that parents demonstrate how to apply the principles of God's Word to everyday living. At the same time, it is also God's plan to teach the characteristics of sin and to demonstrate how to avoid sin.

Therefore, it is obvious that God's plan for training the children has a positive side and a negative side. Positively, God's plan requires parents to understand God's principles and do God's principles. Negatively, God's plan requires parents to understand the principles of sin and purposely seek to avoid committing sin. What good is the first side without the application of the second side of the plan? What good is the ritual of taking vitamins without also practicing hygiene? Here is a person who says she is concerned about her health, which explains why she takes fifteen different vitamins each day. However, it is also obvious that this person is not concerned about hygiene. Her house is a mess, with trash and old moldy food sitting everywhere. She never washes her hands and she takes a bath only once a year on her anniversary. Not surprisingly, this person is sick frequently. What good are vitamins when she exposes herself to so many germs? Likewise we might wonder, "What good are the positive principles of God's Word if we do not also work to avoid the negative problems of sin?"

> God's plan for training has two sides: embrace the principles of God's Word and avoid the principles of sin.

God's plan for training has two sides: embrace the principles of God's Word and avoid the principles of sin. His plan also has two steps. The first step requires parents to teach doctrine. The second step requires parents to teach the practice of doctrine. It is important for children to be familiar with the major doctrines of the Bible. Who will teach them these things? The parents must take this responsibility seriously. It is also very important that the children learn how to make Bible doctrine relevant to life. God's plan for training the children must include teaching doctrine that leads to practice and practice that is built on doctrine.

Therefore, the plan for training children must involve demonstration and illustration. It is not enough to tell the young ones to do right. Parents must show their children what they mean by doing "right." What good is accomplished by teaching the children that God is holy but not showing them how God's holiness works out in everyday living? What good is accomplished by teaching children that Christians have the righteousness of Christ imputed to them without showing them what imputed righteousness looks like in real life? Children rightly say, "Don't just tell me what to do . . . show me how to do it."

Children need both directions and a map or picture. When taking a trip or going somewhere unfamiliar, I often use Google Maps or a similar program to show me how to get to my goal. I just type in my destination, which might be for example my friend's church in Georgia, and the program gives me written directions and a nice map with an obvious blue line to follow. It is also possible to get a satellite picture of the destination. The written directions should be sufficient, but sometimes they are confusing. The map and pictures make the plan very clear. What more do I need?

Likewise, the parents' practice in life should show the children how to make doctrine work. For example, the parent has just taught his son the lesson from the Bible that he needs to love God. That is the doctrine. What is the demonstration of the doctrine in practice? When the woman on the television program takes God's name in vain, which happens with regularity, the parent turns off the program. Why? Because a person who loves God cannot endure to hear a sinner curse His name. Surely, if a guest were visiting in that home and used God's name in vain, the same parent would challenge the guest not to do that. Then is it consistent to allow a guest on television to do the same without "confronting" the situation? Of course it is inconsistent to let it go on, and the children see the inconsistency. Training must be doctrine that results in practice and practice built on doctrine. That is God's way.

It is also very important for the parent to consider the child's way. The phrase "according to his way" can refer to each child's uniqueness. The word translated literally would say "according to the mouth." The Old Testament uses this word to describe a commandment as the "mouth of the Lord." In other words, God's speech reveals His character. So, too, a child's words and ways illustrate what he is. That is what Jesus meant when He taught, "For out of the abundance of the heart the mouth speaketh" (Matthew 12:34). If we listen to a person long enough in various settings, we can generally discern the person's character quite well. The person's character reveals what the person is really like. Children reveal their "way" if parents would just listen to what they are saying.

Each child has a different personality and different needs. The parents are responsible to discern those differences. Parents must determine a child's abilities, gifts, talents, temperament, and such and adjust their training accordingly. That is why it is wrong for a father to demand that his son play football when the boy has no athleticism but is very gifted in music or art. To misunderstand a child's way and, therefore, train him errantly might cause the child to be confused throughout his life about what God planned for him to do. Parents must teach Bible principles, Bible doctrines, and how to live out those truths according to each child's way.

The phrase "according to his way" can also refer to a child's natural way. A child's way, a child's natural bent is expressed well in the retort, "I want to do what I feel like doing!" If a parent trains her daughter according to that way and allows her to expect that she will always get her way, the daughter will never get over it. If parents train their children to live in sin because that is their natural way, they should not be surprised to discover that their children never depart from sin. That is the promise in this proverb. The command requires parents to train the children in godly teaching according to their way. The promise is that the children will generally live their entire lives according to the way they have been trained.

WHILE GROWING OLD, THE CHILDREN WILL STICK TO THE PLAN

The last part of the proverb promises, "Even when he is old he will not depart from it." It is important to understand what is not promised here. This is necessary because of a common misinterpretation of this phrase that many people have proposed or heard for several years. The misinterpretation is that, if a parent trains a child in the right way, the child will return to Christ in old age. This idea says that a child from a Christian home might live in sin for many years, but by middle age or so he will return to his Christian roots. Sadly, the misinterpretation has been used to give parents of non-Christian children false hope. How long must a child live contrary to God's way before he or she is considered departed from it? Also, a person cannot depart from a place he or she has never been. It is obvious that this errant teaching runs contrary to the doctrine of perseverance of the saints.

Another misunderstanding of this verse is the idea that a child reared in a Christian home will automatically become a Christian. It would be nice if that were true, but that idea cuts across the grain of God's truth throughout the Bible. Salvation is not the result of human effort. If it were, some sincere believer would develop a foolproof plan that would guarantee the salvation of all children.

What is promised? In order to understand the promise, we must realize that wisdom literature is not law. A few examples from the Proverbs will prove this point. Proverbs 3:9–10 states that the person who honors God with his wealth will have full barns. Generally that is true. Often God does reward faithful obedience with greater blessing. However, that is not a law; and because it is not law, there are faithful servants who honor God with their income and still have financial need. Likewise, one of the proverbs states that righteous lips are a king's delight (16:13). The world is familiar with too many kings, dictators, and presidents who did not illustrate this truth at all. Also, not everyone who digs a pit falls into it (26:27). These are not laws. They are general statements of truth.

A law is nonnegotiable and should be enforced. For example, "The soul that sinneth, it shall die" (Ezekiel 18:20) is God's law. There is no exception to it, and it cannot be circumvented. Also, God visits "the iniquity of the fathers upon the children unto the third and fourth generation of them that hate me" (Exodus 20:5*b*). That is a practical law that one can observe being worked out every day. The only antidote to that law is God's mercy and kindness, which is explained in verse 6: "showing steadfast love to thousands of those who love me and keep my commandments." "The righteous shall live by faith" (Habakkuk 2:4; Romans 1:17; Galatians 3:11; Hebrews 10:38) is another law. There are no exceptions to this. This is God's immutable standard. God's Word contains many similar laws, such as the promise that a prophecy must come to pass. Laws must be fulfilled. Wisdom sayings may not always come to pass.

> God not only requires parents to train the children in biblical truth but He also connects promises with the training.

Wisdom sayings are excellent guides, are generally true in normal circumstances, and help shape God's people according to God's wisdom. Therefore, it is generally true that the parent who trains a child in Bible principles according to his way will have a child that will not depart from that standard while he is growing old. But, at the same time, the son of wise parents might be too opinionated to learn (13:1). Or a good home might produce a slacker (10:5). It is possible that a foolish child might despise his mother's training in wisdom (15:20). Sincere parents might have a child who mocks them (30:17). Wisdom sayings are generally true, but they are not law.

At the same time, we must concede that this principle that says that right training leads to right living is repeated throughout the Bible. God does require parents to train their children in godliness. It is a general requirement in that God commands, "Ye fathers, provoke not your children to wrath: but bring them up in the nurture and admonition of the Lord" (Ephesians 6:4). It is a specific or special requirement for those who would be leaders of God's people. Paul instructed Pastor Timothy that if anyone would be an elder, he must rule "well his own house, having his children in subjection with all gravity; (for if a man know not how to rule his own house, how shall he take care of the church of God?)" (1 Timothy 3:4–5). He told Timothy that the same requirement was true for men who desired to be deacons: "Let the deacons be the husbands of one wife, ruling their children and their own houses well" (1 Timothy 3:12). Paul repeated that qualification for elders when he told Titus to appoint elders that are "blameless, the husband of one wife, having faithful children not accused of riot or unruly" (Titus 1:6).

Human wisdom wonders how God can expect parents to meet such requirements in light of the children's free will. God not only requires parents to train the children in biblical truth but He also connects promises with the training. This truth was illustrated when God stated that the fulfillment of His promise to Abraham was contingent on Abraham's children keeping the way of the Lord. He concluded, "For I know him, that he will command his children and his household after him, and they shall keep the way of the Lord, to do justice and judgment; that the Lord may bring upon Abraham that which he hath spoken of him" (Genesis 18:19). Furthermore, according to God's plan, making God's testimony known to the children was connected with long life for the children. Moses told the Israelites,

> Only take care, and keep your soul diligently, lest you forget the things that your eyes have seen, and lest they depart from your heart all the days of your life. Make them known to your children and your children's children—how on the day that you stood before the Lord your God at Horeb, the Lord said to me, "Gather the people to me, that I may let them hear my words, so that they may learn to fear me all the days that they live on the earth, and that they may teach their children so." (Deuteronomy 4:9–10 ESV)

As a result, children whose parents teach them God's way set their hope in God. The psalmist commanded parents to teach their children so

> that the generation to come might know them, even the children which should be born; who should arise and declare them to their children: that they might set their hope in God, and not forget the works of God, but keep his commandments: and might not be as their fathers, a stubborn and rebellious generation; a generation that set not their heart aright, and whose spirit was not stedfast with God. (Psalm 78:6–8)

Over 150 years ago, Ralph Wardlaw drew a conclusion on this matter that is pertinent today:

If that which I have mentioned be an extreme, it is, as has been already said, incomparably less injurious than the other; namely, that of lulling the conscience to repose on the incessantly reiterated sentiment of the freedom and sovereignty of grace. When their children "rise up a seed of evildoers," they are grieved no doubt; but they shake their heads and say—with a great deal more self-complacency than of self-reproach, Ah! you see, we cannot command grace:—grace is free; God has "mercy on whom he will have mercy;" we have done what we could; but God has not seen meet to give the blessing. And it is wonderful how very easy reflections like these make them; when, if matters were duly and scripturally examined, the saying "we have done what we could" might be found far short of truth,—both as to the duty itself and the manner of it.[1]

Parents train trees, dogs, and horses. Parents must train children. Godly parents must train their children in righteousness according to each child's way. God has given unique children to each set of parents with the expectation that the parents will train the children how to love Him. Take care how you train them because they will almost certainly reveal the method you used in training for all the world to see.

PUT IT TO WORK

1. Name a few traits about each of your children that might indicate their "way."

2. Name a couple of ways in which your children are different from each other.

3. Which Bible truth do you need to work on in your own life so that you can demonstrate it better to your children?

4. If you appeal to the Bible to back up your argument, do your children think that you are a hypocrite?

5. Discuss with your spouse the unique ways that God has gifted your children and how you think those "ways" can be used for God's service and glory.

NOTES

Principle 1

1. These examples are taken from James B. Pritchard, *The Ancient Near East*, vol. 1 (Princeton, NJ: Princeton University Press, 1973).

Principle 4

1. Centers for Disease Control and Prevention. "Cohabitation, Marriage, Divorce, and Remarriage in the United States." Vital Health and Statistics Series 23, Number 22, Department of Health and Human Services, 2002.

2. U.S. Census Bureau, 2000.

3. U.S. Census Bureau, 2000.

4. Alternatives to Marriage Project, www.unmarried.org.

Principle 5

1. Derek Kidner. "Proverbs" in *Tyndale Old Testament Commentary* (Downers Grove, IL: Inter-Varsity Press, 1964), 443.

2. Robert Leighton [1611–84], quoted in C. H. Spurgeon, *The Treasury of David*, vol. 3 (McLean VA: MacDonald Publishing Company, n.d.), 101.

Principle 7

1. www.time.com/time/magazine/article/0,9171,959163,00.html.

2. Ibid.

Principle 8

1. T. V. Moore, quoted in Walter C. Kaiser Jr. *Malachi* (Grand Rapids: Baker Book House, 1984), 70.

Principle 10

1. http://en.wikipedia.org/wiki/Point_man.

2. http://www.lkwdpl.org/history/vietnam.html.

3. Jerry Lyons, Vietnam veteran, Hammond, Louisiana, USA, http://americanradioworks.publicradio.org/features/vietnam/scrapbook/entries.

Principle 13

1. Marion Soards. "First Corinthians" in *New International Biblical Commentary* (Peabody, MA: Hendrickson Publishers, 2003), 224.

Principle 14

1. http://www.traditioninaction.org/HotTopics/d006htPapalPreacher_Obedience.htm.

2. "The Buzz, Quotables," *World Magazine* (May 12, 2007), 12.

Principle 18

1. http://www.theatre.ubc.ca/dress_decor/ancient_world_dress_rome.htm.

2. Philo, *On the Sacrifices of Cain and Able* quoted in John MacArthur, "1 Timothy" in *The MacArthur New Testament Commentary* (Chicago: Moody, 1995), 80–81.

Principle 19

1. William Barclay. "Letters to Timothy, Titus and Philemon" in *The Daily Bible Study* (Philadelphia: Westminster Press, 1975), 107.

2. Ibid., 106.

3. Ibid., 107.

4. Ibid.

Principle 20

1. D. Edmond Hiebert, "Titus" in *The Expositors Bible Commentary*, ed. Frank E. Gaebelein and J. D. Douglas (Grand Rapids, MI: Zondervan Publishing House, 1978), 437.

Principle 21

1. Alfred Edersheim, *Sketches of Jewish Social Life* (Peabody, MA: Hendrickson Publishers, 1994), 130.

2. "The Letters of James and Peter" in William Barclay. *The Daily Study Bible Series* (Philadelphia: Westminster Press, 1976), 219.

3. Philip Schaff, ed., "The Confessions of St. Augustine" in *The Nicene and Post Nicene Fathers*, vol. 1, trans. J. G. Pilkington (Grand Rapids: Wm. B. Eerdmans Publishing Company, 1979), 136–37.

Principle 22

1. Tim Harford, "Is the Wife Valuable Property" in *The Undercover Economist*, July 1, 2006.

Principle 24

1. *Poems About Baal, Ancient Near Eastern Texts Relating to the Old Testament.* Edited by J. B.Pritchard, 1955. Quoted in J. A. Thompson, "Deuteronomy" in *Tyndale Old Testament Commentaries* (Downers Grove, IL: Inter-Varsity Press, 1974), 121.

Principle 25

1. W. H. Grispen, "Exodus" in *Bible Study Commentaries* (Grand Rapids: Zondervan, 1982), 192.

Principle 26

1. C.H. Spurgeon. *The Treasury of David*, vol. 2 (McClean, VA: MacDonald Publishing, n.d.), 330.

Principle 27

1. C. H. Spurgeon, *The Treasury of David*, vol. 3 (McClean, VA: MacDonald Publishing Company, n.d.), 85.

Principle 30

1. Ralph Wardlaw, *Lectures on the Book of Proverbs*, vol. 3 (1861; repr., Minneapolis: Klock & Klock, 1982), 38.